Seattle
Subtext

Seattle

SUBTEXT

PAUL BERGER

VISUAL STUDIES WORKSHOP PRESS, ROCHESTER

THE REAL COMET PRESS, SEATTLE————1984

Seattle Subtext is a co-publication of
Visual Studies Workshop Press
&
The Real Comet Press
A division of Such a Deal Corporation

Designed and printed by
Visual Studies Workshop Press
31 Prince Street
Rochester, New York 14607

Distributed by
The Real Comet Press
932 18th Avenue East
Seattle, Washington 98112
(206) 328-1801

Publication of this book was made
possible by a grant from the National
Endowment for the Arts, a federal agency.

Library of Congress Cataloging in Publication Data

Berger, Paul, 1951-
    Seattle subtext.

    1. Photography, Journalistic—Miscellanea.
I. Title.
TR820.B46 1984   700'.92'4   83-26047
ISBN 0-89822-037-8
ISBN 0-941104-09-5 (Real Comet Press)

First Printing 1984

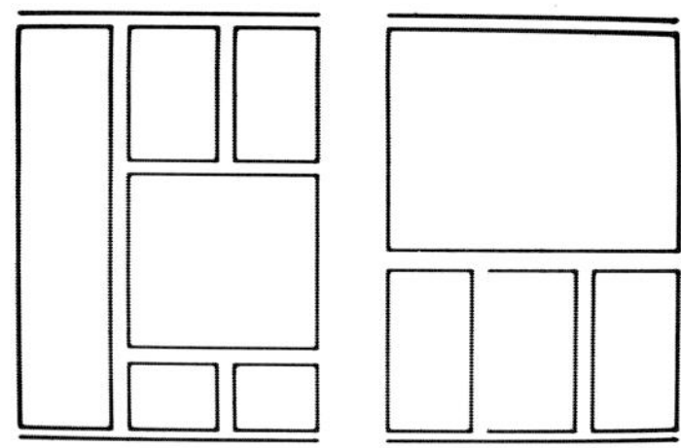

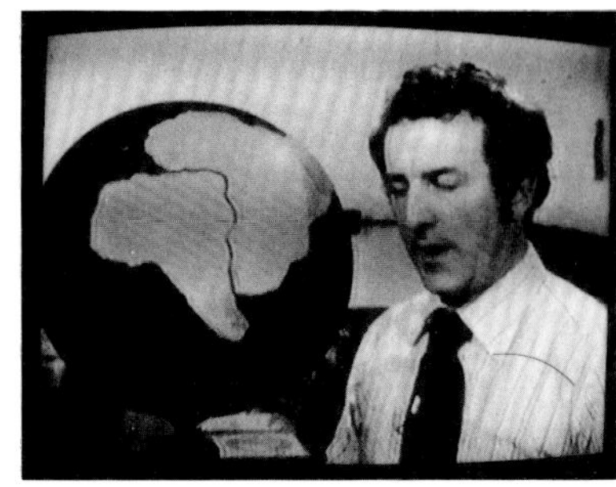

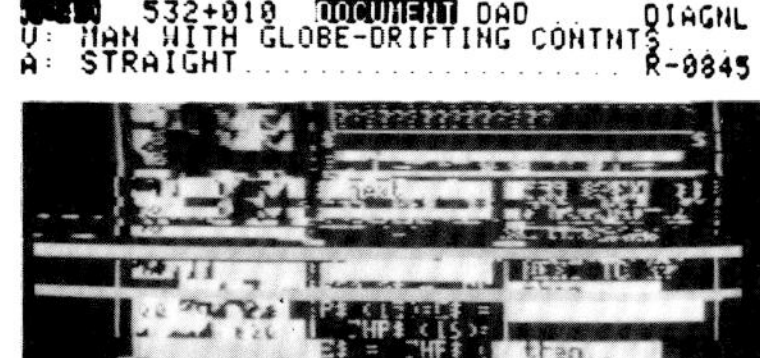

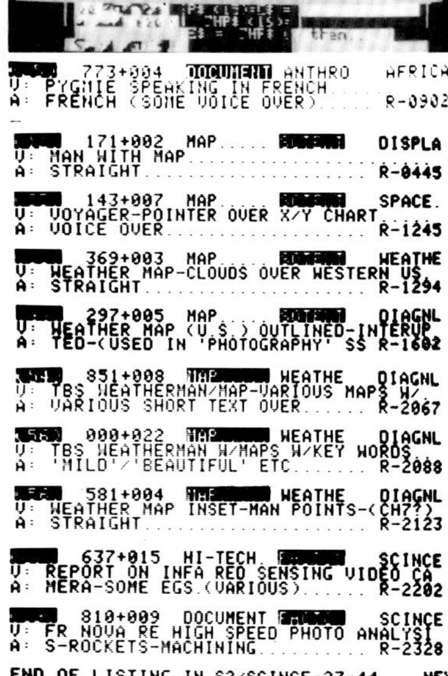

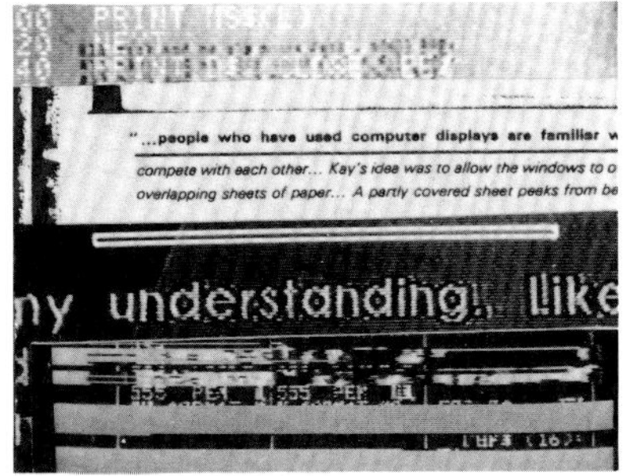

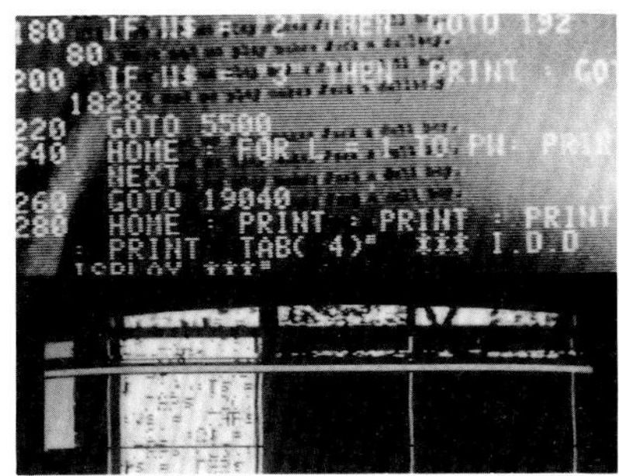

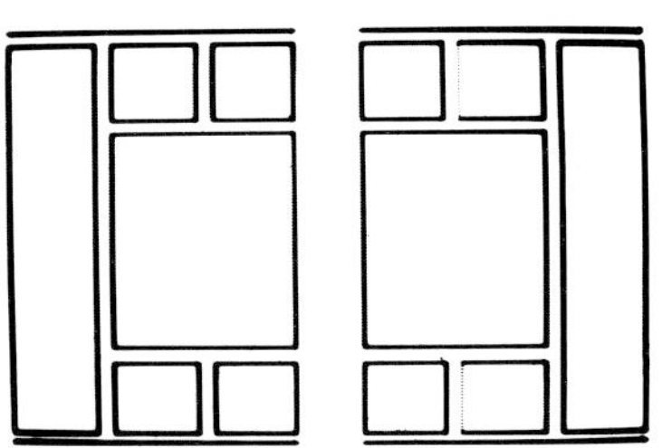

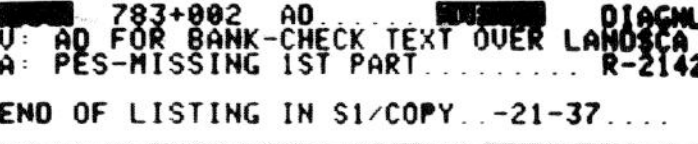

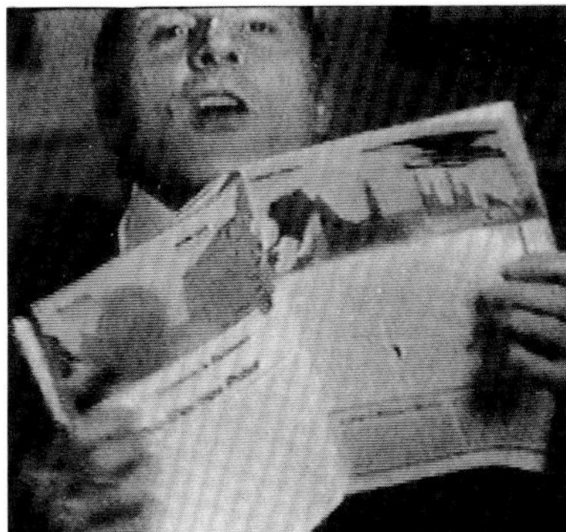

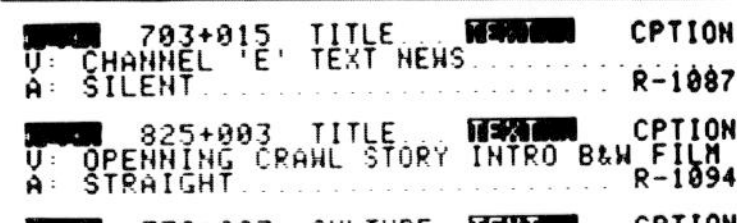

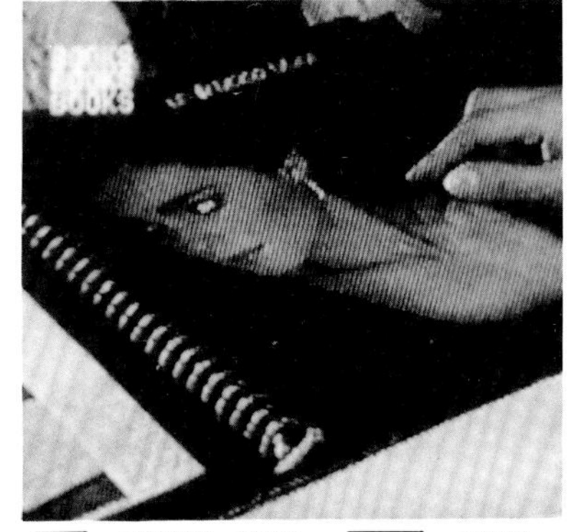

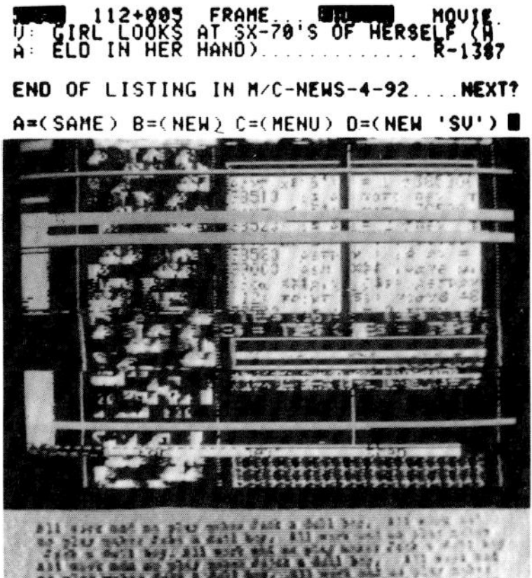

INTRODUCTION

Photographs are seldom solitary or reclusive; they most often gather in groups along with their uneasy ally, text. Together, they are the cohabiters of the most common "picture" of all, the printed page.

This book begins with the arena of the printed page as a format and a context. Consequently, the "shape" of its pages invokes the magazine double-page spread, but departs from it in at least the following ways: (1) Columns of text have been replaced by columns of overlapped television imagery; (2) The topics of the pages shift from the normal magazine section headlines ("Nation", "Show Business", etc.) to more generalized or personalized areas ("Writing", "Memory"); (3) Pages labeled "Display" contain annotated versions of the pages that both precede and follow them, displaying or listing alternatives and "out-takes"; and (4) The visual cadence of the imagery becomes more akin to film, television, or computer display than to the static printed page.

Seattle Subtext is an imaginary and reordered magazine, a hypothetical alteration of the context and composition of all the "information" that pours into ones home. By drawing on the conventions of "layout", it becomes possible to construct complex relationships among still photographs and television imagery, typeset captions and computer text. These relationships posit a personalized environment of great density and simultaneity in a format usually thought of as fixed when received—the magazine.

Paul Berger, Seattle Washington, October 1983

SEAMLESS	RECURSIVE	AUTONOMA

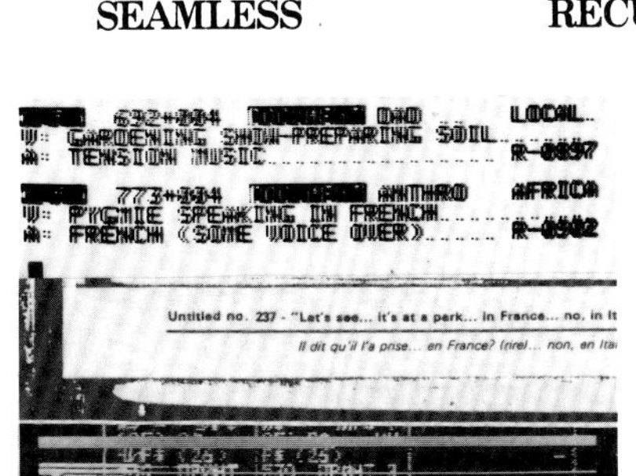

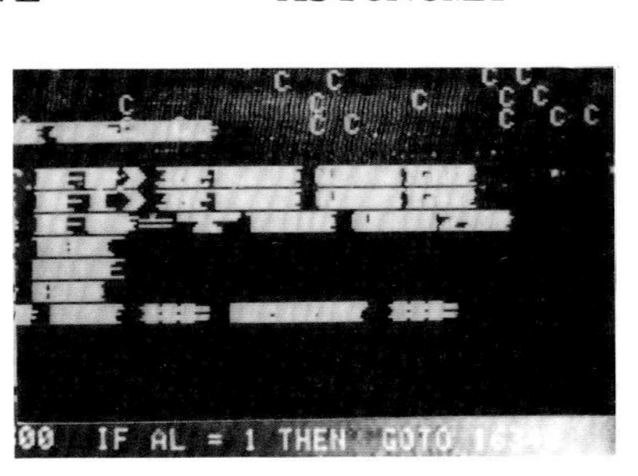

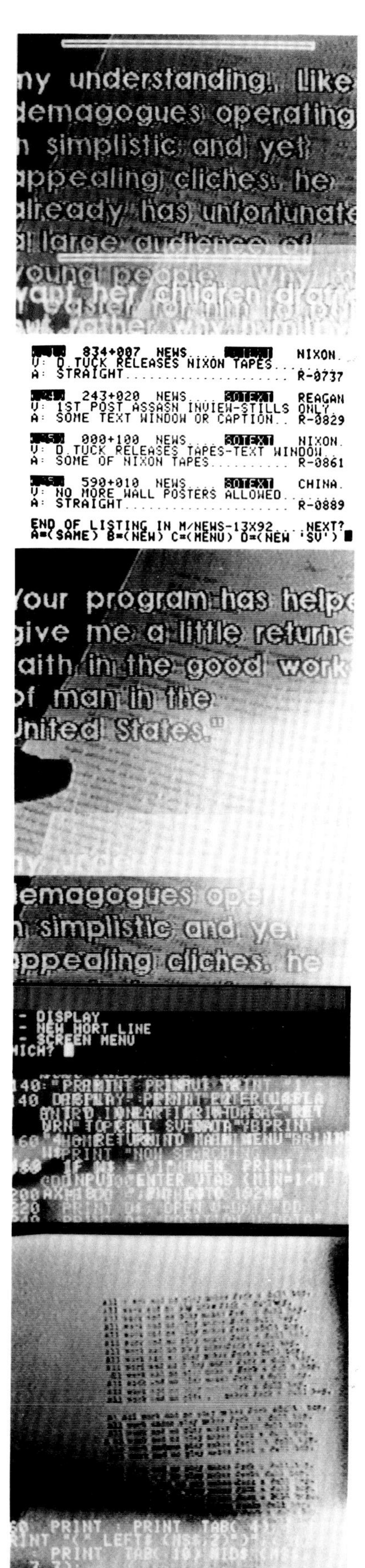

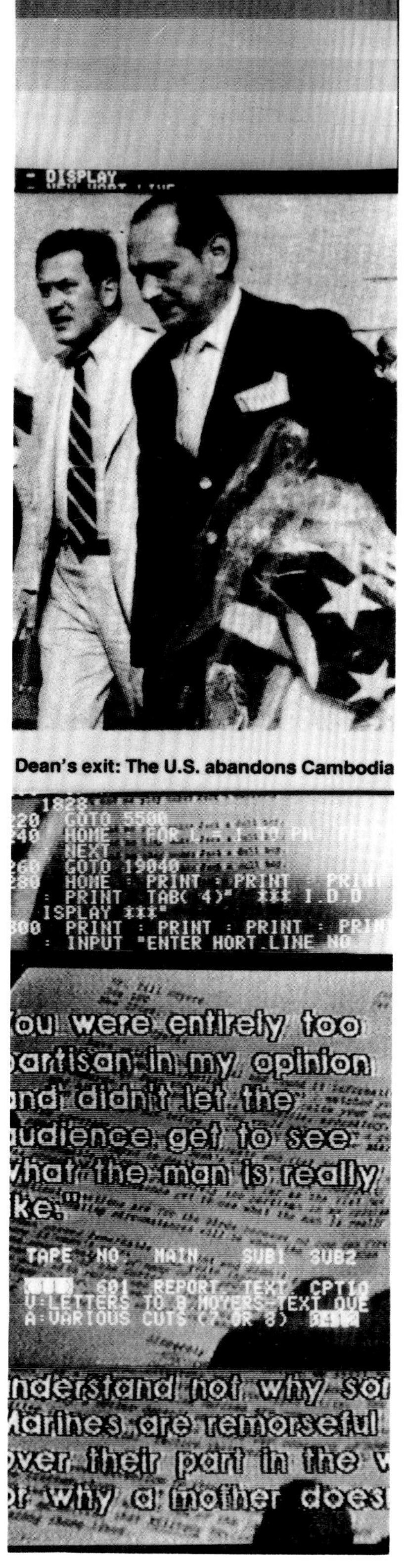

Dean's exit: The U.S. abandons Cambodia

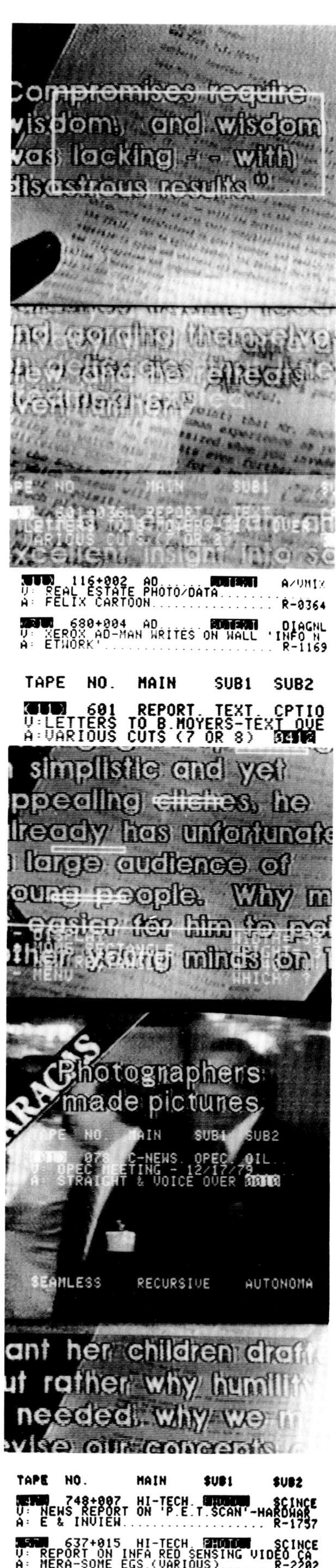

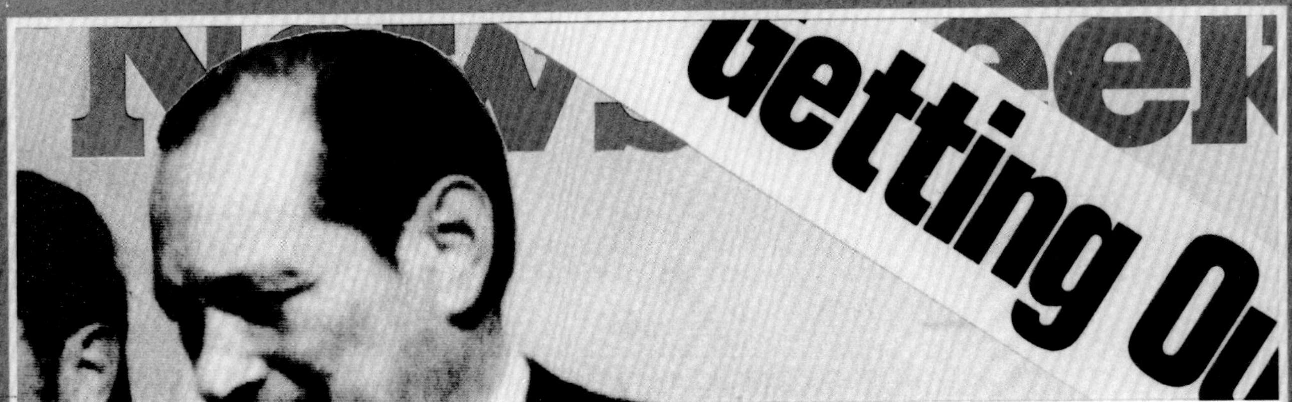

SEATTLE
SUBTEXT

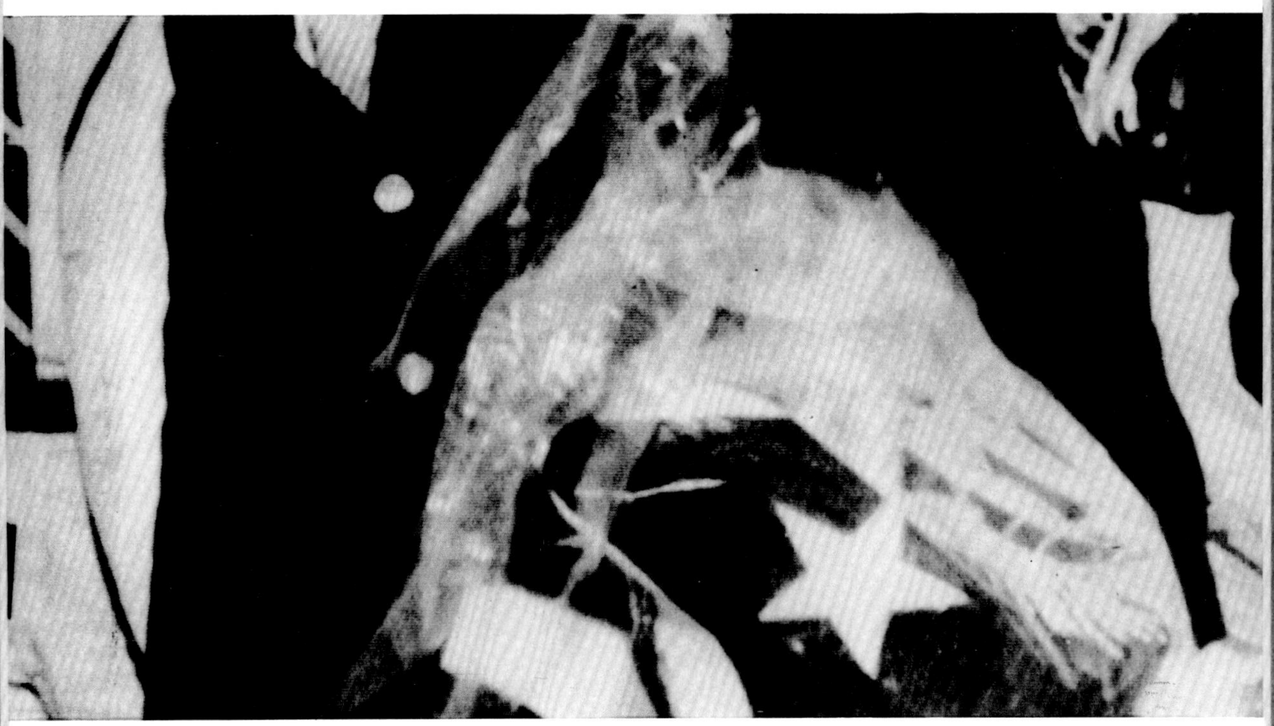

SEAMLESS   **RECURSIVE**   **AUTONOMA**

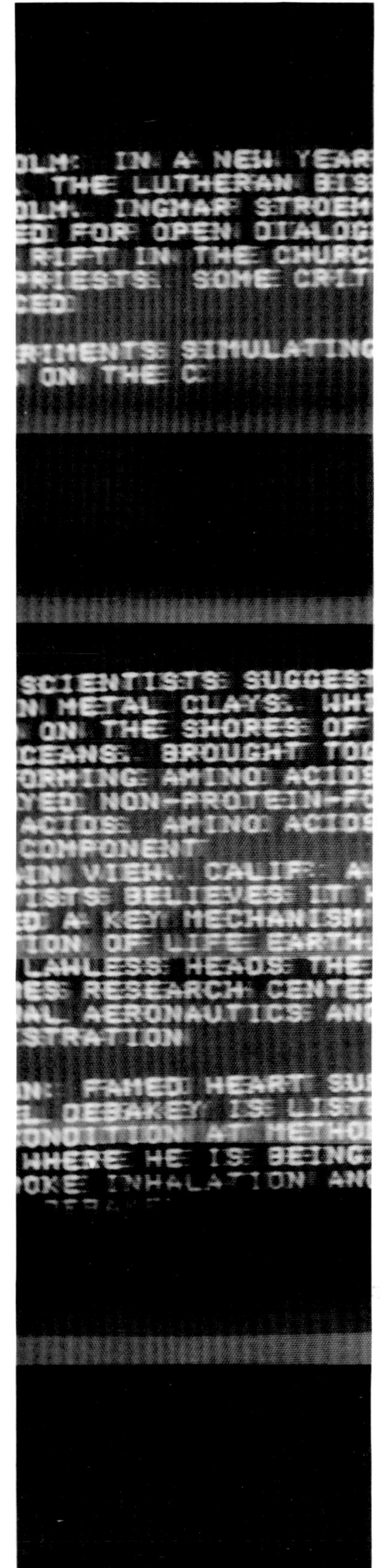
OLM: IN A NEW YEAR
THE LUTHERAN BIS
OLM. INGMAR STROEH
ED FOR OPEN DIALOG
RIFT IN THE CHURC
PRIESTS SOME CRIT
CED
RIMENTS SIMULATING
ON THE C
SCIENTISTS SUGGEST
N METAL CLAYS WHI
ON THE SHORES OF
CEANS BROUGHT TOG
FORMING AMINO ACIDS
YED NON-PROTEIN-FO
ACIDS AMINO ACIDS
COMPONENT
IN VIEW CALIF A
TISTS BELIEVES IT
ED A KEY MECHANISM
TION OF LIFE EARTH
LAWLESS HEADS THE
ES RESEARCH CENTE
AL AERONAUTICS AND
STRATION
N: FAMED HEART SU
L DEBAKEY IS LIST
CONDITION AT METHO
WHERE HE IS BEING
OKE INHALATION AND

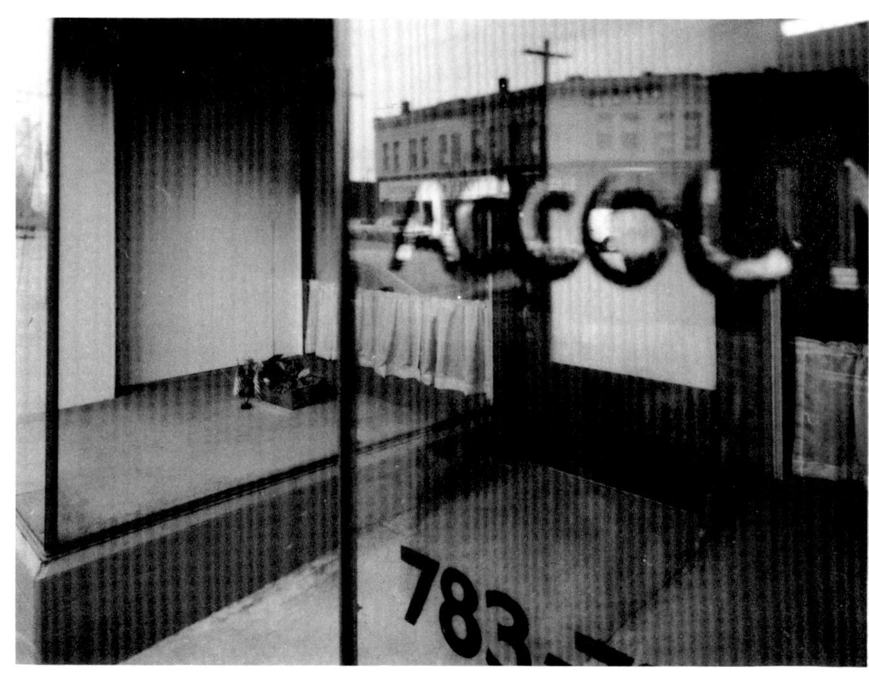
ACCOU
783-

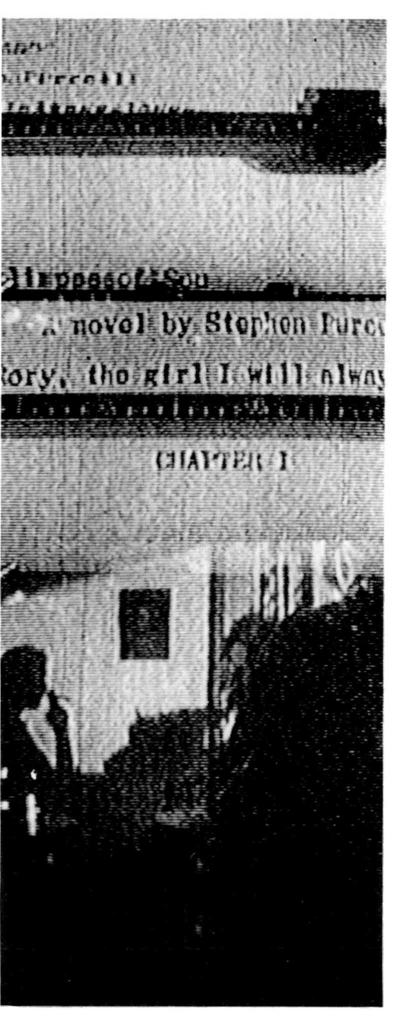
A novel by Stephen Purc
ory, the girl I will alway
CHAPTER I

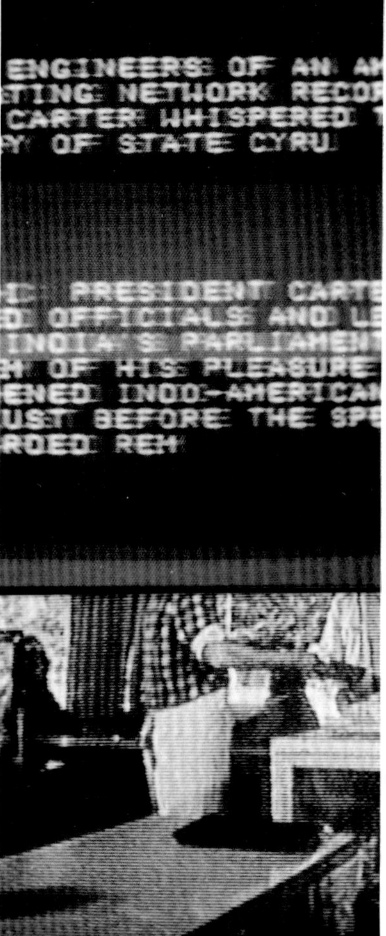
ENGINEERS OF AN AM
TING NETWORK RECOR
CARTER WHISPERED
Y OF STATE CYRU
PRESIDENT CARTE
OFFICIALS AND LE
INDIA S PARLIAMEN
H OF HIS PLEASURE
ENED INDO-AMERICAN
UST BEFORE THE SP
RDED REM

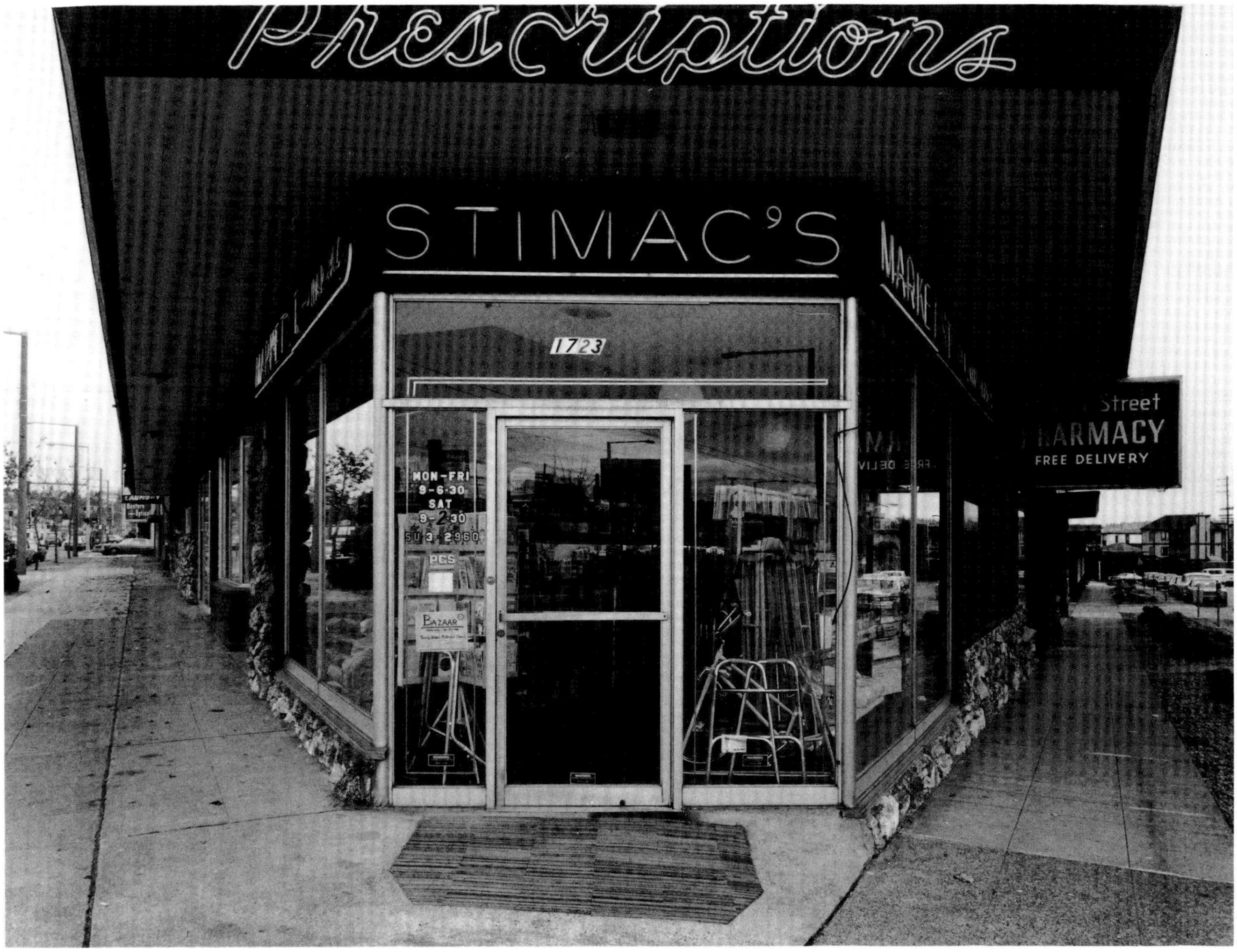

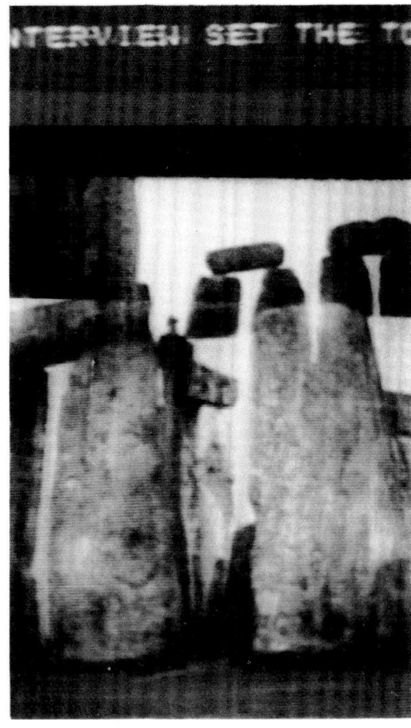

SEATTLE SUBTEXT: Table of Context

(1)"Magazine" format; (2) TV strips as text; (3) Photographs as photographs; (4) Captioned

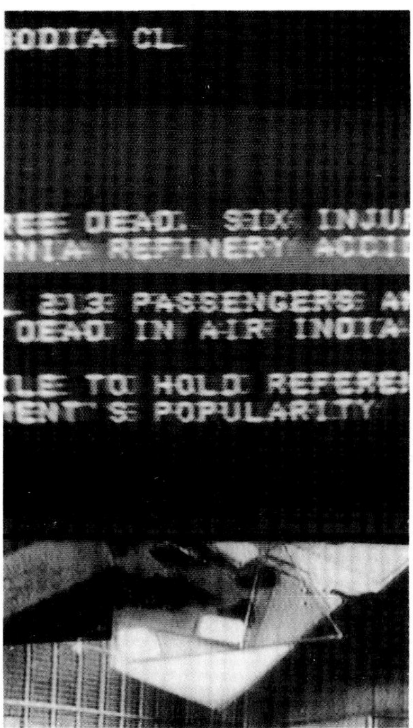

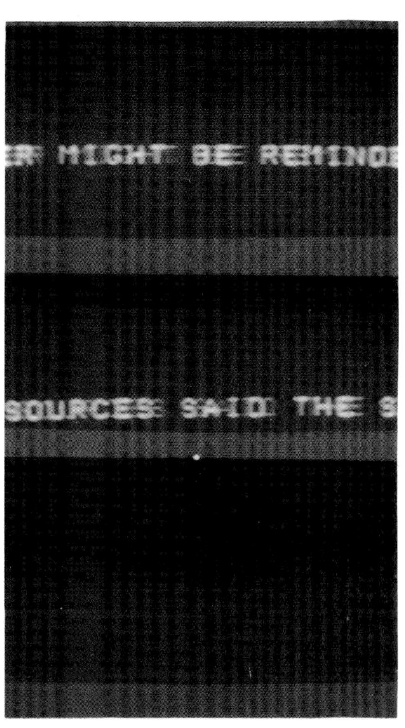

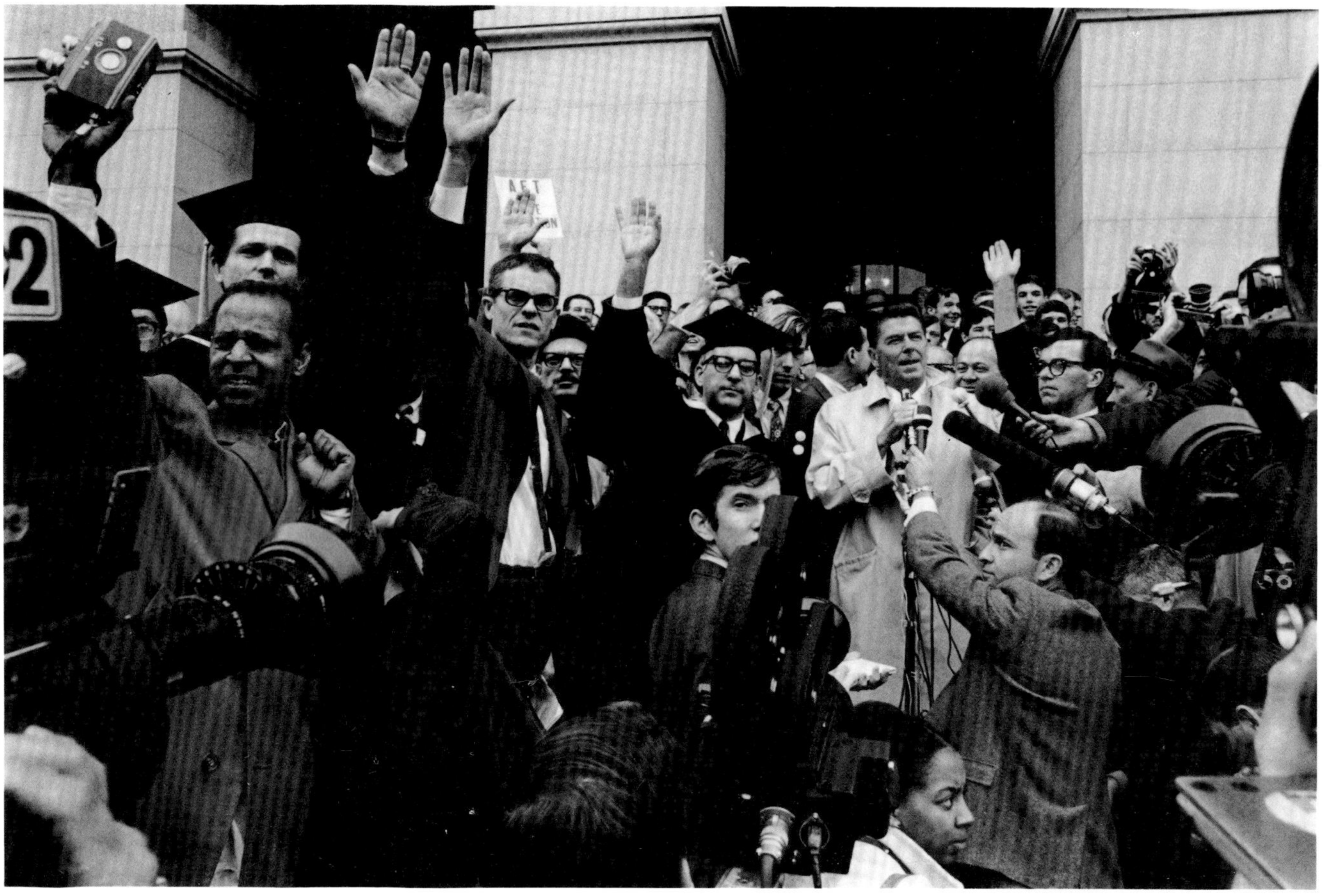

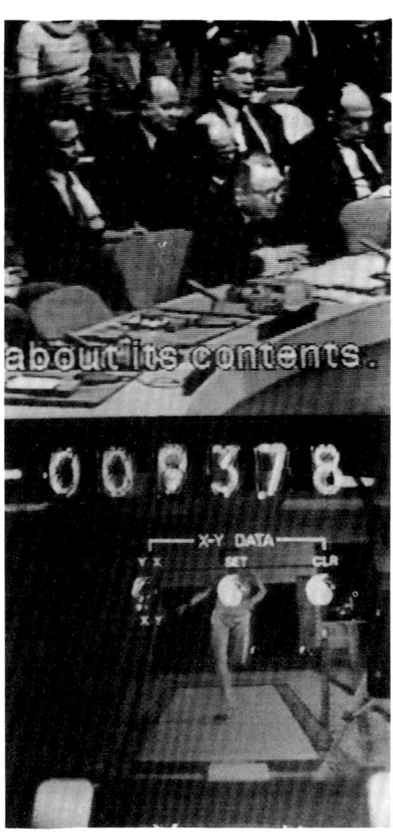

Ronald Reagan crashes student/AFT demonstration

2/11/67, Sacramento, Ca. 95814

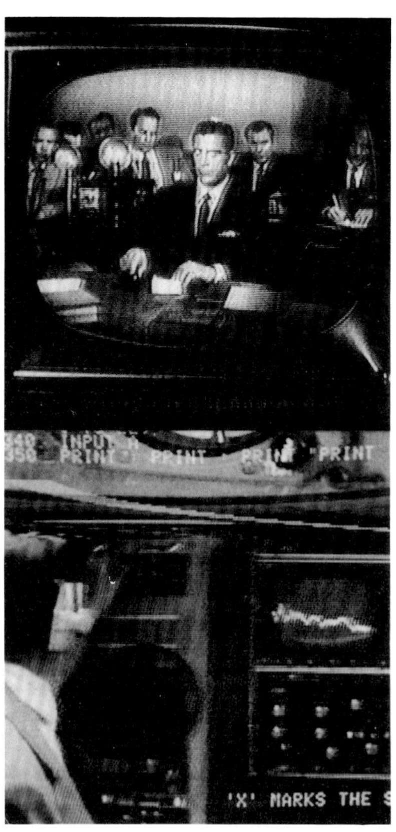

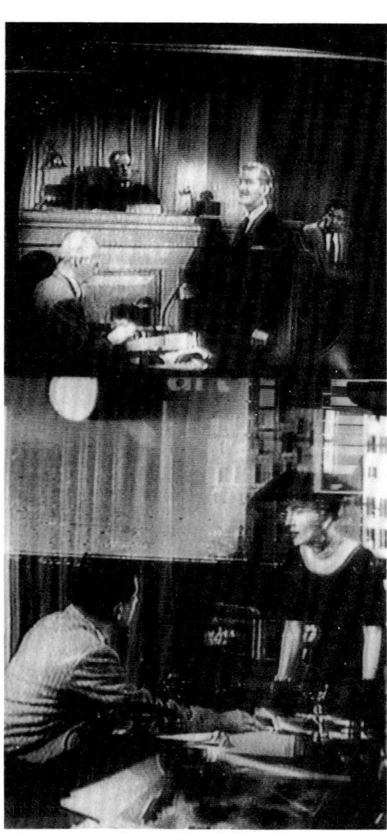

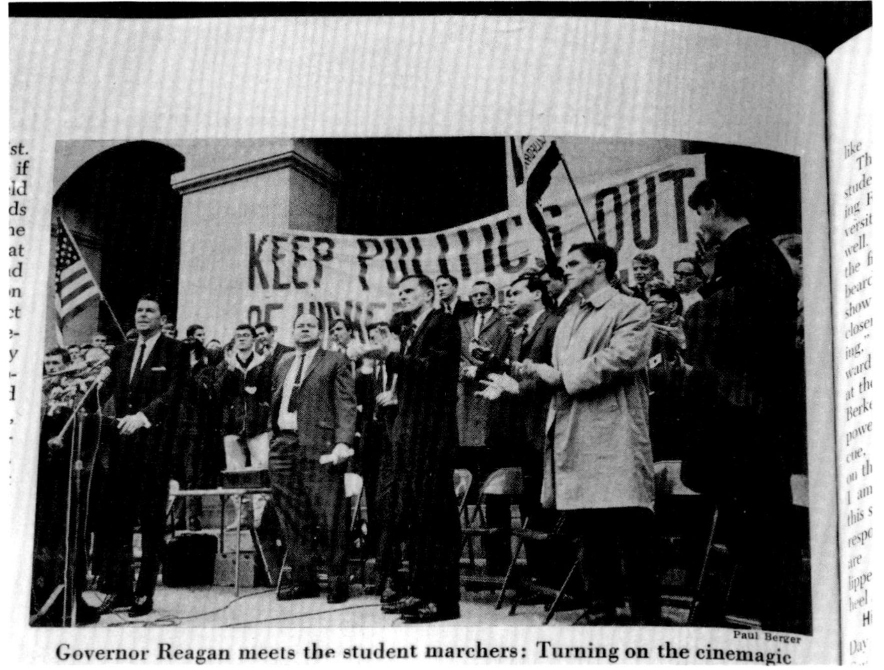

Governor Reagan meets the student marchers: Turning on the cinemagic

Newsweek, Feb. 20, 1967

The Newsweek photographer ran out of film and asked me for mine

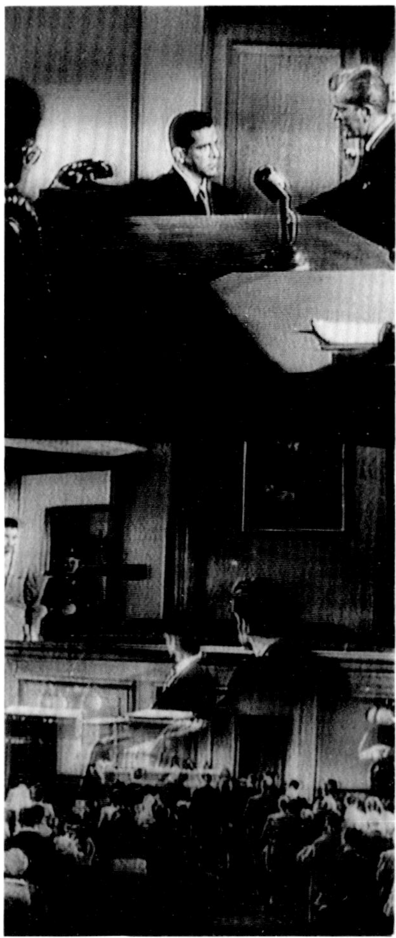

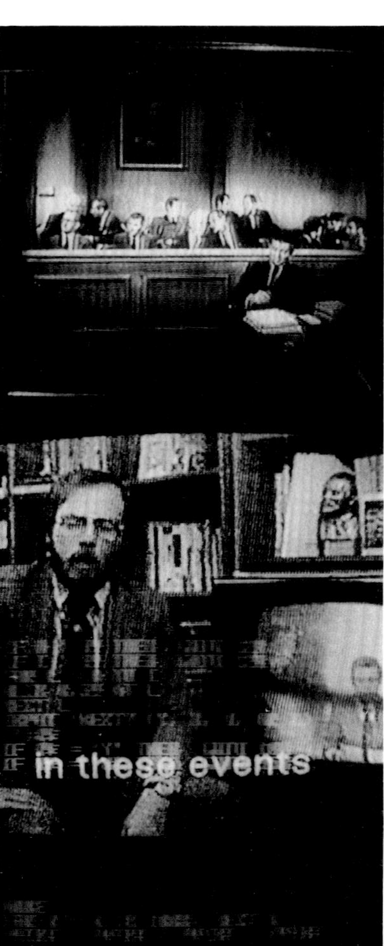

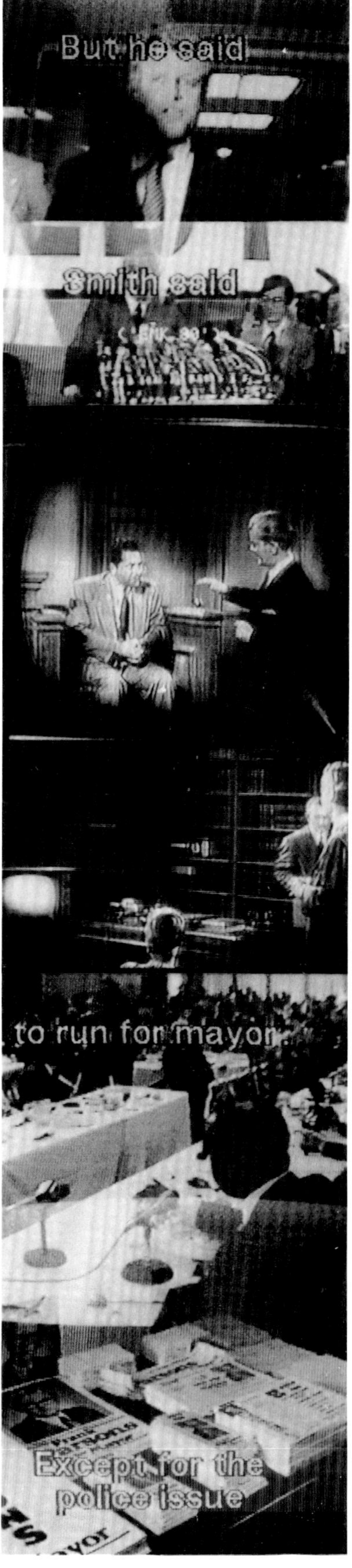

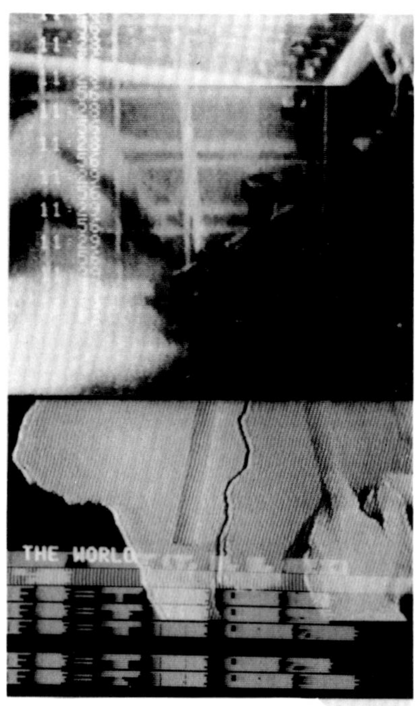

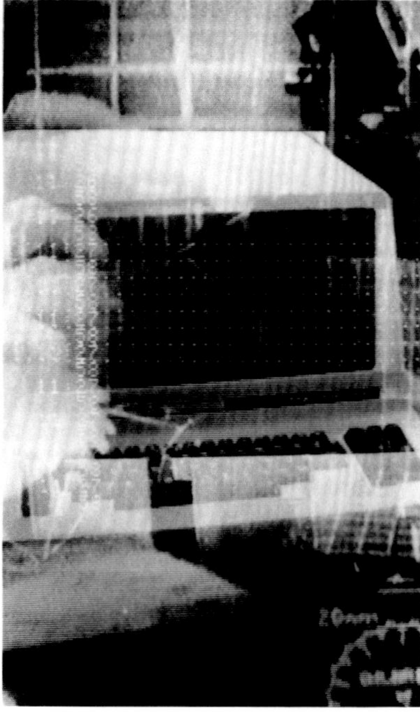

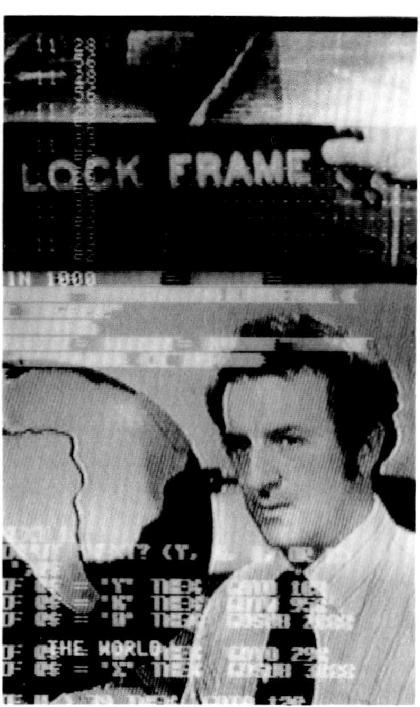

Television

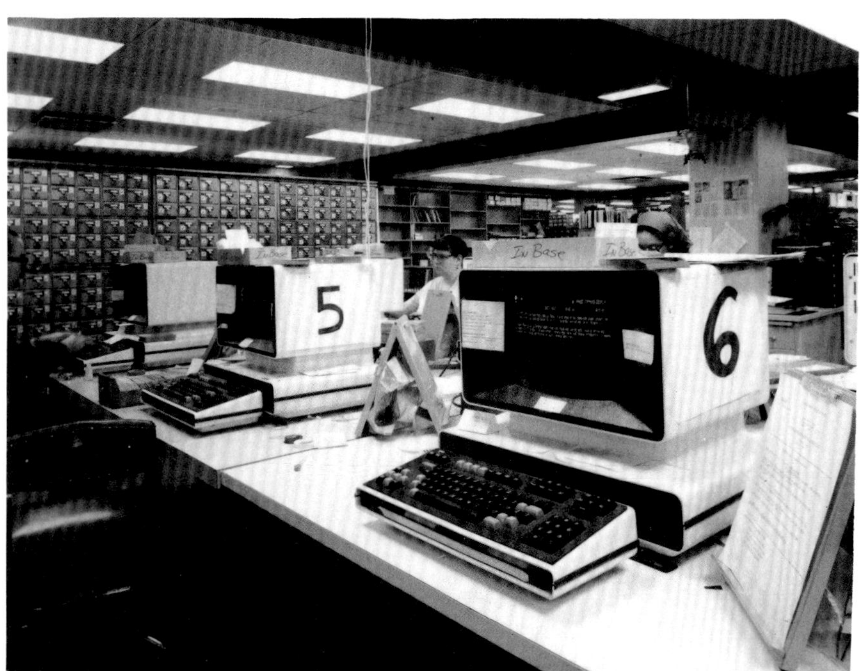

5:00 5 CRT ON THE JOB : TV AT HOME : GOTO WORK

IAT6108 JOB TFO89932,0303 ENDED, COMP CODE=ZERO CN (00)

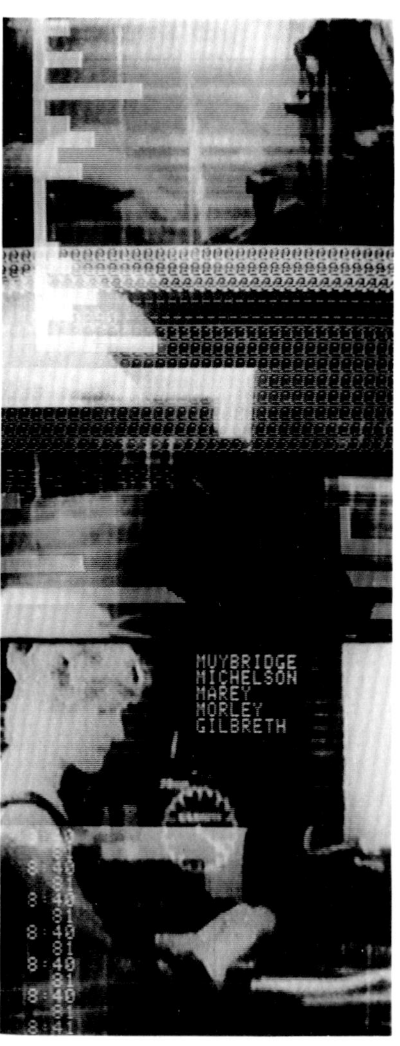

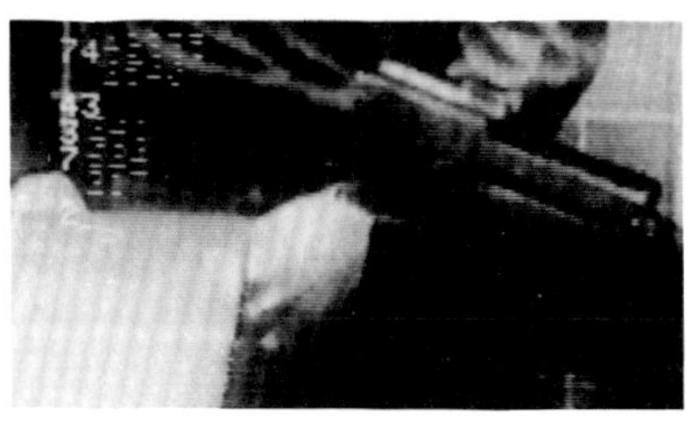

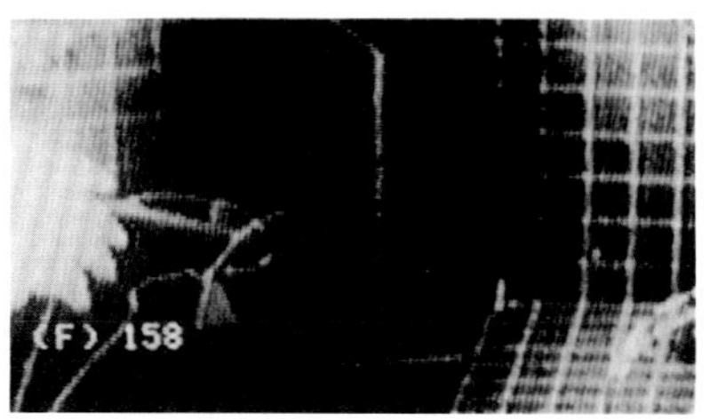

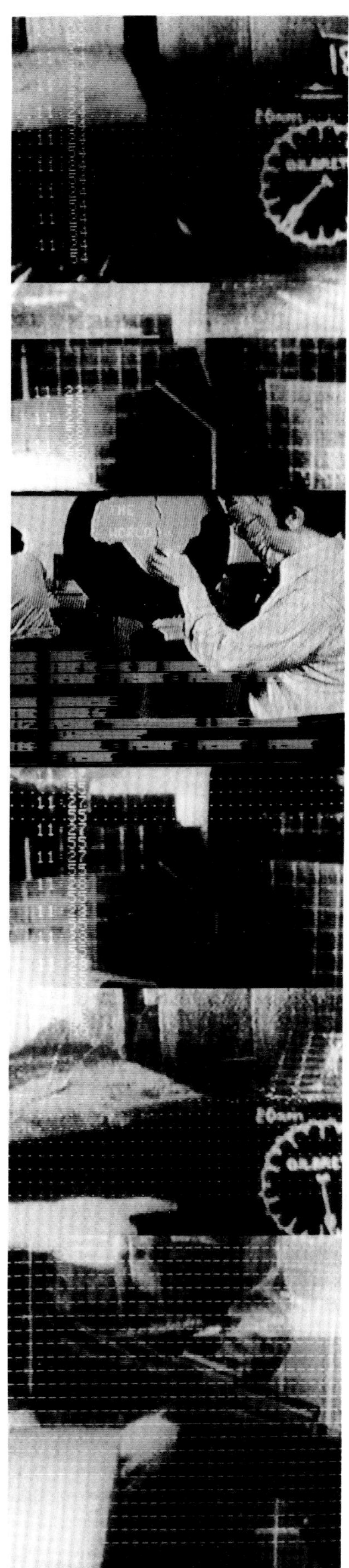

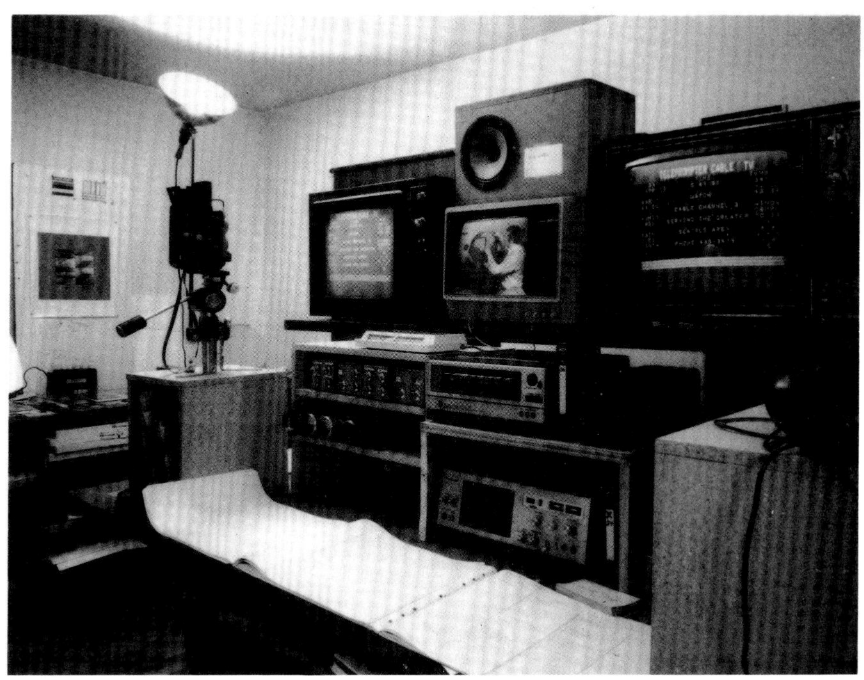

9:00 **9** MUYBRIDGE AND MAREY - SCIENCE FICTION

An alien scientist (Frank Gilbreth) turns M&M'S stop-motion loose on the world.

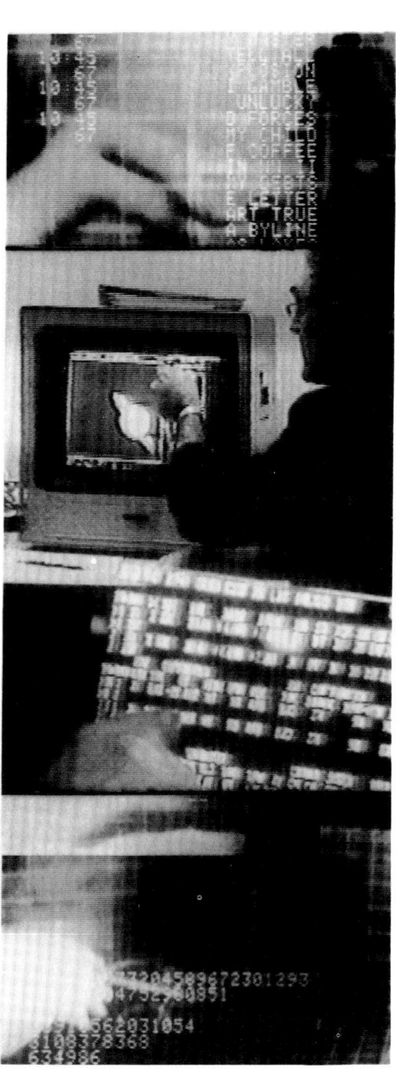

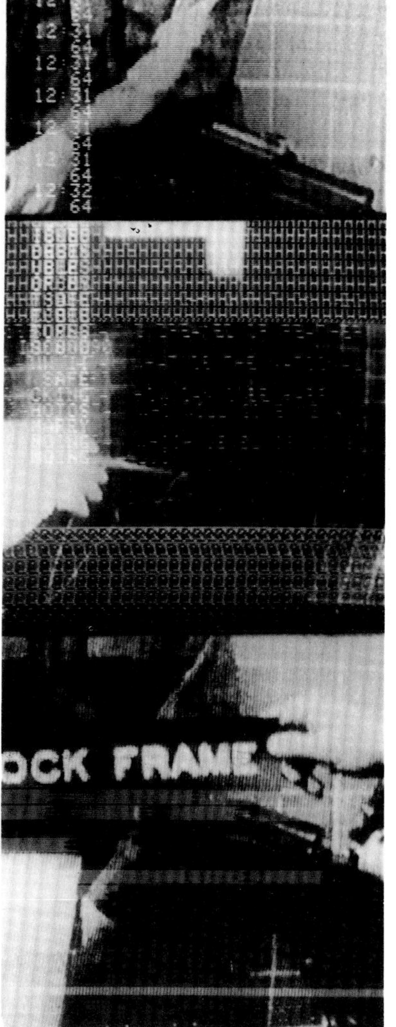

Display

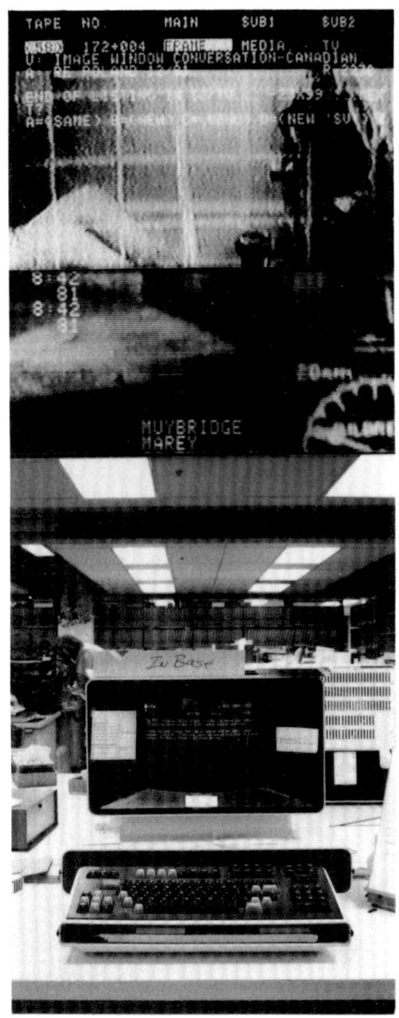

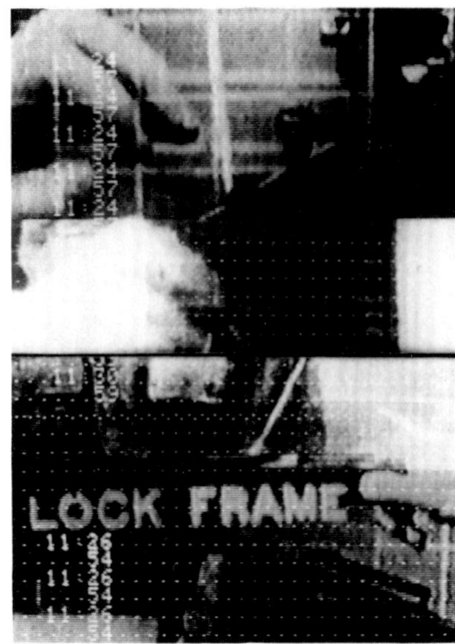

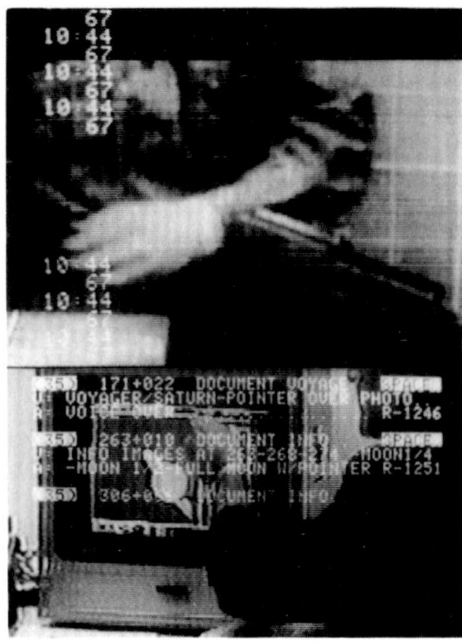

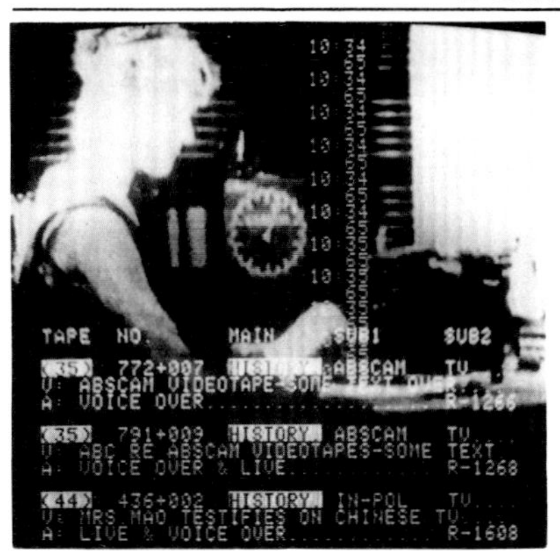

Television

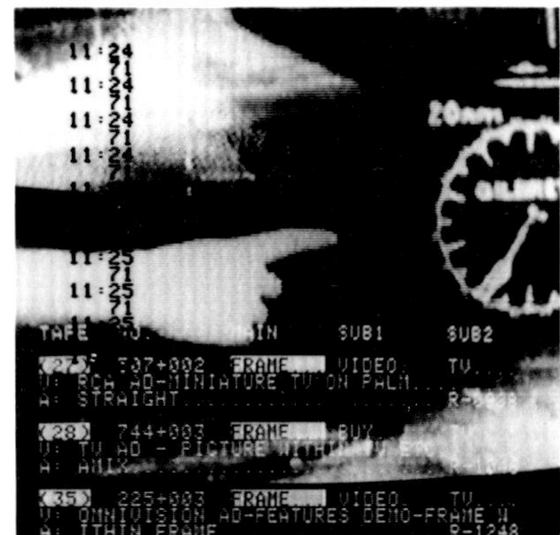

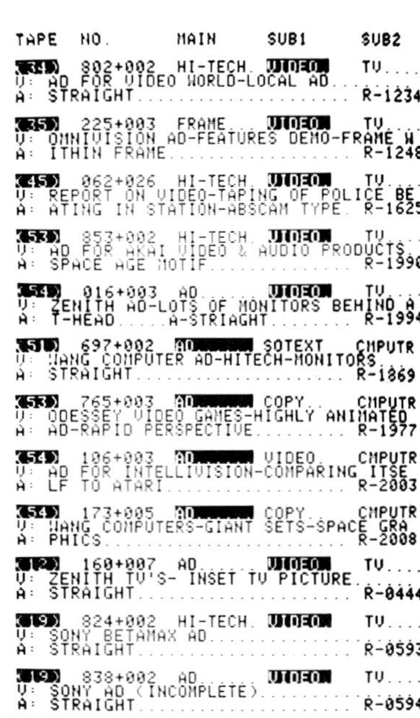

TELEVISION: Print D$"Open Television,L525": Print D$"Read Television,R"X: For L=1 to TV: Input Z$(L): Next: Print D$"Close Tele

A2 00 A0 02 88 B1 3E 4A 3E 00 BC 4A 3E 00 BC 99 00 BB E8 E0 56 90 ED A2 00 98 D0 E8 A2 55 BD 00 BC 29 3F 9D 00 CA 10 F5 60 38 86 27 8E 78 06

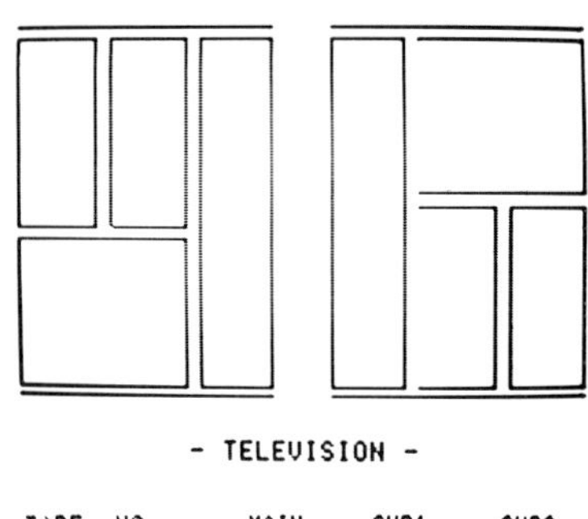

- TELEVISION -

```
TAPE  NO.       MAIN    SUB1    SUB2

(74)  569+002   NEWS....TEXT    CPTION
V: BAGNARIOL TRIAL - LESSER TEXT OVER
A: AMIX.............................R-0713

(22)  620+001   TITLE...TEXT    CPTION
V: END OF SHOW CREDITS TO 'WRITE ON'
A: AMIX.............................R-0754

(22)  677+001   TITLE...TEXT    CPTION
V: AIRLINE AD W/ CITIES OVER LANDING
A: STRAIGHT.........................R-0758

(23)  827+004   TITLE...TEXT    CPTION
V: MUSIC ALBUM AD-CRAWL OF SONGS
A: COUNTRY MUSIC....................R-0811

(48)  684+003   NEWS....TEXT    CPTION
V: ICBM'S-SPLIT SCREEN-W.HOUSE & TEXT
A: STRAIGHT.........................R-1039
```

```
TAPE  NO.       MAIN    SUB1    SUB2

(34)  802+002   HI-TECH VIDEO   TV....
V: AD FOR VIDEO WORLD-LOCAL AD
A: STRAIGHT.........................R-1234

(35)  225+003   FRAME   VIDEO   TV....
V: OMNIVISION AD-FEATURES DEMO-FRAME W
A: ITHIN FRAME......................R-1248

(45)  062+026   HI-TECH VIDEO   TV....
V: REPORT ON VIDEO-TAPING OF POLICE BE
A: ATING IN STATION-ABSCAM TYPE. R-1625

(53)  853+002   HI-TECH VIDEO   TV....
V: AD FOR AKAI VIDEO & AUDIO PRODUCTS
A: SPACE AGE MOTIF..................R-1990

(54)  016+003   AD      VIDEO   TV....
V: ZENITH AD-LOTS OF MONITORS BEHIND A
A: T-HEAD.....A-STRIAGHT............R-1994

(51)  697+002   AD      SOTEXT  CMPUTR
V: WANG COMPUTER AD-HITECH-MONITORS
A: STRAIGHT.........................R-1869

(53)  765+003   AD      COPY    CMPUTR
V: ODESSEY VIDEO GAMES-HIGHLY ANIMATED
A: AD-RAPID PERSPECTIVE.............R-1977

(54)  106+003   AD      VIDEO   CMPUTR
V: AD FOR INTELLIVISION-COMPARING ITSE
A: LF TO ATARI......................R-2003

(54)  173+005   AD      COPY    CMPUTR
V: WANG COMPUTERS-GIANT SETS-SPACE GRA
A: PHICS............................R-2008

(12)  160+007   AD      VIDEO   TV....
V: ZENITH TV'S- INSET TV PICTURE
A: STRAIGHT.........................R-0444

(19)  824+002   HI-TECH VIDEO   TV....
V: SONY BETAMAX AD
A: STRAIGHT.........................R-0593

(19)  838+002   AD      VIDEO   TV....
V: SONY AD (INCOMPLETE)
A: STRAIGHT.........................R-0594
```

```
(51)  697+002   AD      SOTEXT  CMPUTR
V: WANG COMPUTER AD-HITECH-MONITORS
A: STRAIGHT.........................R-1869

(58)  014+005   AD      SOTEXT  CMPUTR
V: AD FOR RADIO SHACK TSR-80 CMPUTR
A: STRAIGHT.........................R-2220
```

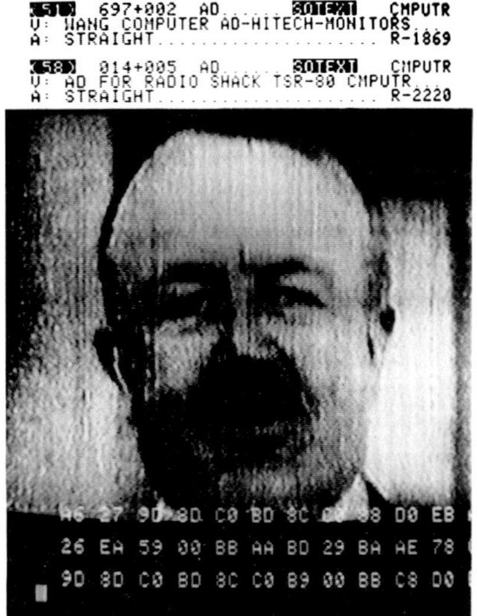

Frank B. Gilbreth - Mr. Digital

"The Robot woke up".

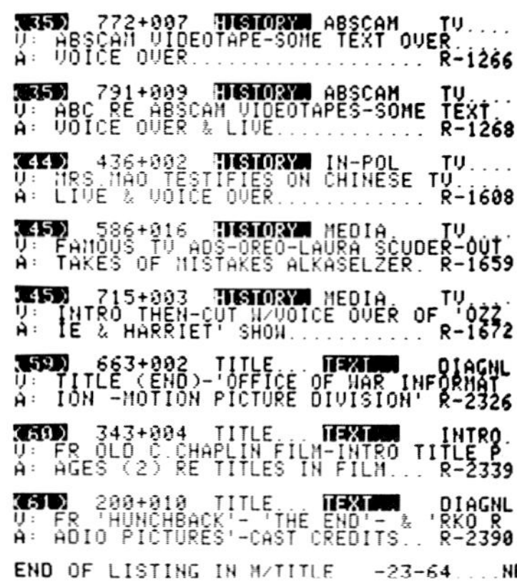

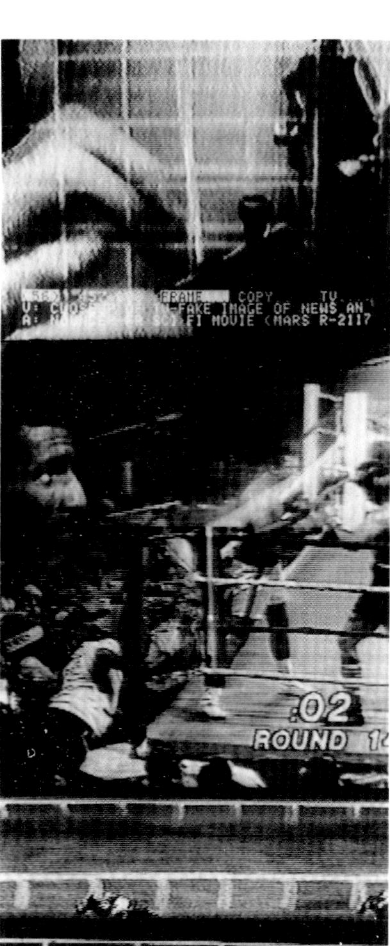


```
(35)  772+007  HISTORY  ABSCAM    TV....
V: ABSCAM VIDEOTAPE-SOME TEXT OVER.
A: VOICE OVER................... R-1266

(35)  791+009  HISTORY  ABSCAM    TV....
V: ABC RE ABSCAM VIDEOTAPES-SOME TEXT.
A: VOICE OVER & LIVE............ R-1268

(44)  436+002  HISTORY  IN-POL    TV....
V: MRS.MAO TESTIFIES ON CHINESE TV.
A: LIVE & VOICE OVER............ R-1608

(45)  586+016  HISTORY  MEDIA.    TV
V: FAMOUS TV ADS-OREO-LAURA SCUDER-OUT.
A: TAKES OF MISTAKES ALKASELZER. R-1659

(45)  715+003  HISTORY  MEDIA.    TV.
V: INTRO THEN-CUT W/VOICE OVER OF 'OZZ.
A: IE & HARRIET' SHOW........... R-1672

(59)  663+002  TITLE... TEXT      DIAGNL
V: TITLE (END)-'OFFICE OF WAR INFORMAT
A: ION -MOTION PICTURE DIVISION' R-2326

(60)  343+004  TITLE... TEXT      INTRO.
V: FR OLD C.CHAPLIN FILM-INTRO TITLE P.
A: AGES (2) RE TITLES IN FILM... R-2339

(61)  200+010  TITLE... TEXT      DIAGNL
V: FR 'HUNCHBACK'- 'THE END'- & 'RKO R
A: ADIO PICTURES'-CAST CREDITS.. R-2390

END OF LISTING IN M/TITLE   -23-64 ...NE
```

```
(03)  197+016  SPORTS  BOXING   DISPLY
V: FIRST ALI/SPINKS FIGHT.......
A: ALI VOICE OVER............... R-0074

(12)  176+012  SPORTS  BOXING   GAME..
V: MIX OF BOXING/WRESTLING......
A: STRAIGHT..................... R-0446

(12)  196+010  SPORTS  BOXING   DISPLY
V: MIX - BOXING & WRESTLING.....
A: STRAIGHT..................... R-0448

(12)  688+005  SPORTS  BOXING   DIAGNL
V: BOXING/KARATE - LAST 21 SECS.
A: STRAIGHT..................... R-0723

(12)  364+016  SPORTS  BOXING   MOVIE.
V: TRIUMPH MATCH - 'RAGING BULL'
A: STRAIGHT..................... R-0834

(03)  203+007  SPORTS  HORSE    DISPLY
V: HORSE RACE (B&W TRANS FROM CTOP)
A: STRAIGHT..................... R-0075

(12)  132+013  SPORTS  HORSE    CPTION
V: INTRO TO HORSERACE-SUBTITLES OFEACH
A: VOICE OVER................... R-0441

(12)  191+005  SPORTS  HORSE    DISPLY
V: HORSE RACE - LAST PART.......
A: STRAIGHT..................... R-0447
```

```
(12)  524+006  HI-TECH  VIDEO    CMPUTR
V: COMPUTER STOREFRONT ** CAMERA **
A: AMBIANT...................... R-0536

(21)  826+002  HI-TECH  VIDEO    CMPUTR
V: LANIER AD WORD PROCESSING (CARTOON)
A: STRAIGHT..................... R-0733

(39)  232+002  AD       VIDEO    CMPUTR
V: AD FOR ATARI VIDEO-GAME (INTERUPTED
A: BY APPLE DISPLAY............. R-1451

(45)  850+005  SPORTS   BOXING   MOVIE
V: 'REQUIEM FOR HEAVYWEIGHT'-WITH CASS
A: IUS CLAY-OLD B&W  A-STRAIGHT R-0909

(43)  663+044  SPORTS   BOXING   ALI
V: FR ALI/SPINKS 2/78 FIGHT-ROUND 10-
A: 15-INTERUPTED. A-VOICE OVER R-1574

(44)  317+022  SPORTS   BOXING   ALI...
V: LAST 2MIN OF 2ND ALI/SPINKS FIGHT
A: ALI WINS. A-VOICE OVER... R-1603

(58)  026+029  SPORTS   BOXING   RELIGN
V: G.FOREMAN EX-BOXER NOW CHRISTIAN MI
A: NISTER-BOXING & PREACHING. R-2222

END OF LISTING IN M/SPORTS -22-86 ...NE
XT?
A=(SAME) B=(NEW) C=(MENU) D=(NEW 'SV')
```

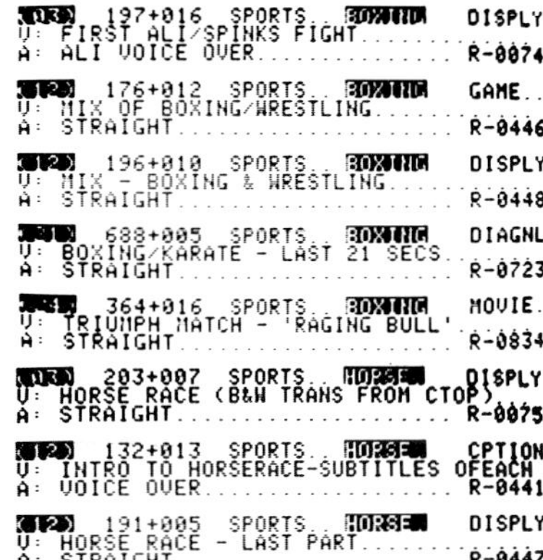

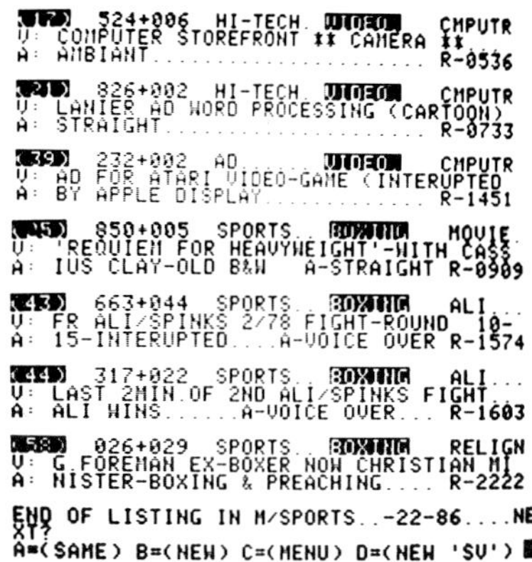

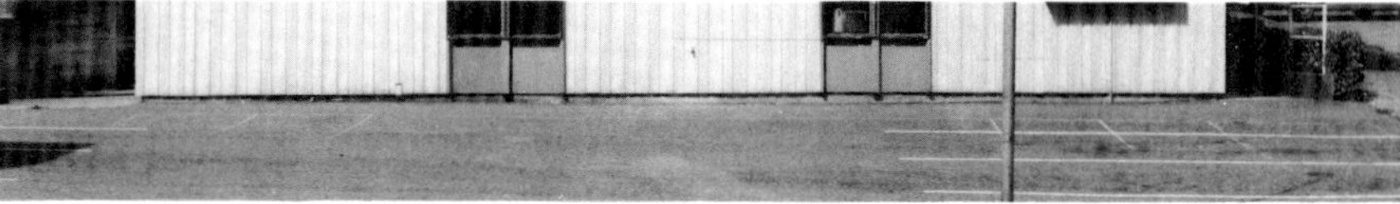

I pledge allegiance, to the flag, of the United States of America. And to the Republic,

God of God, Light of Light, very God of very God, begotten, not made, being of one substance

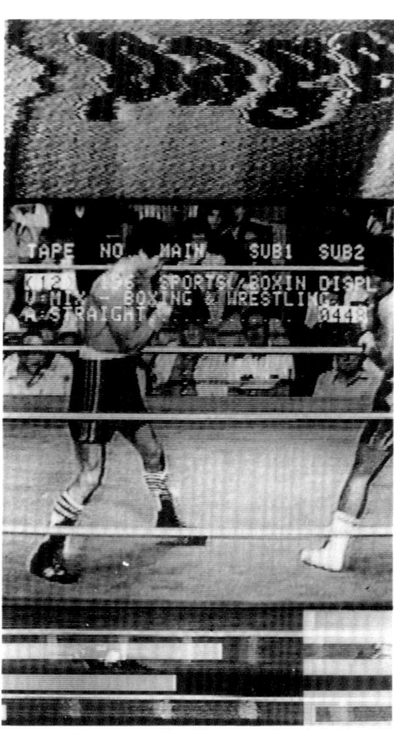

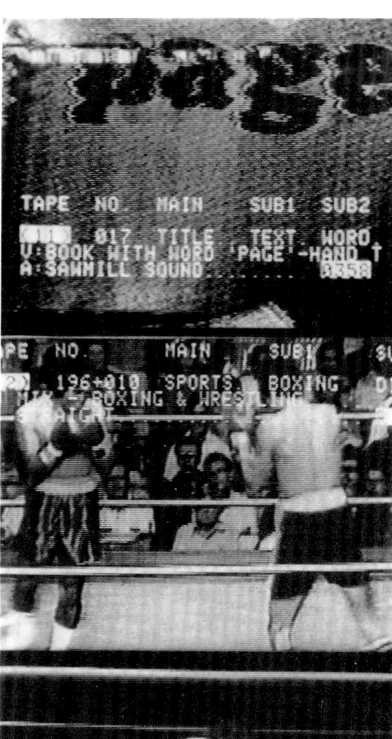

RELIGION: Print D$"Open Religion,L666": Print D$"Read Religion,R"X: For L= 1 to RA: Input Z$(L): Next: Print D$"Close Religion": Re

88 B1 3E 4A 3E 00 BC 4A 3E 00 BC 99 00 BB E8 E0 56 90 ED A2 00 98 D0 E8 A2 55 BD 00 BC 29 EB 20 B8 B8 A9 FF 20 B8 B8 BD 8E C0 BD 8C

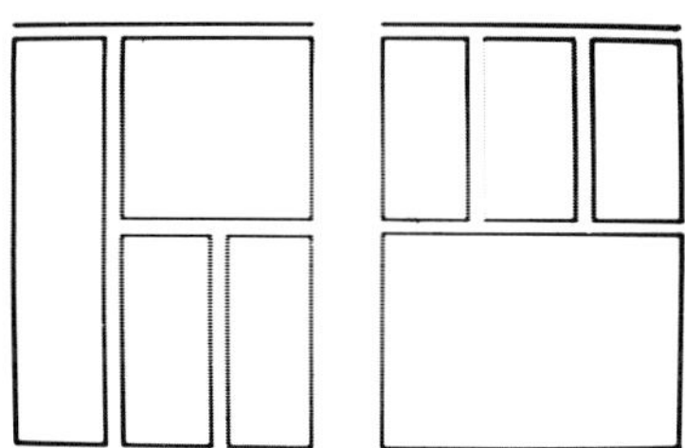

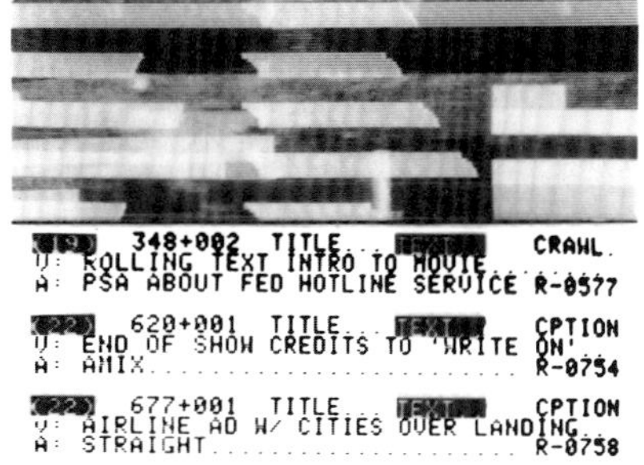

```
(19)  348+002  TITLE...          CRAWL.
V: ROLLING TEXT INTRO TO MOVIE
A: PSA ABOUT FED HOTLINE SERVICE R-0577

(12)  620+001  TITLE...          CPTION
V: END OF SHOW CREDITS TO 'WRITE ON'
A: AMIX........................ R-0754

(12)  671+001  TITLE...          CPTION
V: AIRLINE AD W/ CITIES OVER LANDING
A: STRAIGHT.................... R-0758
```

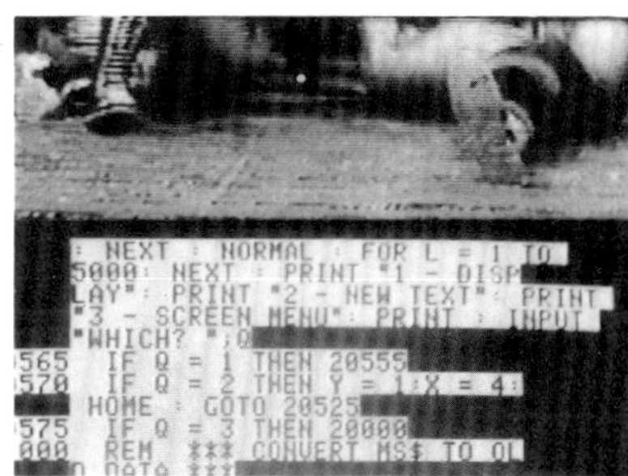

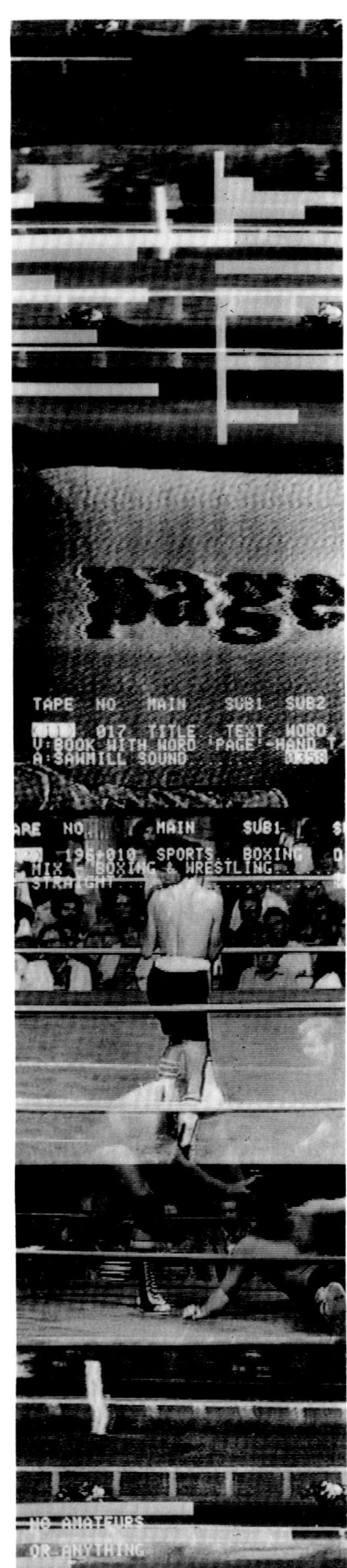

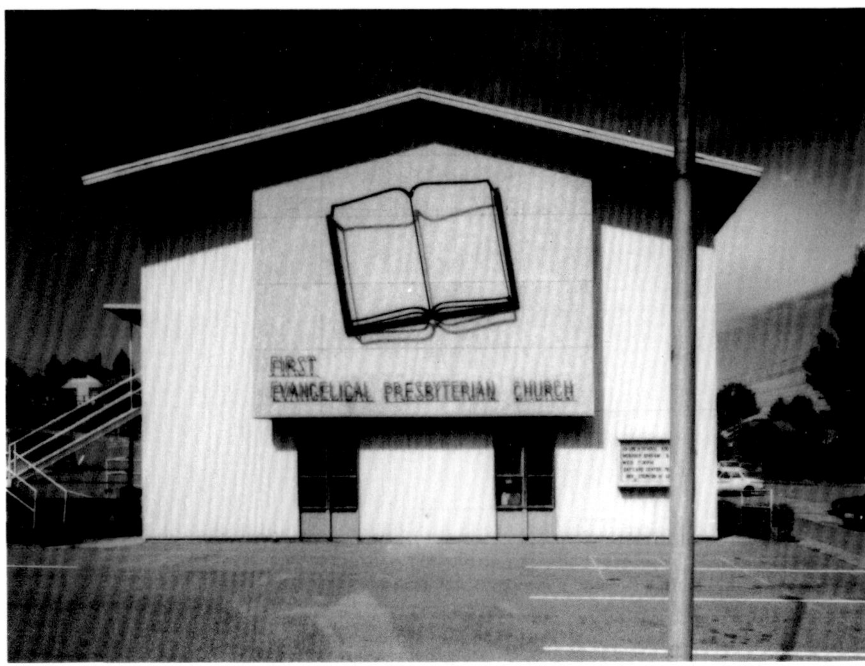

First Church of the Transparent Book in Seattle, Washington

Is the United States the city of Babylon referred to in Revelation 18?

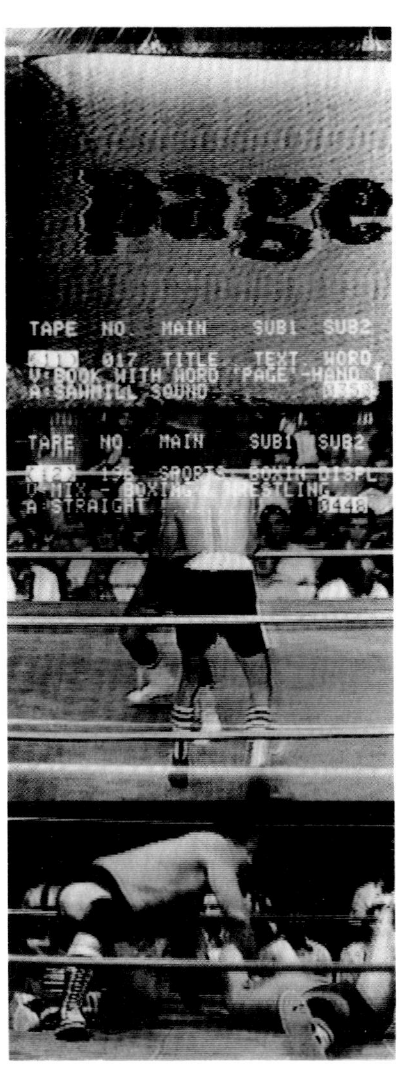

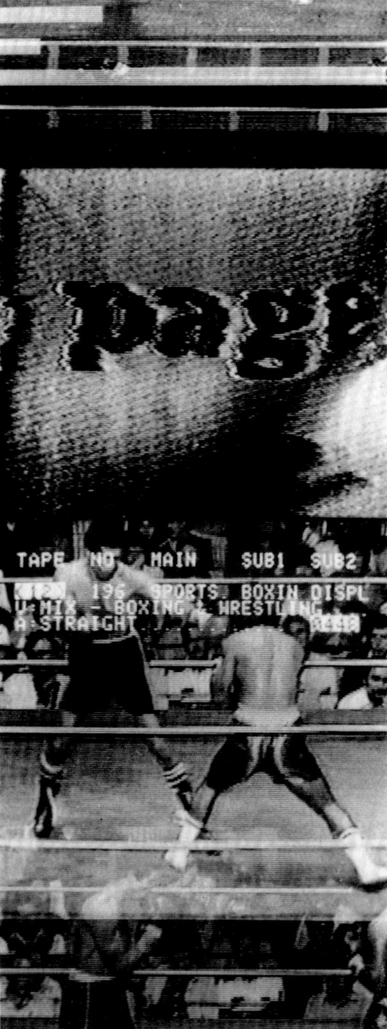

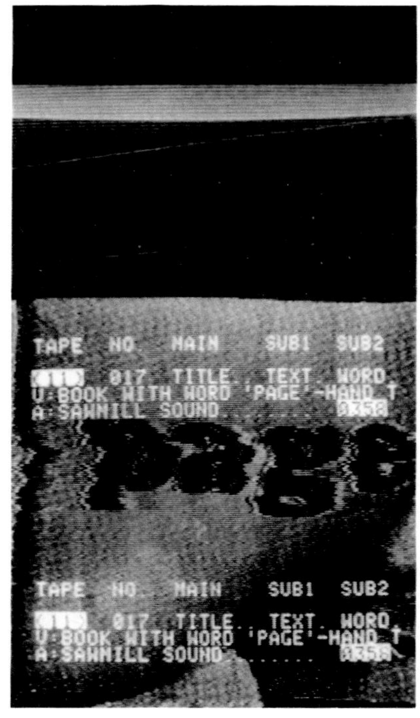

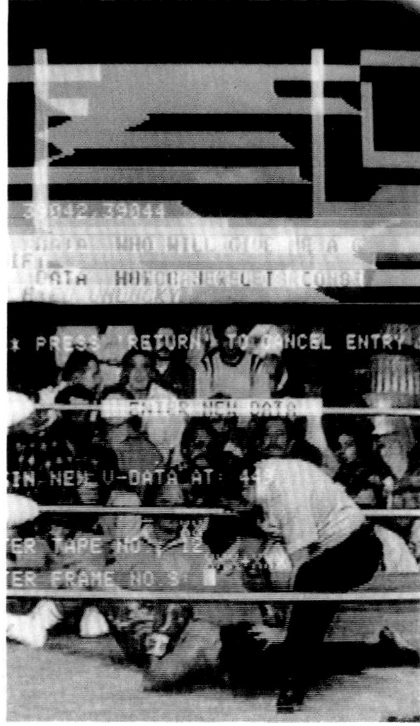

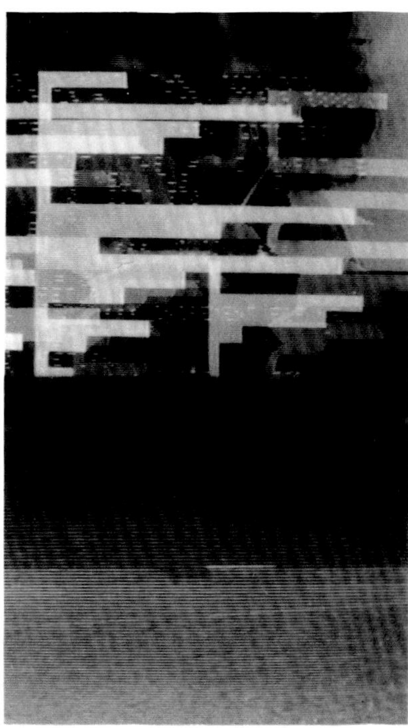

Religion

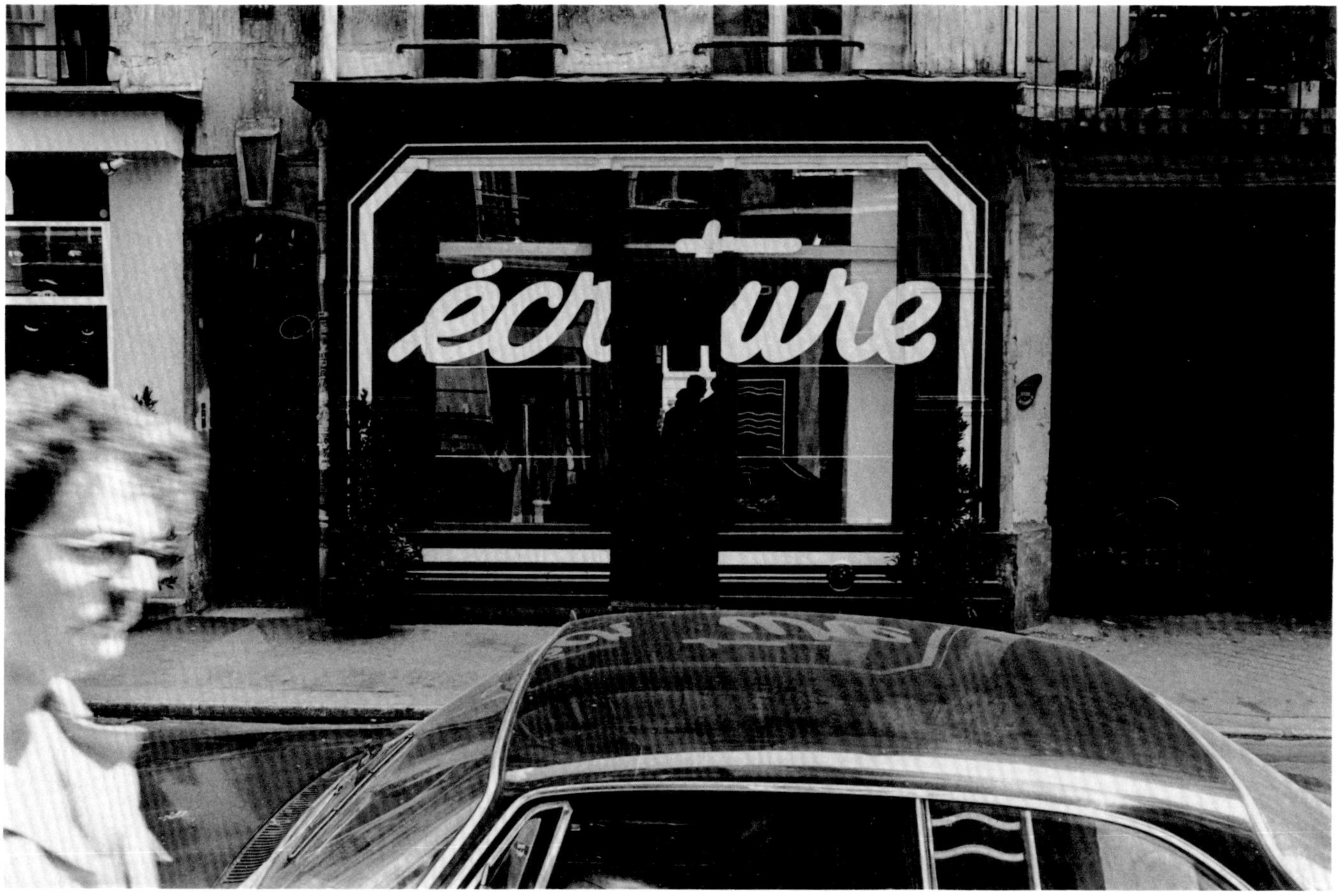

Temple of Reason, in Paris, France, 1976

Disguised as stationery stores, these metaphysical temples and their flocks draw no distinction between a sheet of paper and a "page".

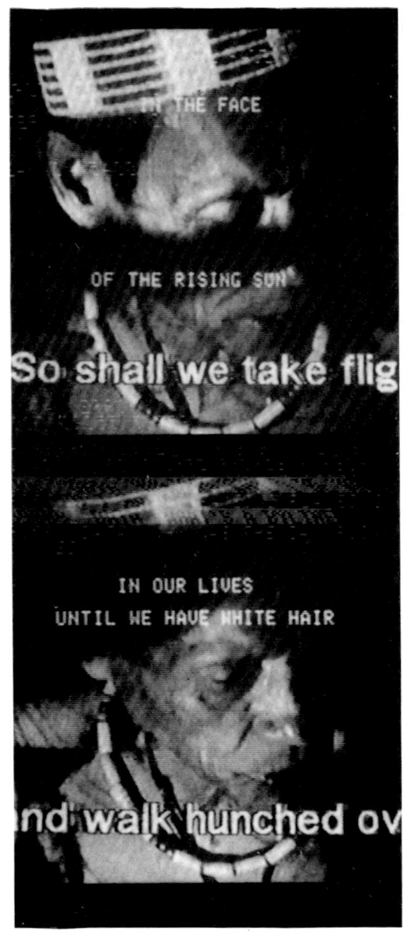

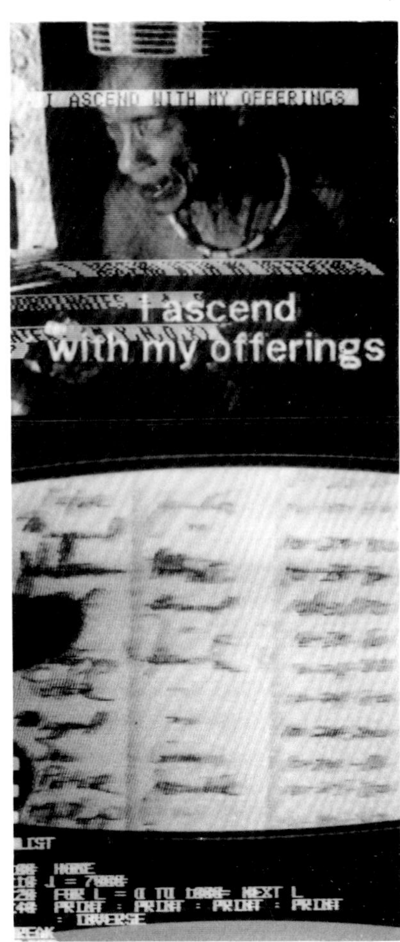

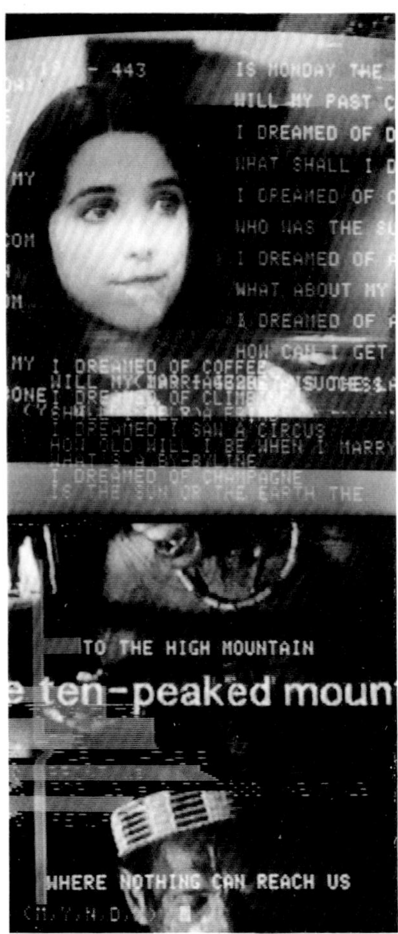

Show Business

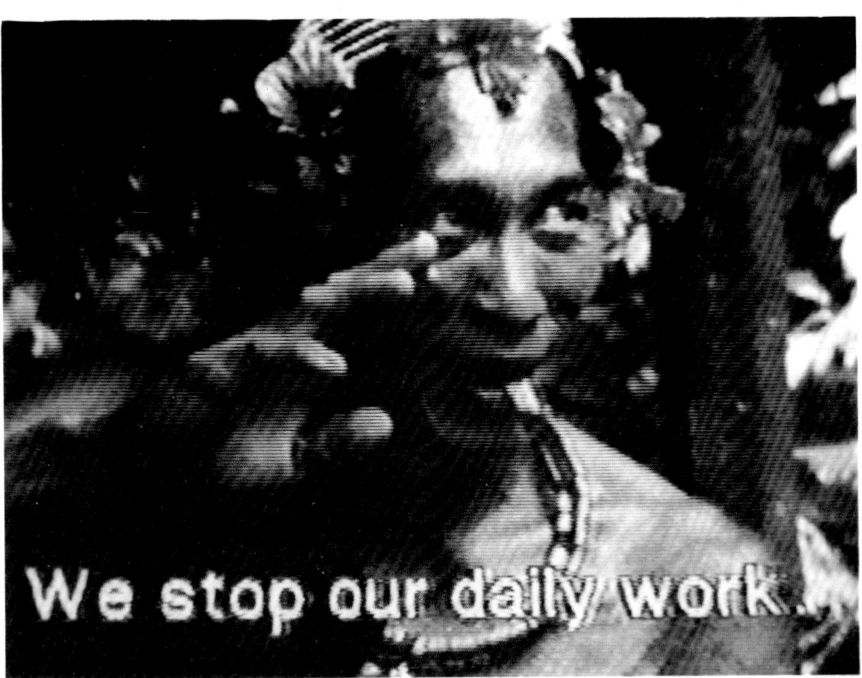

Sakuddei tribesman offers his now-recorded prayer: I ascend with my offerings / to

the high mountain / the ten-peaked mountain / where nothing can reach us / evil can't reach

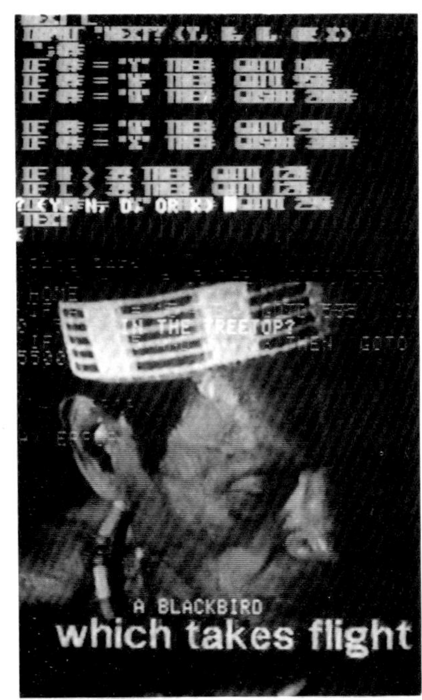

us / What crowns its top? / a Begeget

tree / leaves waving happily / so our hearts

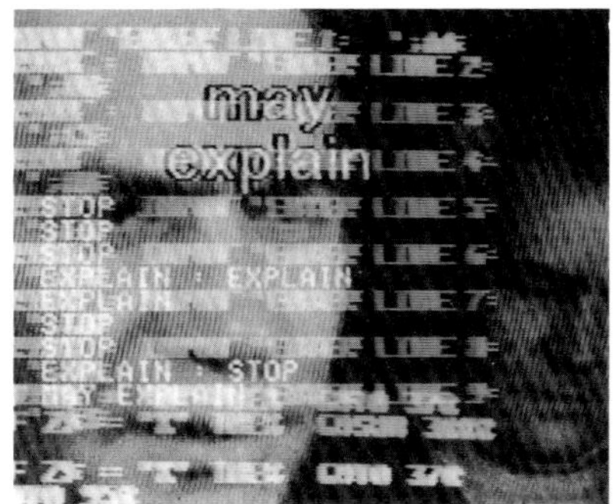

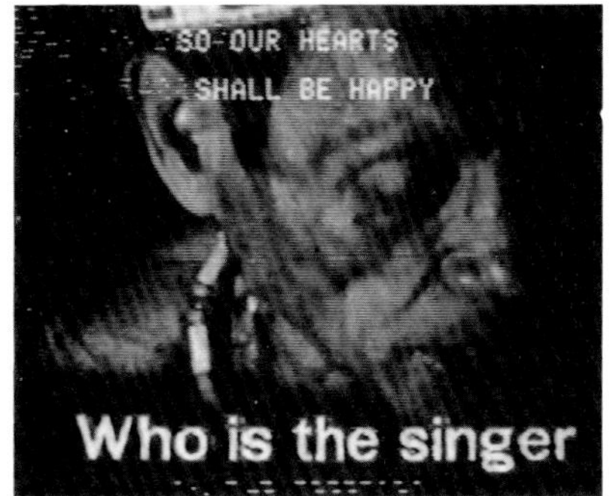

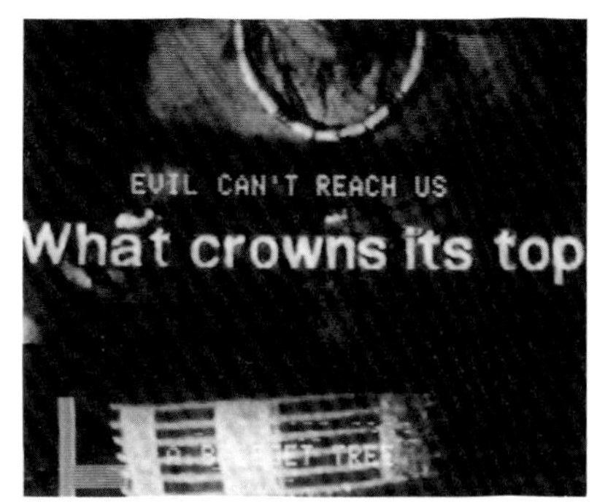

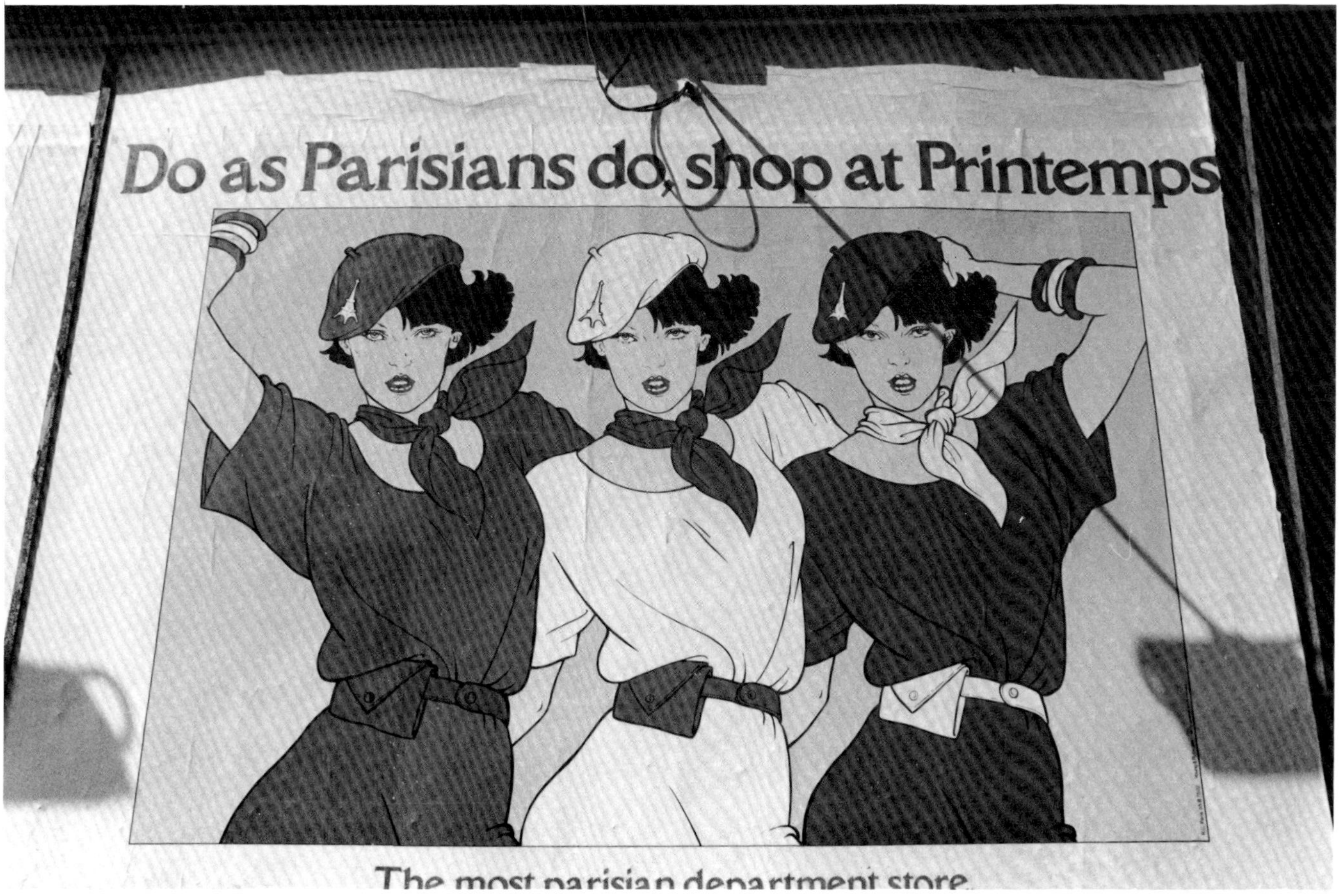

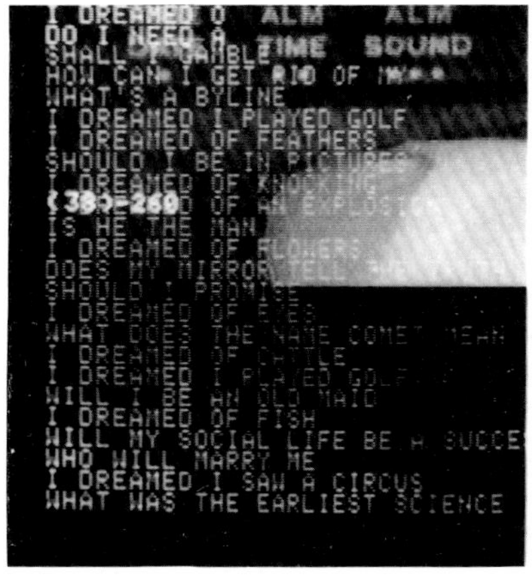

too / shall be happy / Who is the singer/ in the treetop? / A blackbird / which takes flight in the face of the rising sun

/ so shall we take flight / in our lives / until we have white hair / and walk hunched over.

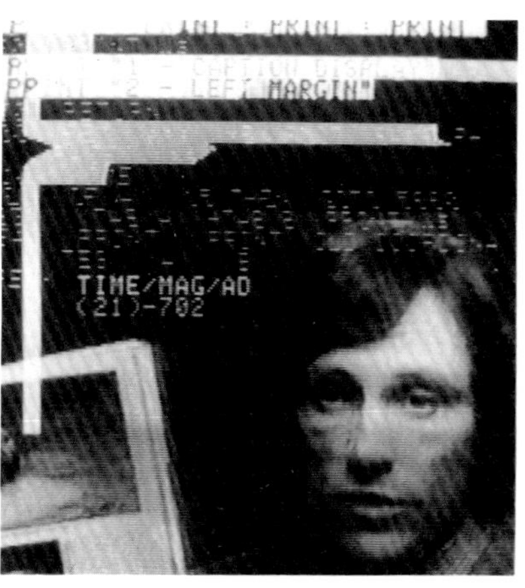

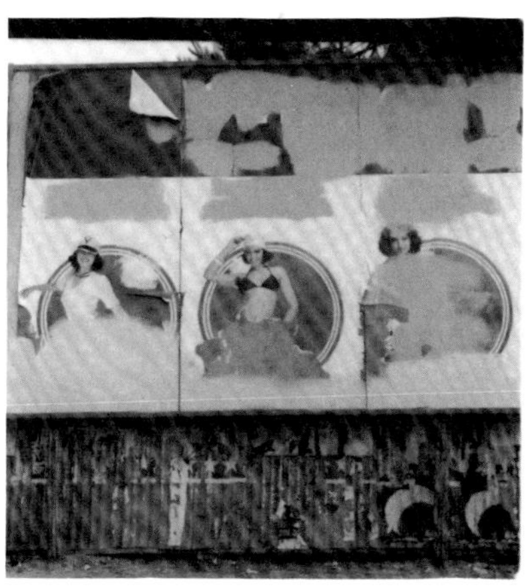

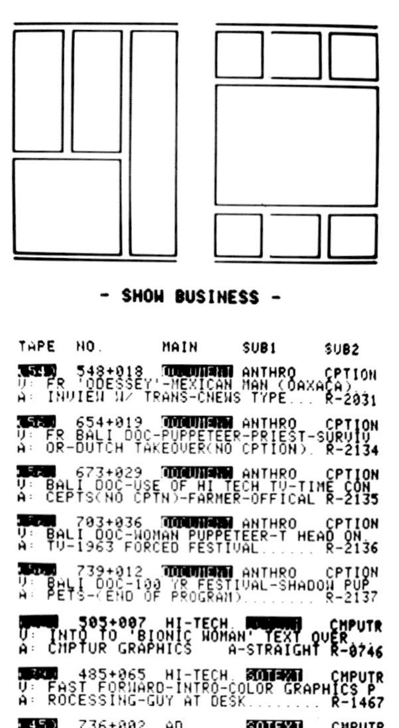

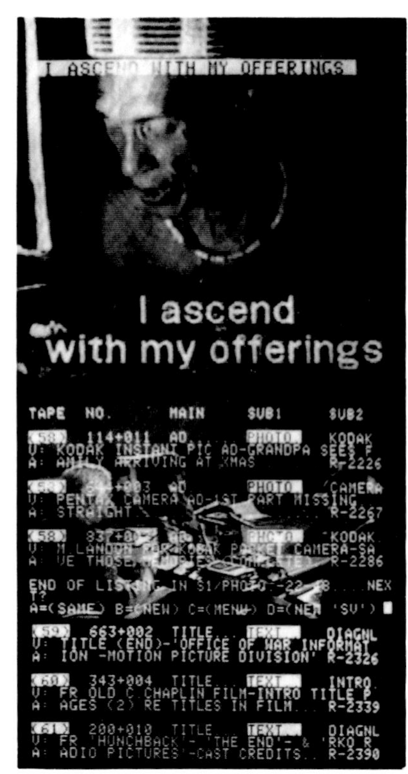

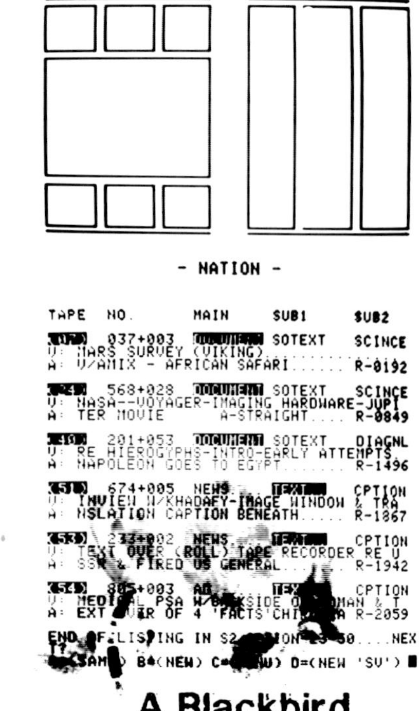

Display

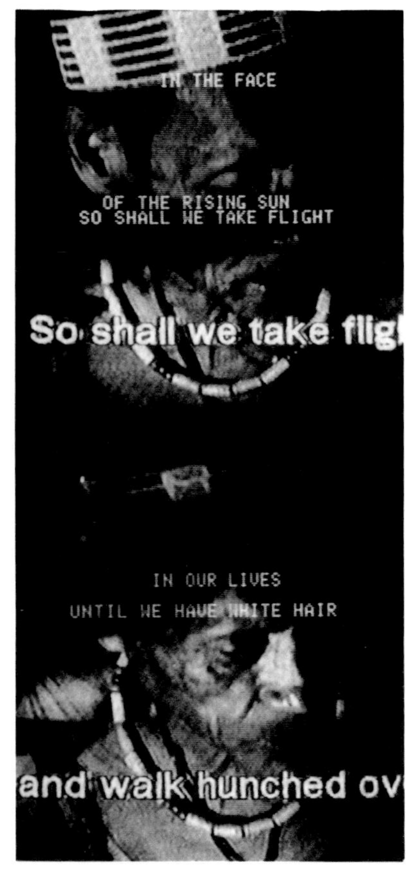

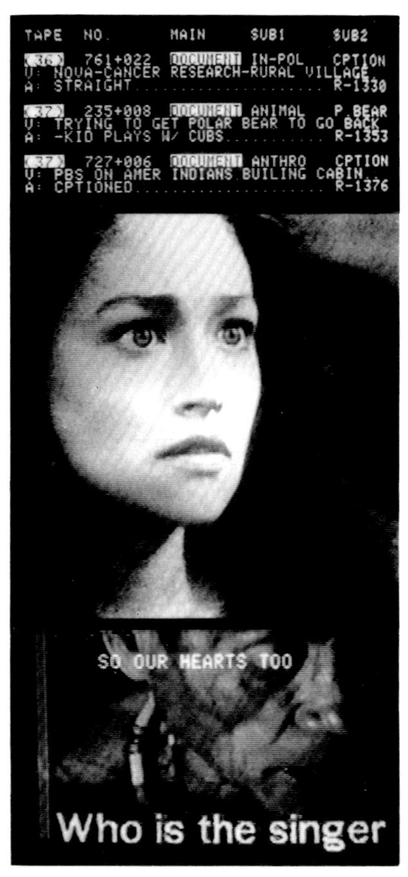

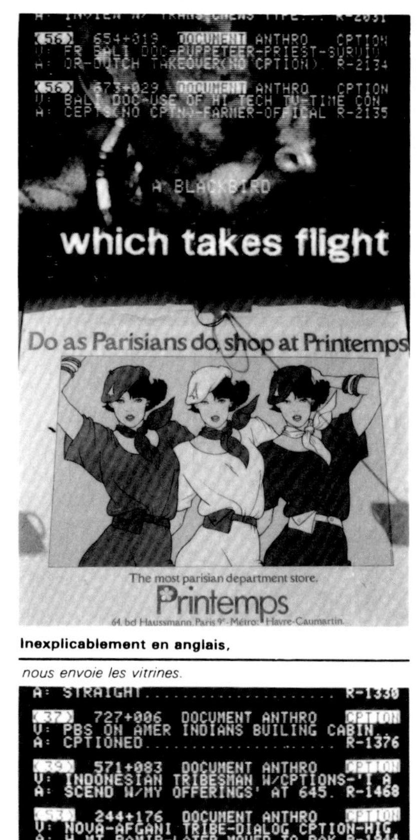

SHOW BUSINESS: Print D$"Open Showbiz,L70": Print D$"Read Showbiz,R"X: For L=1 to CA: Input Z$(L): Next: Print D$"Close Sh

A6 27 9D 8D C0 BD 8C C0 88 D0 EB A5 26 EA 59 00 BB AA BD 29 BA AE 78 06 9D 8D C0 BD 8C C0 B9 00 BB C8 D0 EA BB C8 D0 EA AA BD 29 BA

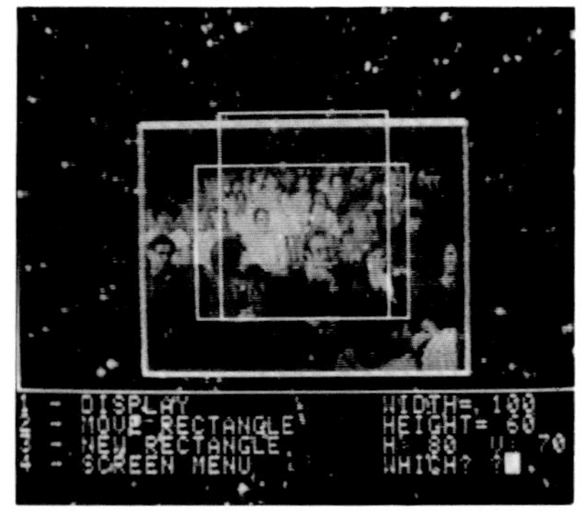

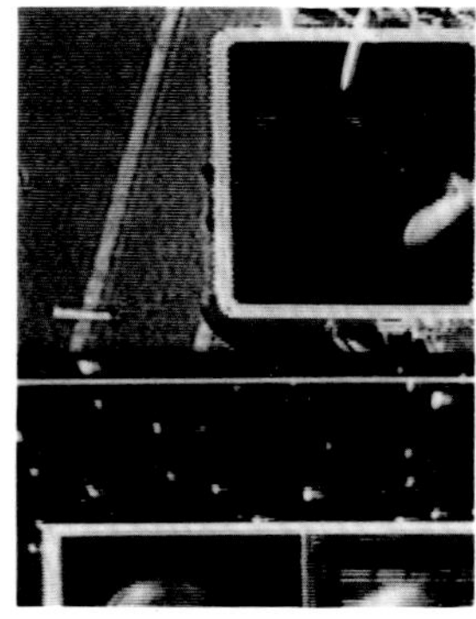

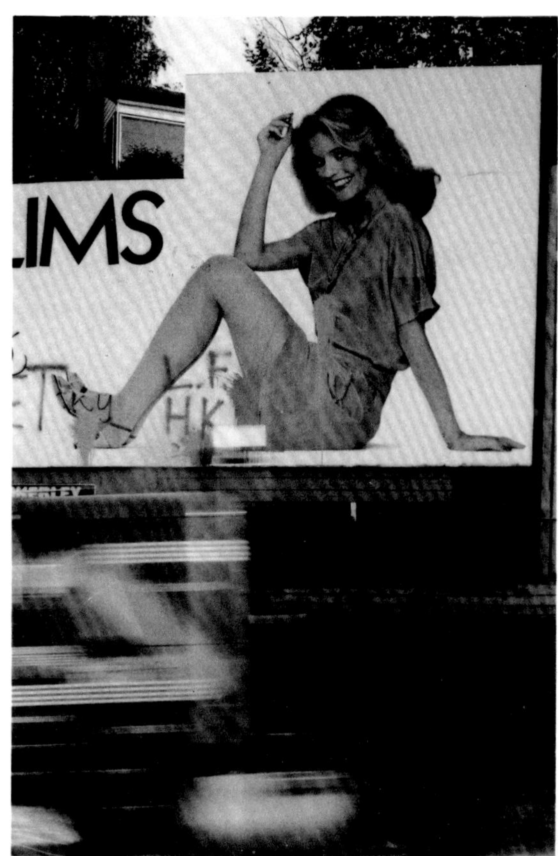

Nation

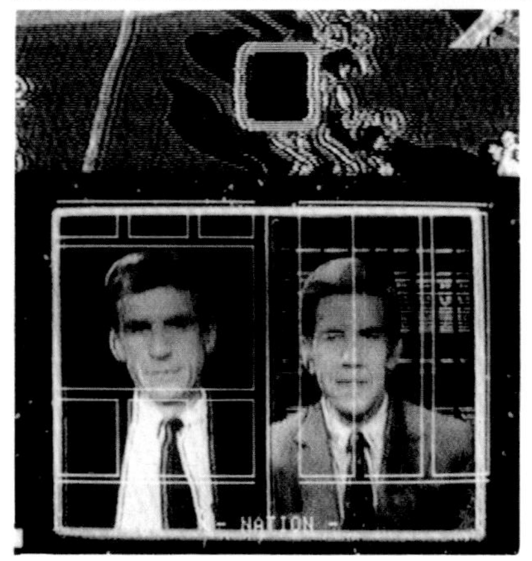

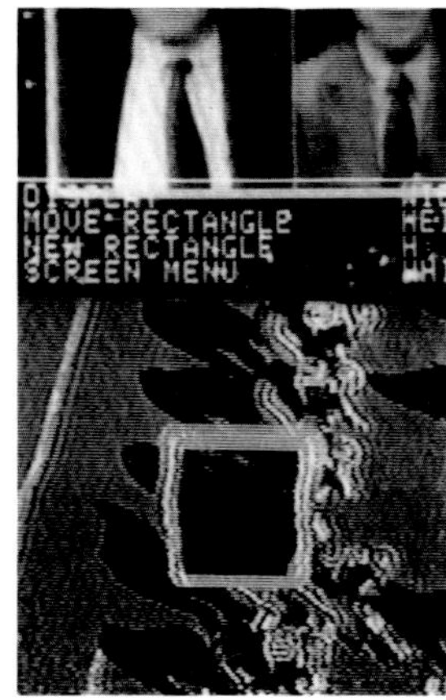

NATION: Print D$"Open Nation,L50": Print D$"Read Nation,R"X: For L=1 to US: Input Z$(L): Next: Print D$"Close Nation": Return

EB 20 B8 B8 A9 FF 20 B8 B8 BD 8E C0 BD 8C C0 60 18 48 68 9D 8D C0 1D 8C C0 60 A0 00 A2 56 CA 30 FB B9 00 BB 5E B9 00 BB 5E 00 BC 2A 5E 00

708+001 FRAME COPY NITELI
FROM ABC NIGHTLINE NEWS-BIG SCREEN
INVIEW W/OTHER REPORTER...... R-1965

781+002 FRAME F-BALL PROMO
PROMO FOR SPORTS COVERAGE-NITELINE
TYPE IMAGE WINDOW............ R-1981

166+004 FRAME NEWS DIAGNL
NITELINE INTRO IMAGE WINDOW-RE SCHO
OLS CLOSING.................. R-2006

220+008 FRAME NEWS DIAGNL
BUSINESS SHOW-LARGE SCREEN BIT
INVIEW...................... R-2014

657+003 FRAME NEWS DIAGNL
INTRO TO NIGHTLINE NEWS-IMAGE WINDO
W-SPACE SHUTTLE PREP-11/81... R-2039

801+013 FRAME NEWS DIAGNL
MCNIEL/LEHRER- BIG TV INVIEW
STRAIGHT.................... R-1091

275+004 FRAME NEWS DIAGNL
MCNEIL/LEHRER - GIANT SCREEN
STRAIGHT.................... R-1455

787+004 FRAME NEWS LOCAL
LOCAL STATION MCNIEL/LEHRER BIG SCR
EEN IMITATION......A-STRAIGHT R-1516

373+003 FRAME NEWS NITELI
INTRO TO NITELINE - WINDOW INSETS
VOICE OVER.................. R-1841

568+002 FRAME NEWS DIAGNL
INTRO WINDOW TO NITELINE NEWS
STRAIGHT.................... R-1855

303+005 FRAME F-BALL DIAGNL
WATCHING F-BALL MOVIES-N.DALLAS 40
STRAIGHT.................... R-1132

604+004 FRAME SOTEXT NEWS
INTRO TO NITELINE NEWS W/REAGAN & C
ARTER DEBATE................ R-1157

225+003 FRAME VIDEO TV
OMNIVISION AD-FEATURES DEMO-FRAME W
ITHIN FRAME................. R-1248

711+005 FRAME TEXT DIAGNL
FILM INTRO CREDITS OVER HAND TURNIN
G PAGES OF BOOK-ITALIAN TEXT. R-1261

507+001 FRAME TEXT CRAWL
TEXT OVER HELD OPEN BIBLE
STRAIGHT.................... R-1310

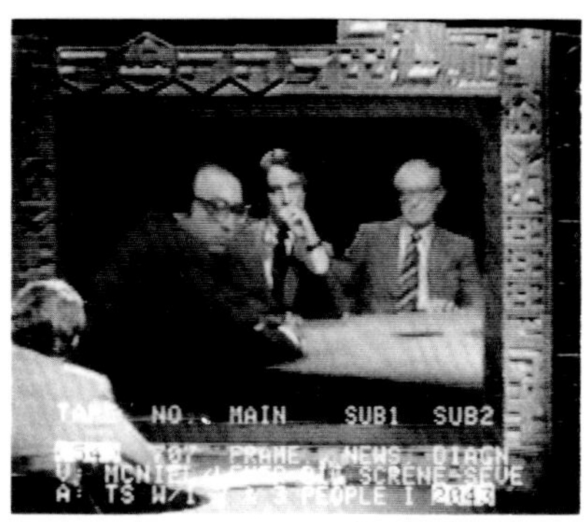

801+013 FRAME NEWS DIAGNL
MCNIEL/LEHRER- BIG TV INVIEW
STRAIGHT.................... R-1091

166+004 FRAME NEWS DIAGNL
NITELINE INTRO IMAGE WINDOW-RE SCHO
OLS CLOSING................. R-2006

220+008 FRAME NEWS DIAGNL
BUSINESS SHOW-LARGE SCREEN BIT
INVIEW..................... R-2014

657+003 FRAME NEWS DIAGNL
INTRO TO NIGHTLINE NEWS-IMAGE WINDO
W-SPACE SHUTTLE PREP-11/81.. R-2039

707+019 FRAME NEWS DIAGNL
MCNIEL/LEHER BIG SCRENE-SEVERAL SHO
TS W/1 2 & 3 PEOPLE IN SCREEN R-2043

275+004 FRAME NEWS DIAGNL
MCNEIL/LEHRER - GIANT SCREEN
STRAIGHT.................... R-1455

787+004 FRAME NEWS LOCAL
LOCAL STATION MCNIEL/LEHRER BIG SCR
EEN IMITATION......A-STRAIGHT R-1516

373+003 FRAME NEWS NITEL
INTRO TO NITELINE - WINDOW INSETS
VOICE OVER.................. R-1841

568+002 FRAME NEWS DIAGNL
INTRO WINDOW TO NITELINE NEWS
STRAIGHT.................... R-1855

298+006 TITLE TEXT SHOWTI
V: INTRO TO SHOWTIME MOVIE-TEXT-RATING
A: LION MGM LOGO MOVIE INTRO.... R-1702

279+001 TITLE TEXT TV
V: SIGN OFF-LOGO OF NAT'L TELEVISION C
A: ODE SEAL OF GOOD PRACTICE.... R-1737

808+005 TITLE TEXT DIAGNL
V: INTRO CREDITS TO B.LEE FILM-MOSTLY
A: IN CHINESE CHARACTERS COLLAGE R-2060

368+010 TITLE TEXT FRIDAY
V: END THEME & SX-70'S AT END OF FRIDA
A: MUSIC & VOICE OVER.......... R-2109

480+005 TITLE TEXT CRAWL
V: FR SNL-CRAWL TEXT INTRO EXPLANATION
A: OF HUGH HEFNER SKIT......... R-2178

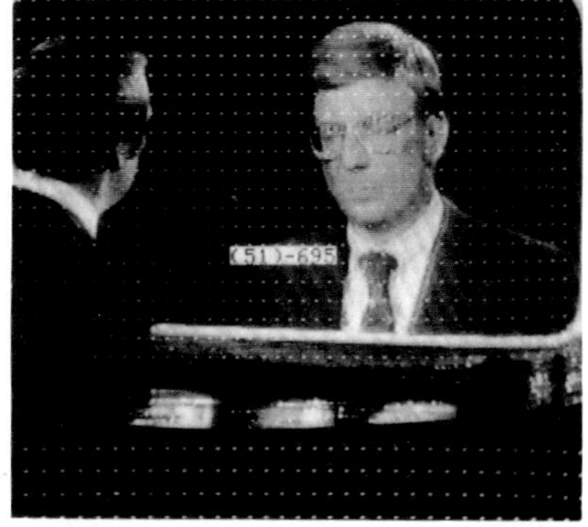

829+008 DOCUMENT MUSIC
V: ON SINGER 'PIAF'-ENG.SUBTITLES
A: STRAIGHT (FRENCH)........... R-0488

761+022 DOCUMENT IN-POL
V: NOVA-CANCER RESEARCH-RURAL VILLAGE
A: STRAIGHT................... R-1330

727+006 DOCUMENT ANTHRO
V: PBS ON AMER INDIANS BUILING CABIN
A: CPTIONED.................. R-1376

571+083 DOCUMENT ANTHRO
V: INDONESIAN TRIBESMAN W/CPTIONS-'I A
A: SCEND W/MY OFFERINGS' AT 645. R-1468

244+176 DOCUMENT ANTHRO
V: NOVA-AFGANI TRIBE-DIALOG CPTION-HIG
A: H MT.PAMIR-LATER MOVED TO PAK R-1944

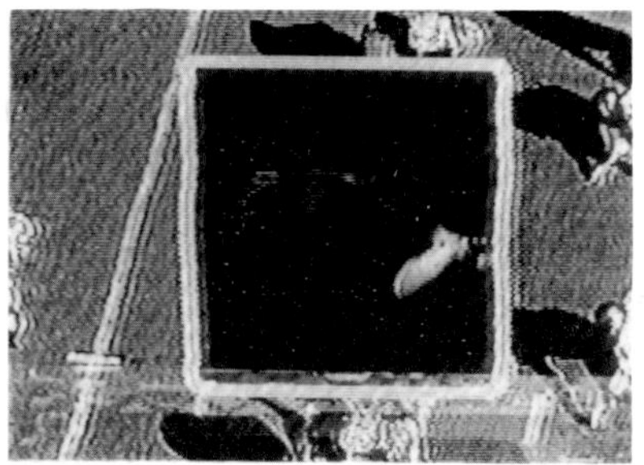

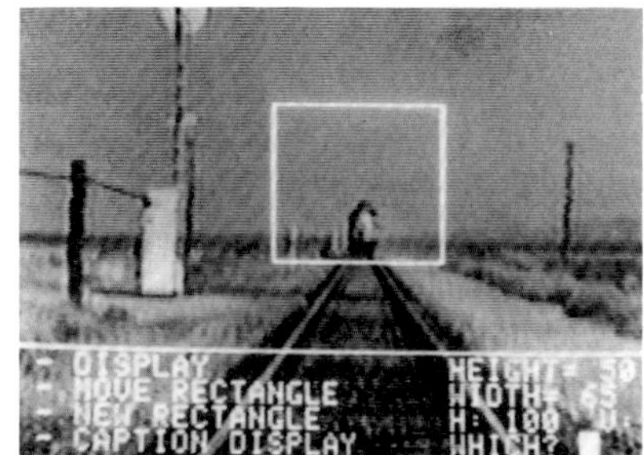

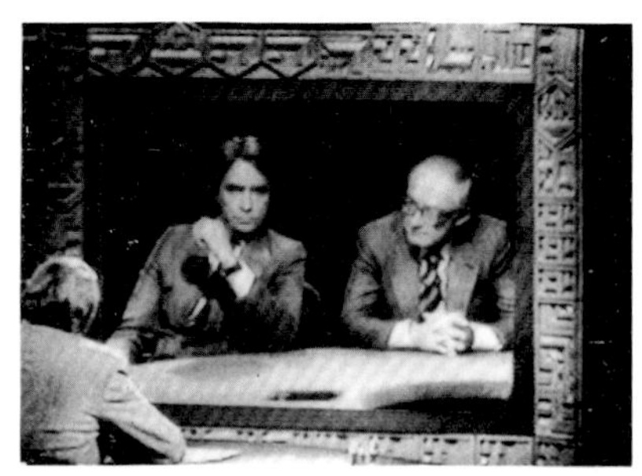

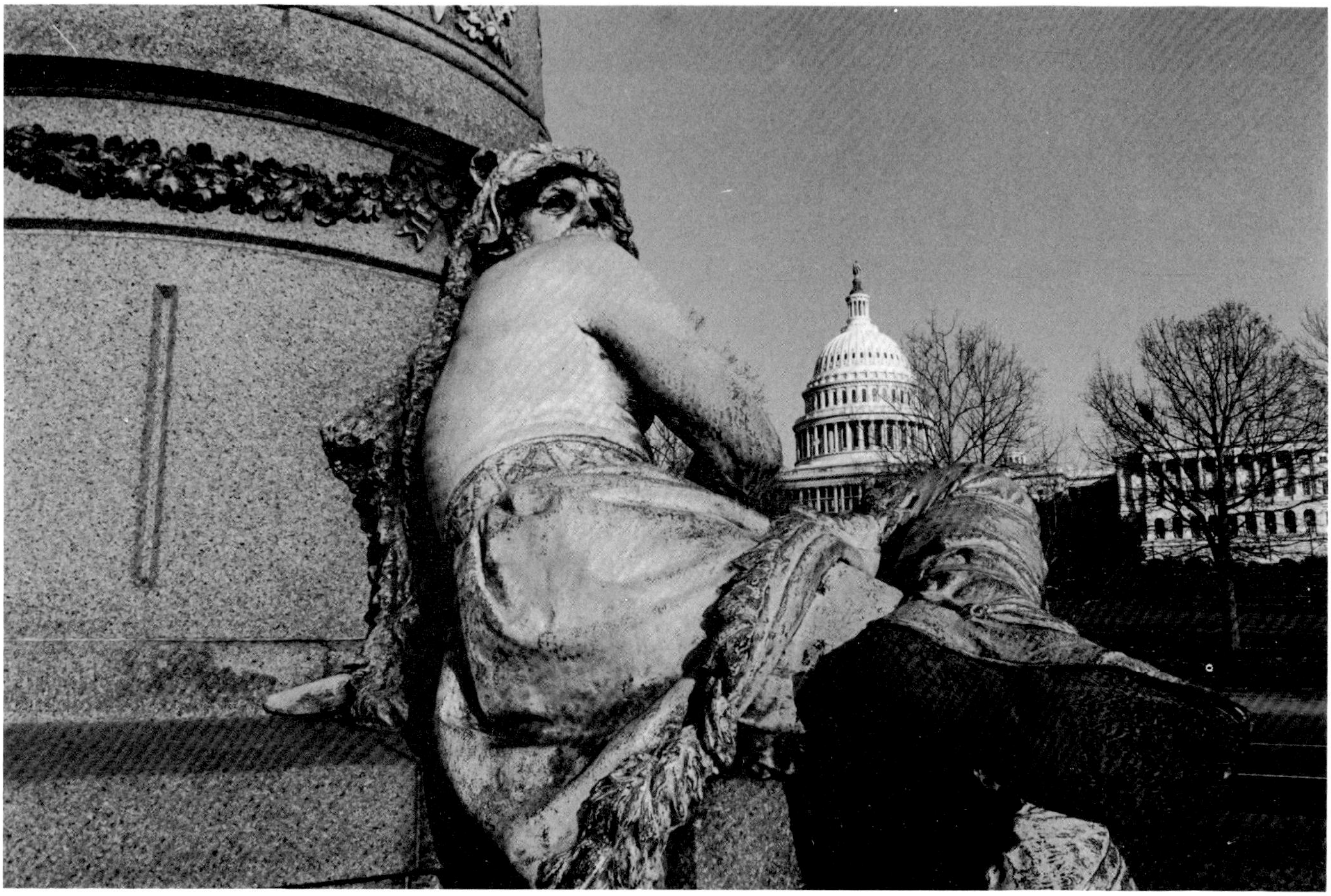

I pledge allegiance, to the flag, of the United States of America. And to the Republic, for which it stands, one nation, under God,

God of God, Light of Light, very God of very God, begotten, not made, being of one substance with the Father, by whom all things were made.

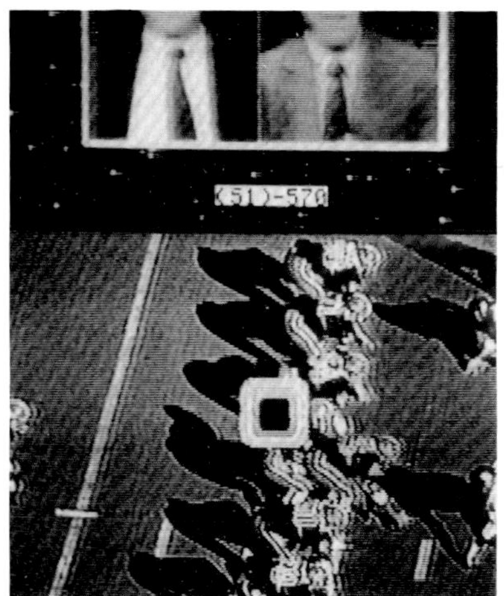

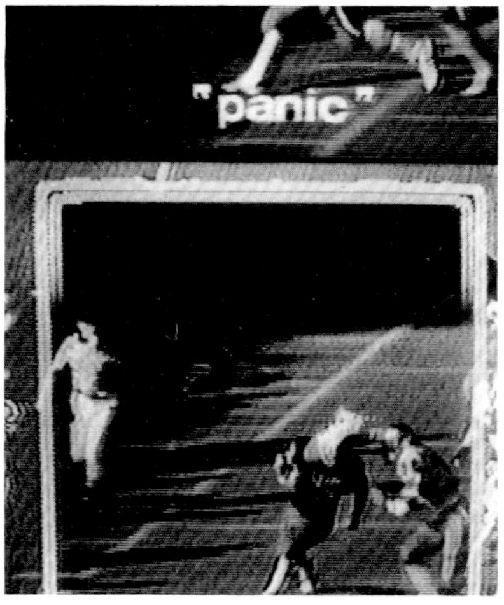

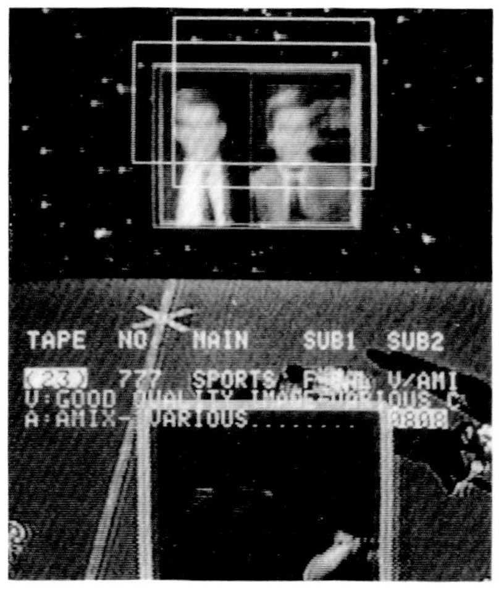

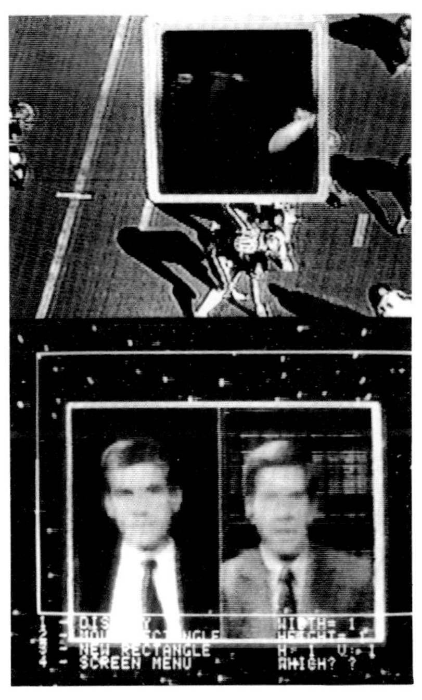

DISPLAY   WIDTH= 1
                         HEIGHT= 1
NEW RECTANGLE   H: 1   V: 1
SCREEN MENU   AHIGH? ?

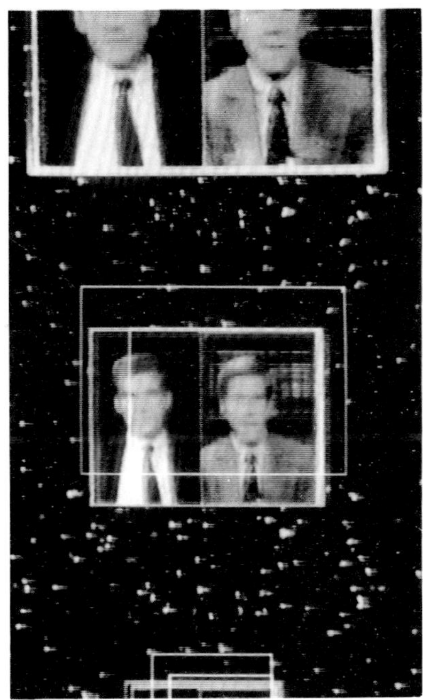
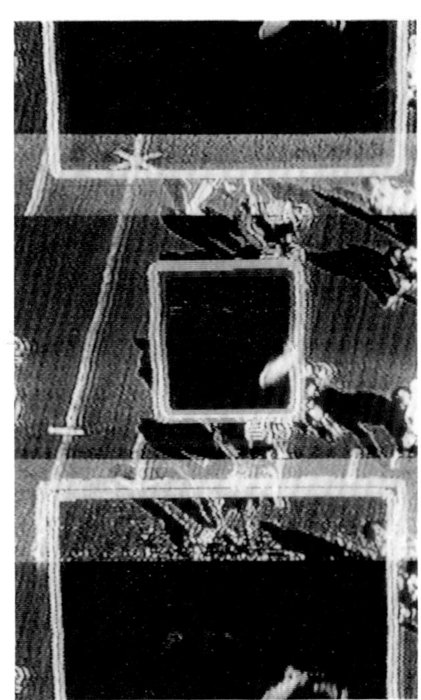

Nation

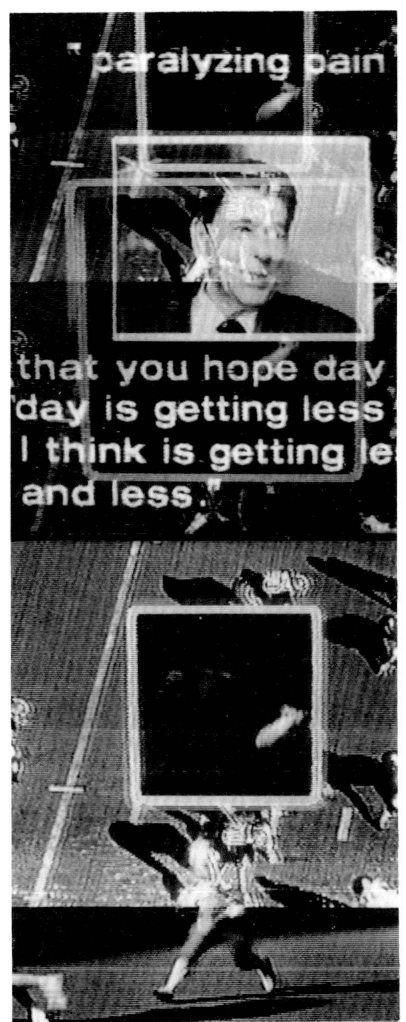

paralyzing pain
that you hope day
day is getting less
I think is getting le
and less.

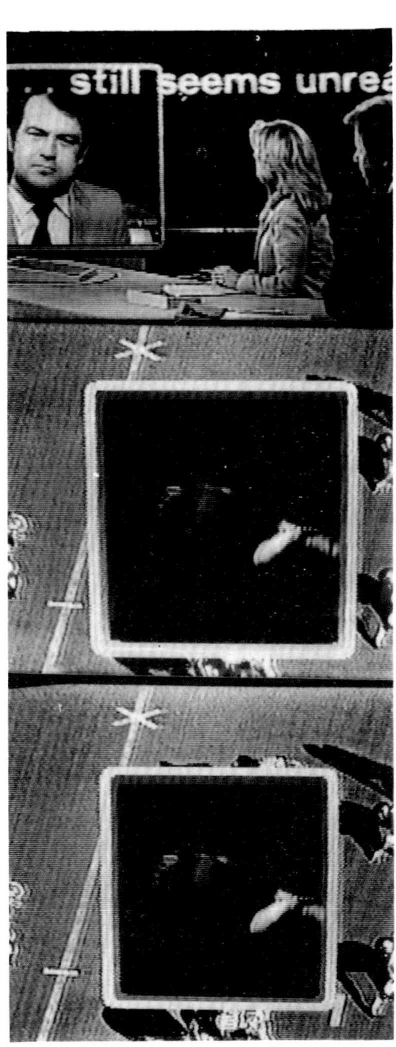

. . . still seems unrea

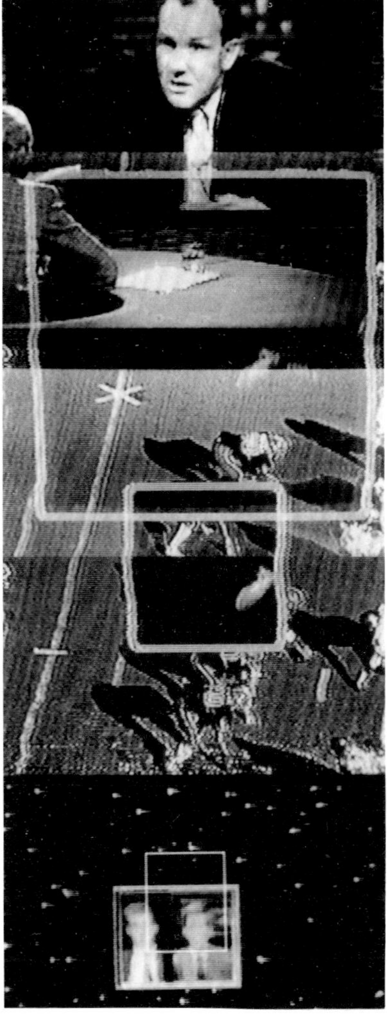

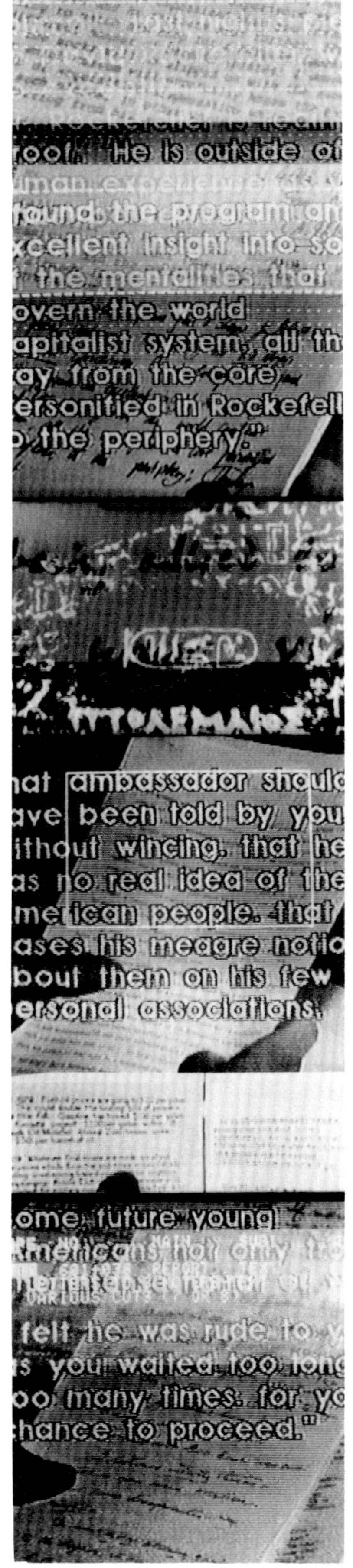

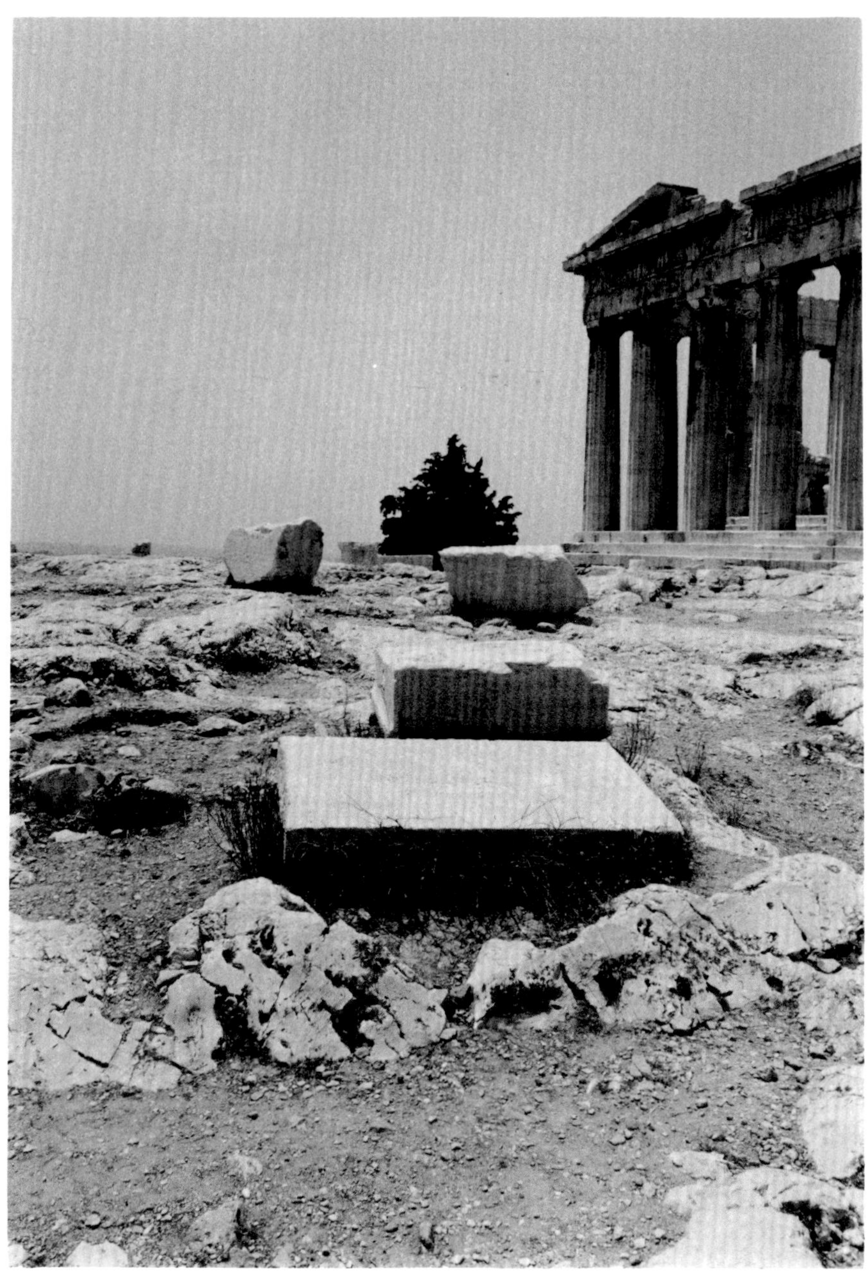

In 1798 Napoleonic naval forces, accompanied by scholars, invade Egypt; however,

their sea link is cut by the British Navy. In 1799, while assembling stone blocks robbed from ancient buildings to enlarge their fort, Napoleon's men uncover the Rosetta Stone.

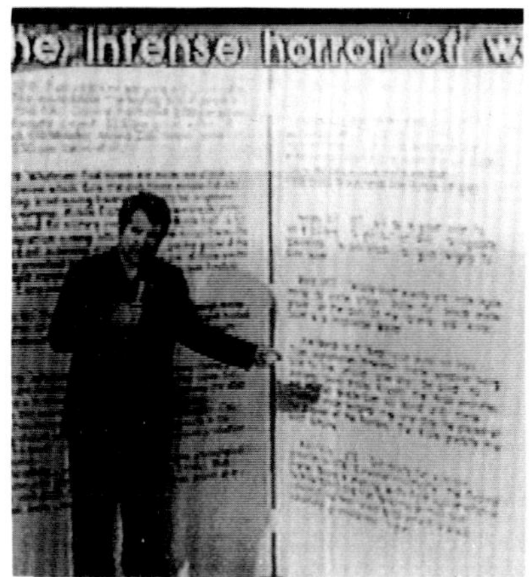

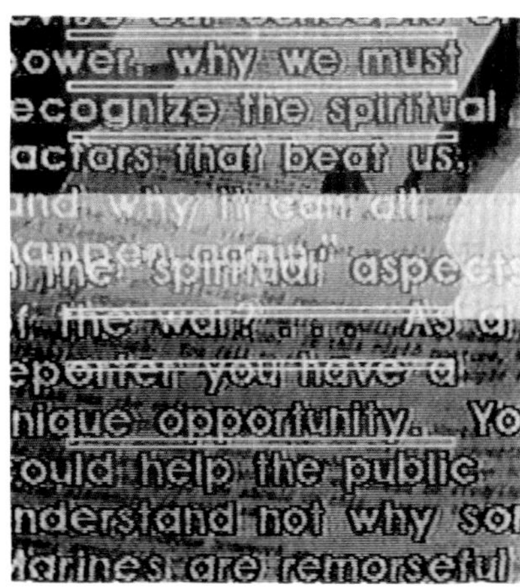

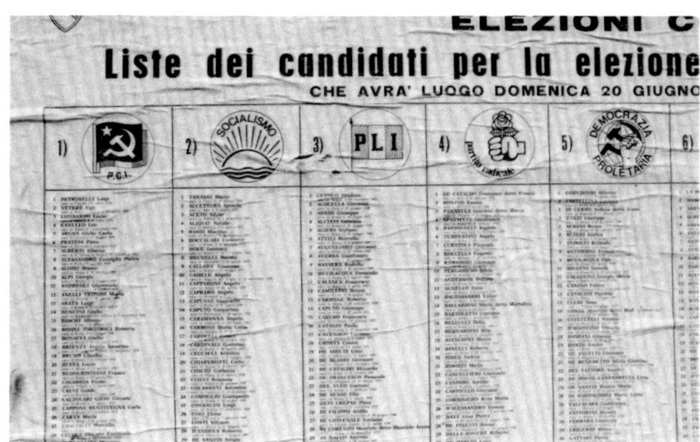

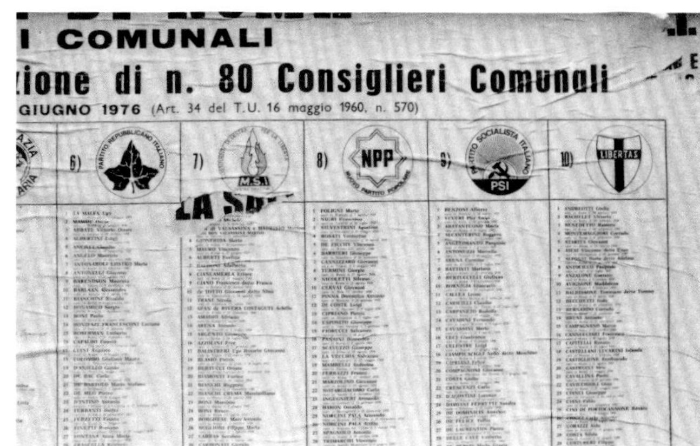

In 1801, the French surrender Egypt and the Rosetta Stone, which is placed in the British Museum. Englishman Tom Young's work

on the Stone is superceded by Frenchman Jean-Francois Champollion, who declares, "...I shall never recognize originality of any alphabet but my own.", and completes his translation in 1822. In 1828, Champollion visits Egypt for the first time, and is welcomed as a national hero.

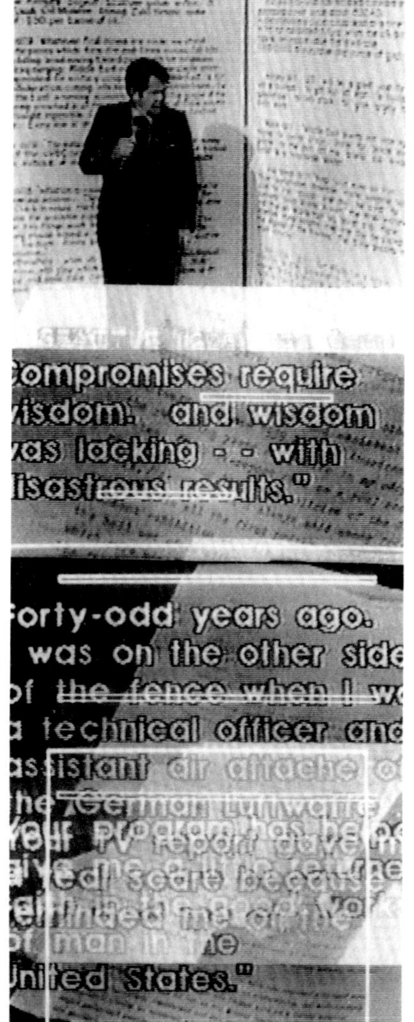

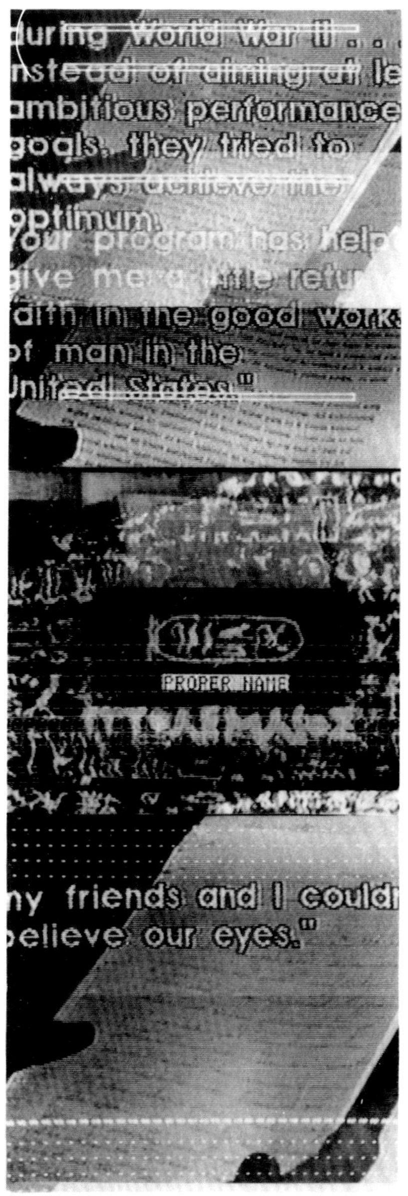

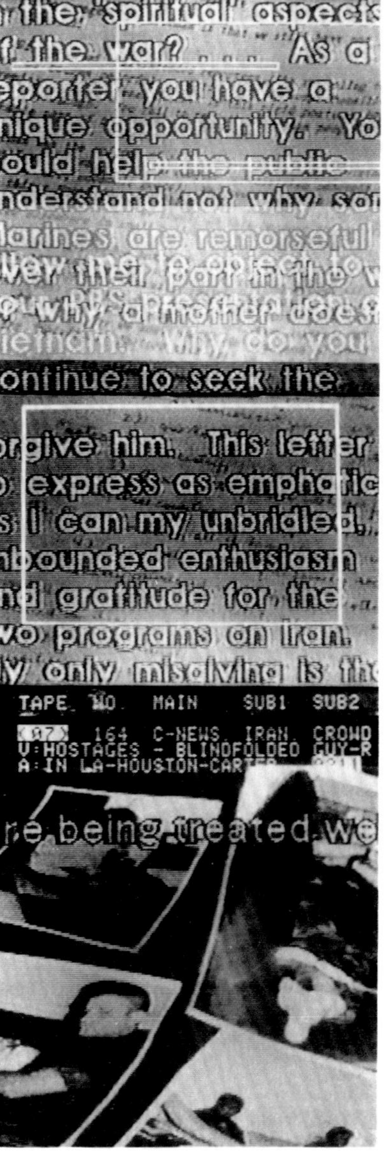

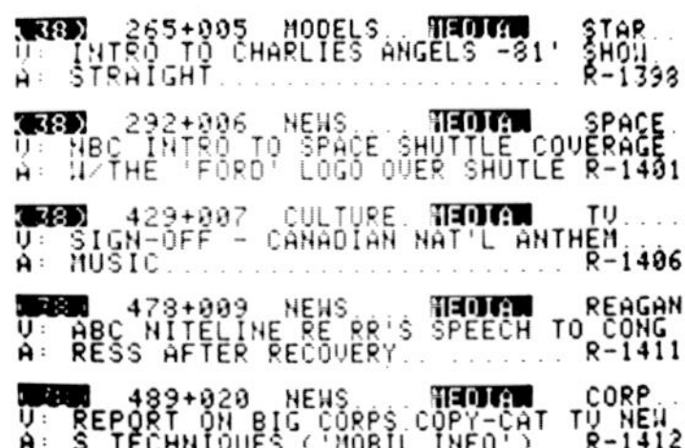

```
(38)  265+005  MODELS...[MEDIA]    STAR
V: INTRO TO CHARLIES ANGELS -81' SHOW
A: STRAIGHT................... R-1398

(38)  292+006  NEWS.....[MEDIA]    SPACE
V: NBC INTRO TO SPACE SHUTTLE COVERAGE
A: W/THE 'FORD' LOGO OVER SHUTLE R-1401

(38)  429+007  CULTURE..[MEDIA]    TV
V: SIGN-OFF - CANADIAN NAT'L ANTHEM
A: MUSIC...................... R-1406

(38)  478+009  NEWS.....[MEDIA]    REAGAN
V: ABC NITELINE RE RR'S SPEECH TO CONG
A: RESS AFTER RECOVERY........ R-1411

(38)  489+020  NEWS.....[MEDIA]    CORP
V: REPORT ON BIG CORPS COPY-CAT TU NEW
A: S TECHNIQUES ('MOBIL INFO').. R-1412
```

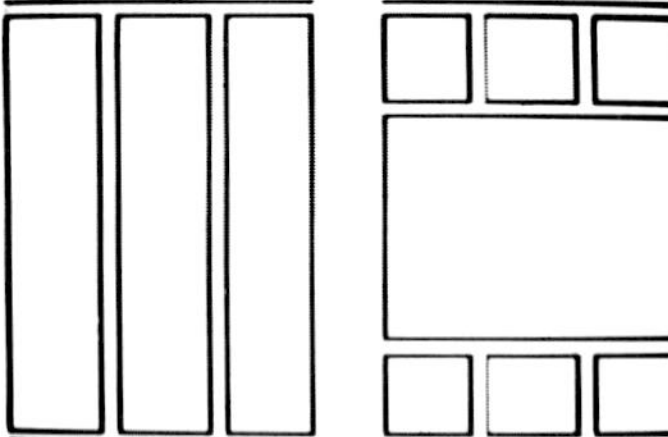

- READING -

```
(53)  616+011  DRAMA....[MEDIA]    STAR
V: CPTN.KIRK AS PAUL REVERE-FIGHT SCEN
A: CE FR 'THE BASTARD'........ R-1957

(53)  829+004  NEWS.....[MEDIA]    REAGAN
V: REAGAN'S AWAC VOTE VICTORY COMPARED
A: TO THE DODGER'S WORLDSERIES.. R-1985
```

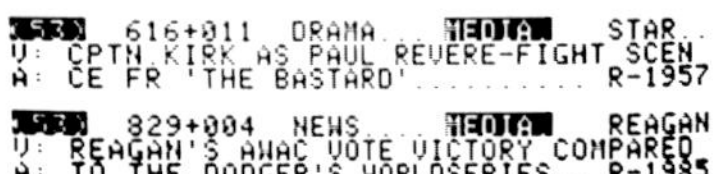

```
(22)  620+001  TITLE....[TEXT]     CPTION
V: END OF SHOW CREDITS TO 'WRITE ON'
A: AMIX....................... R-0754

(22)  677+001  TITLE....[TEXT]     CPTION
V: AIRLINE AD W/ CITIES OVER LANDING
A: STRAIGHT................... R-0758

(23)  033+002  TITLE....[TEXT]     DISPLY
V: NEWSPAPER HEADLINE.........
A: STRAIGHT................... R-0771
```

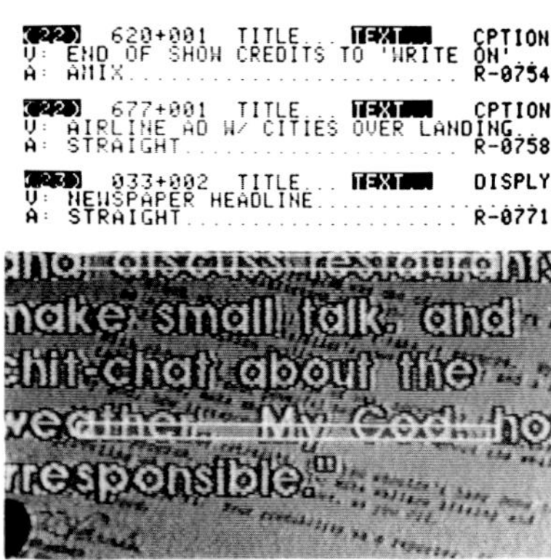

Reading

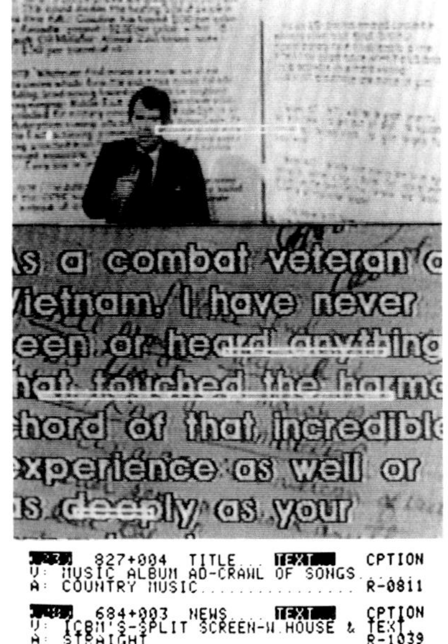


```
(38)  827+004  TITLE....[TEXT]     CPTION
V: MUSIC ALBUM AD-CRAWL OF SONGS
A: COUNTRY MUSIC.............. R-0811

(38)  684+003  NEWS.....[TEXT]     CPTION
V: ICBM'S-SPLIT SCREEN-W HOUSE & TEXT
A: STRAIGHT................... R-1039
```

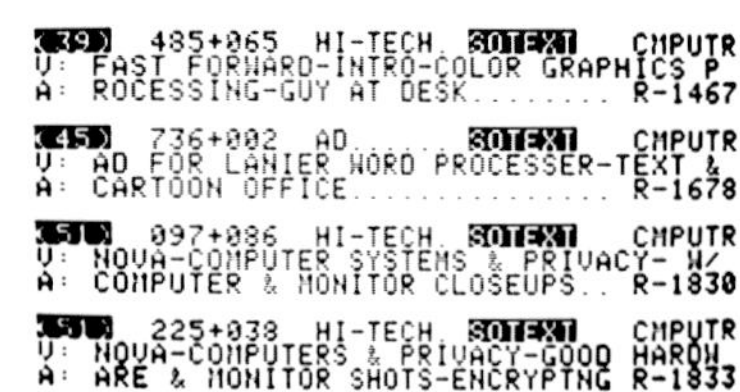


```
(47)  279+001  TITLE....[TEXT]     TV
V: SIGN OFF-LOGO OF NAT'L TELEVISION C
A: ODE SEAL OF GOOD PRACTICE.... R-1737
```

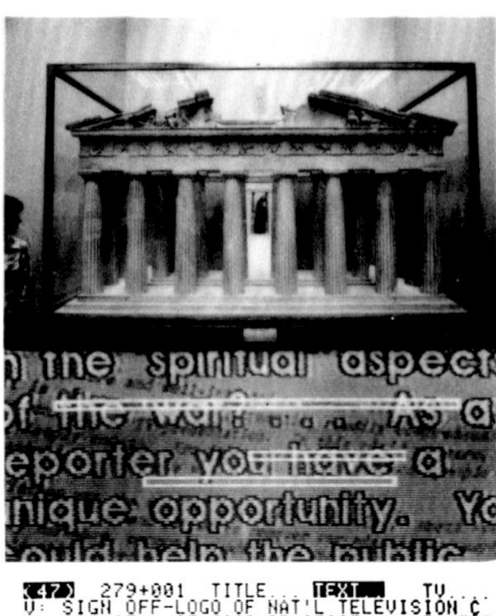

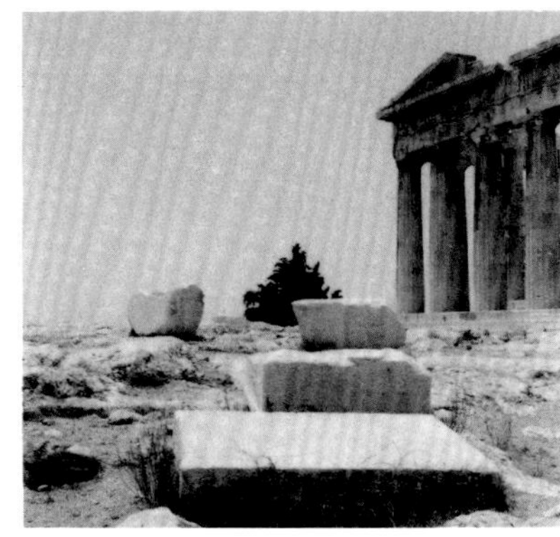

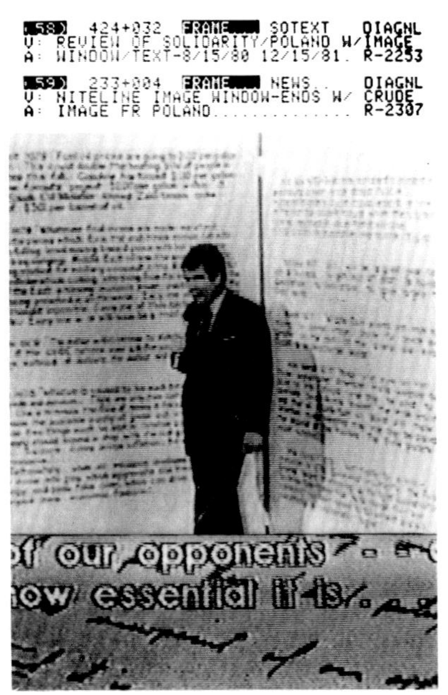


```
(58)  424+032  [FRAME]   SOTEXT    DIAGNL
V: REVIEW OF SOLIDARITY/POLAND W/IMAGE
A: WINDOW/TEXT-8/15/80 12/15/81. R-2253

(59)  233+004  [FRAME]   NEWS      DIAGNL
V: NITELINE IMAGE WINDOW-ENDS W/ CRUDE
A: IMAGE FR POLAND............ R-2307
```

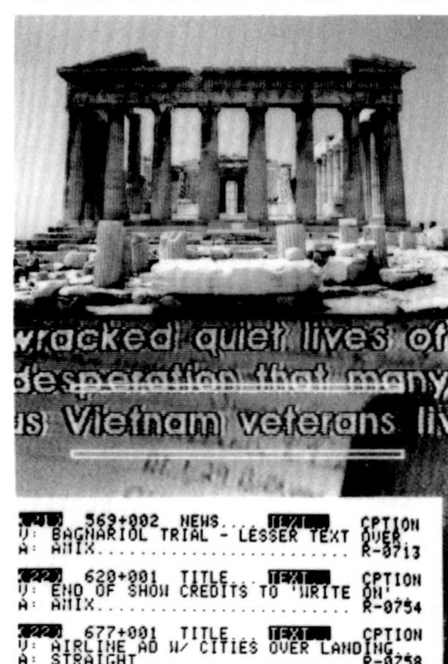


```
(22)  569+002  NEWS.....[TEXT]     CPTION
V: BAGNARIOL TRIAL - LESSER TEXT OVER
A: AMIX....................... R-0713

(22)  620+001  TITLE....[TEXT]     CPTION
V: END OF SHOW CREDITS TO 'WRITE ON'
A: AMIX....................... R-0754

(22)  677+001  TITLE....[TEXT]     CPTION
V: AIRLINE AD W/ CITIES OVER LANDING
A: STRAIGHT................... R-0758
```

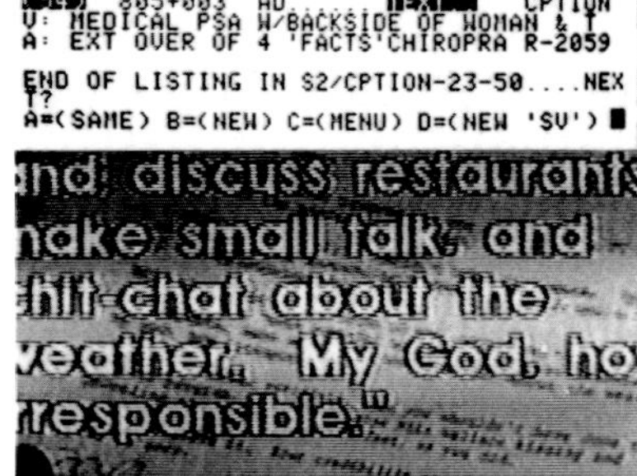


```
(53)  233+002  NEWS.....[TEXT]     CPTION
V: TEXT OVER (ROLL) TAPE RECORDER RE U
A: SSR & FIRED US GENERAL..... R-1942

(54)  805+003  AD.......[TEXT]     CPTION
V: MEDICAL PSA W/BACKSIDE OF WOMAN & T
A: EXT OVER OF 4 'FACTS'CHIROPRA R-2059

END OF LISTING IN S2/CPTION-23-50....NEXT?
A=(SAME) B=(NEW) C=(MENU) D=(NEW 'SV') ■
```

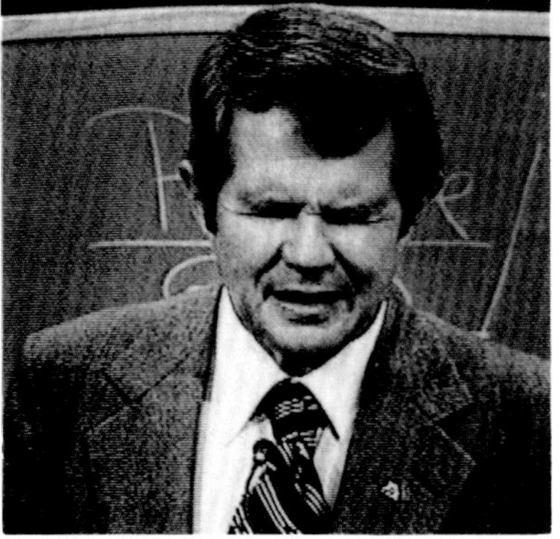


```
(25)  636+002  DRAMA....[RELIGN]   700CLU
V: 700 CLUB GUY ON GOD & ENTROPY
A: STRAIGHT................... R-0893
```

The top right column entries:

```
(50)  663+002  [TITLE]   TEXT      DIAGNL
V: TITLE (END)-'OFFICE OF WAR INFORMAT
A: ION -MOTION PICTURE DIVISION' R-2326

(50)  343+004  [TITLE]   TEXT      INTRO
V: FR OLD C.CHAPLIN FILM-INTRO TITLE P
A: AGES (2) RE TITLES IN FILM... R-2339
```

The top middle column entries:

```
(39)  485+065  HI-TECH  [SOTEXT]   CMPUTR
V: FAST FORWARD-INTRO-COLOR GRAPHICS P
A: ROCESSING-GUY AT DESK...... R-1467

(45)  736+002  AD.......[SOTEXT]   CMPUTR
V: AD FOR LANIER WORD PROCESSER-TEXT &
A: CARTOON OFFICE............. R-1678

(38)  097+086  HI-TECH  [SOTEXT]   CMPUTR
V: NOVA-COMPUTER SYSTEMS & PRIVACY- W/
A: COMPUTER & MONITOR CLOSEUPS.. R-1830

(38)  225+038  HI-TECH  [SOTEXT]   CMPUTR
V: NOVA-COMPUTERS & PRIVACY-GOOD HARDW
A: ARE & MONITOR SHOTS-ENCRYPTNG R-1833
```

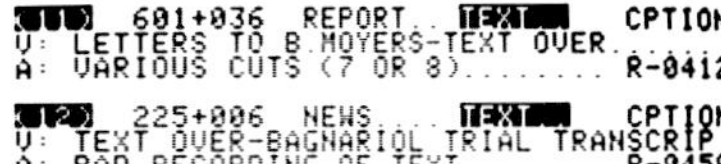

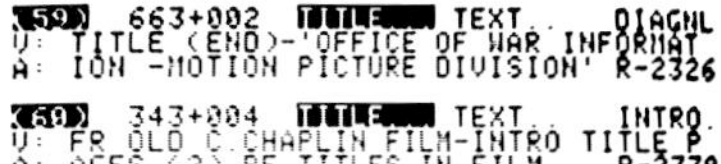

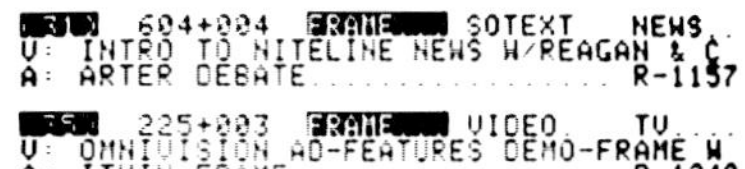

Display

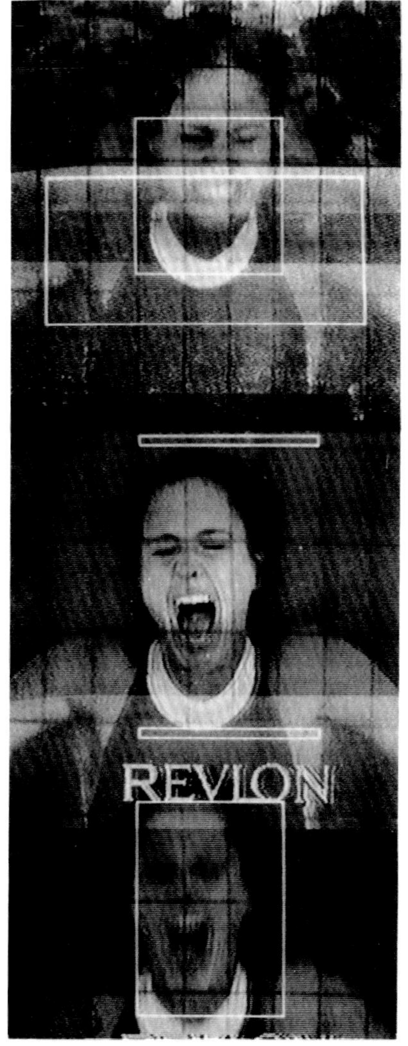

Cinema

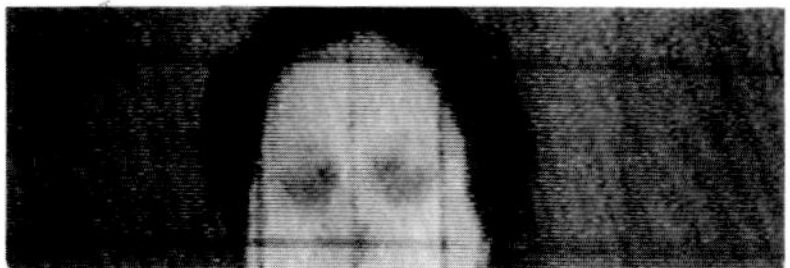

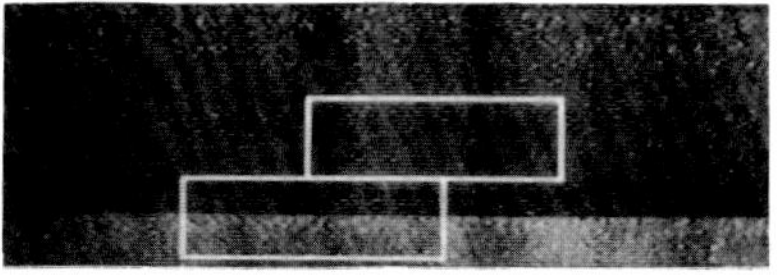

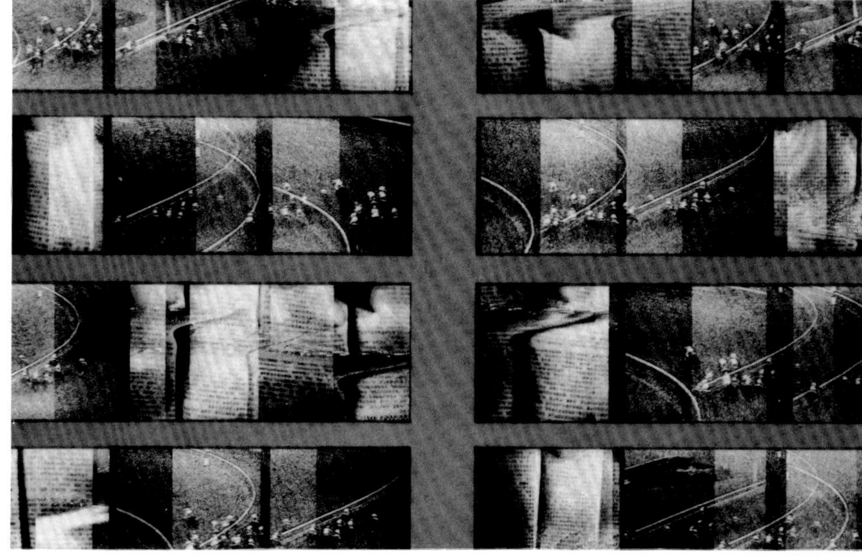

SEATTLE SUBTEXT: Table of Context

(1)"Magazine" format; (2) TV strips as text; (3) Photographs as photographs; (4) Captioned

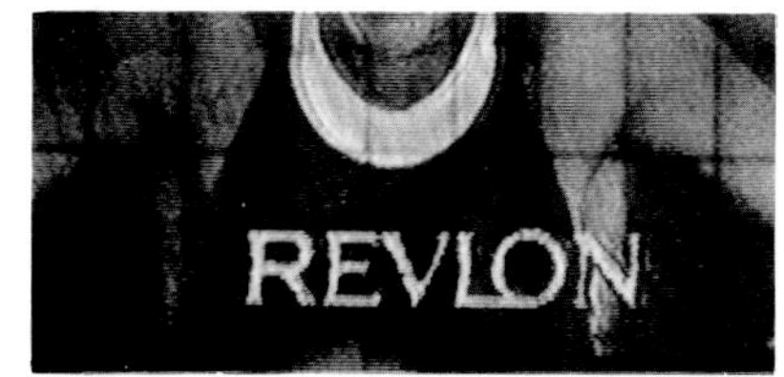

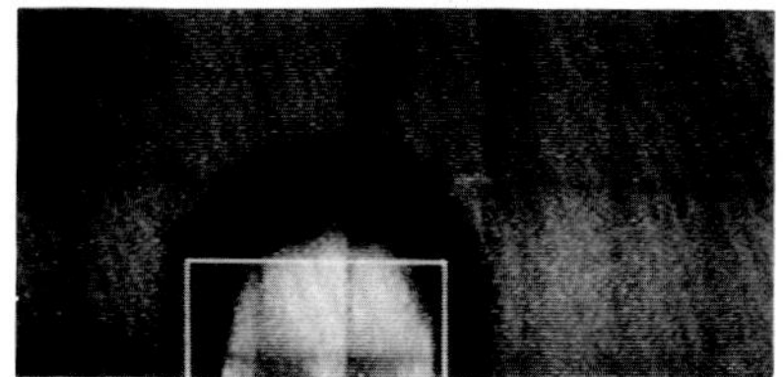

CINEMA: Print D$"Open Cinema,L70": Print D$"Read Cinema,R"X: For L=1 to EF: Input Z$(L): Next: Print D$"Close Cinema": Return

FB 59 00 BA A4 26 99 00 BC D0 EE 84 26 BC 8C C0 10 FB 59 00 BA A4 26 99 00 BB C8 D0 EE BC 8C C0 10 FB D9 00 BA D0 13 BD 8C C0 10 FB C9

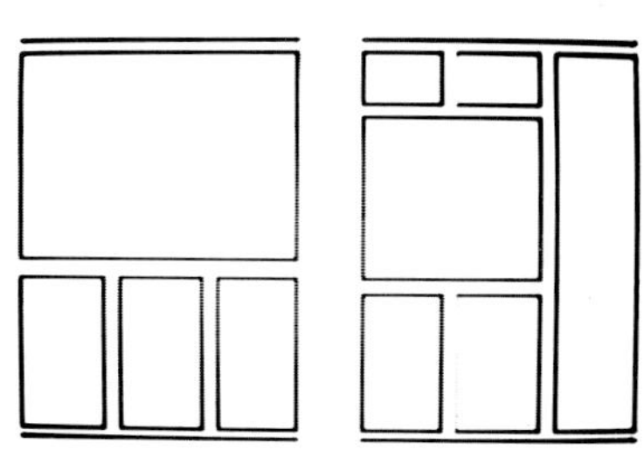

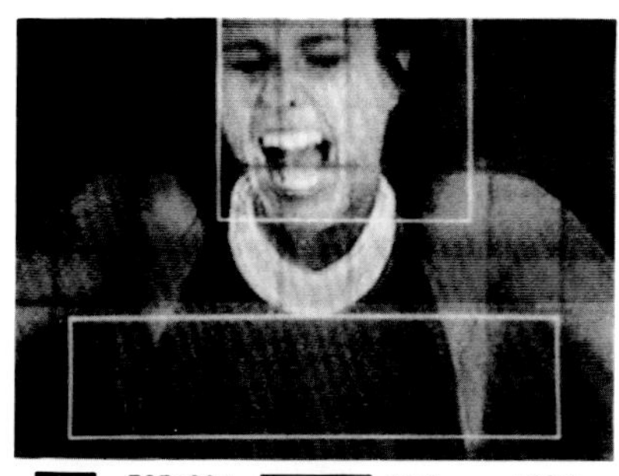

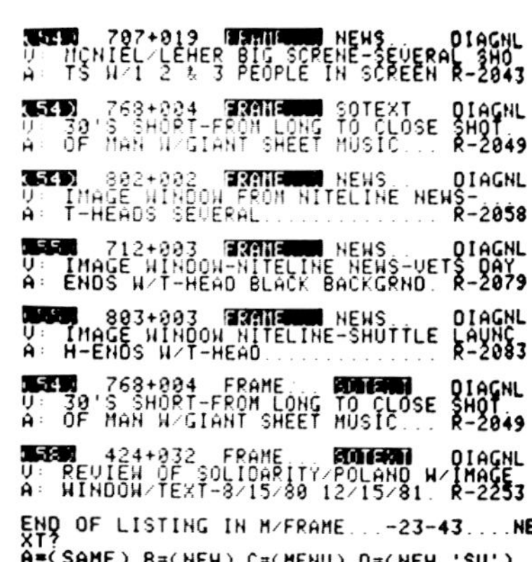

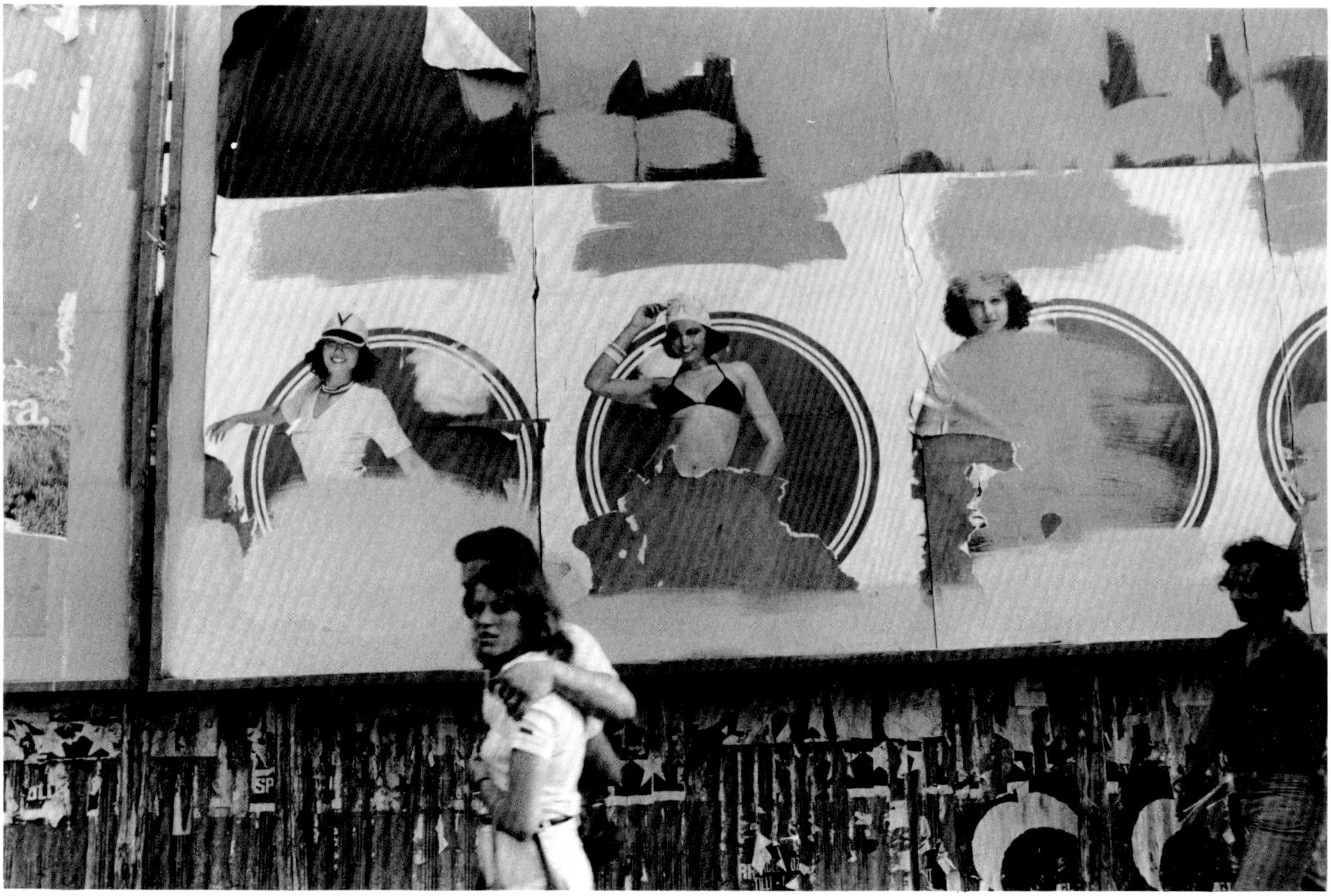

In modern physics, motion is treated as a functional relationship between points of space and instants of time..............

In the modern image-world, consciousness is mapped by points of attention along a continuum of desire.......................

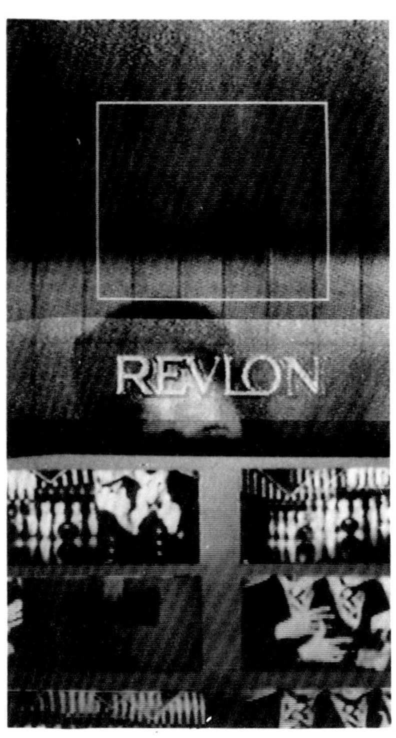

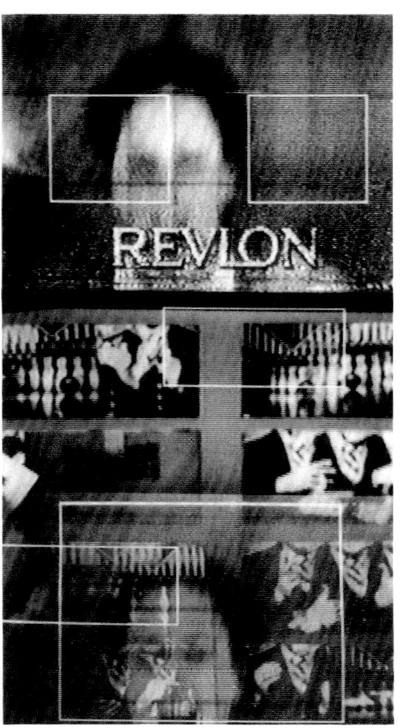

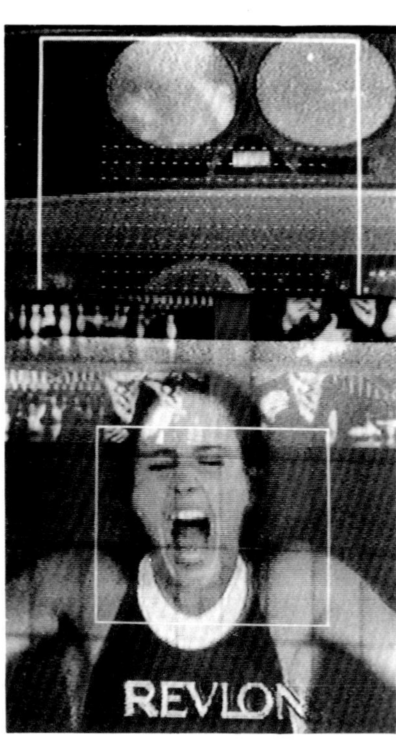

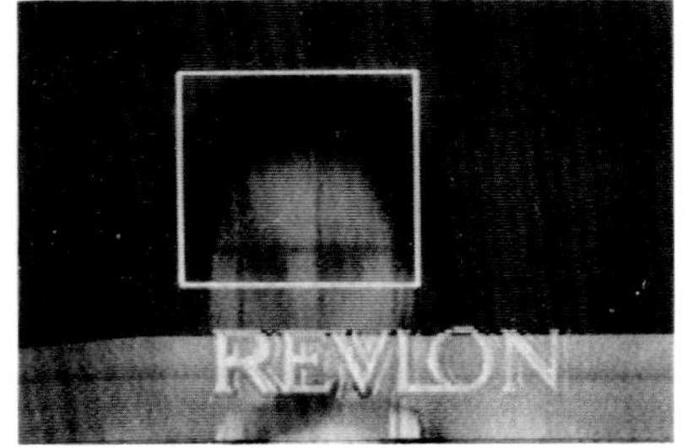
REVLON

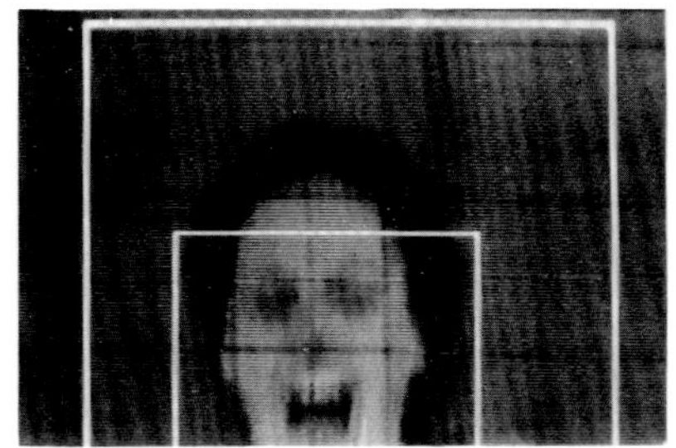

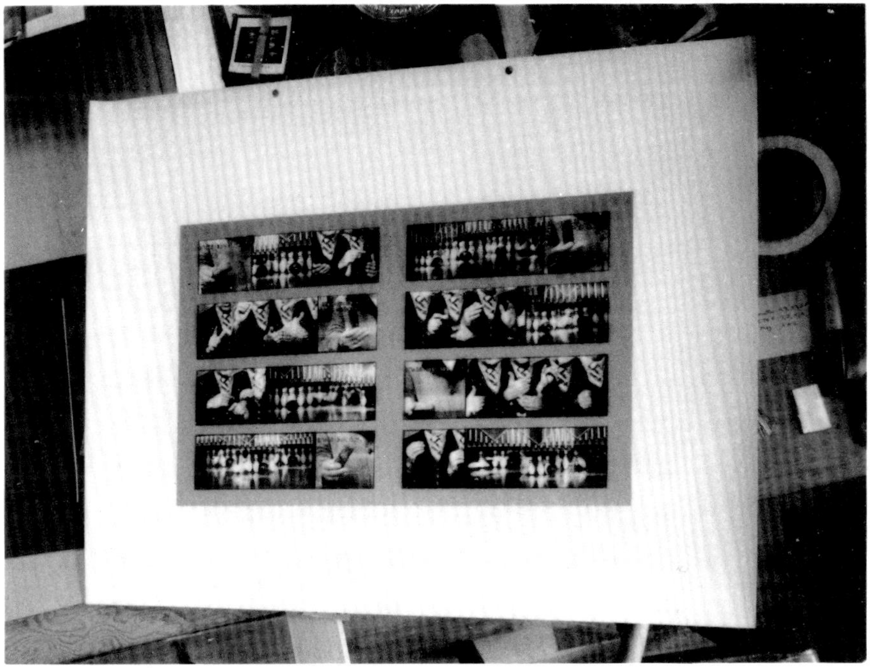

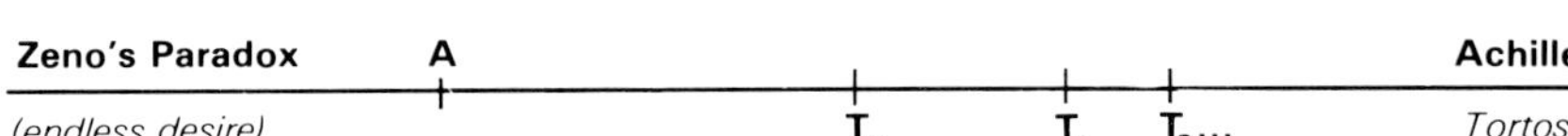

Zeno's Paradox   A   Achilles
(endless desire) T_0 T_1 T_2...   Tortose

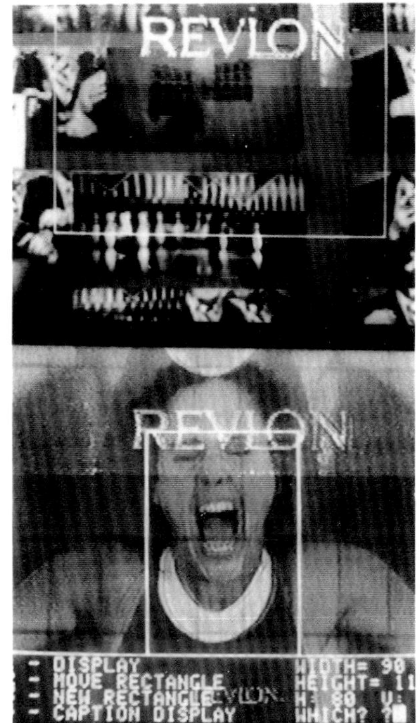

REVLON
REVLON
DISPLAY   WIDTH= 90
MOVE RECTANGLE   HEIGHT= 1
NEW RECTANGLE REVLON H: 80   V:
CAPTION DISPLAY   WHICH?

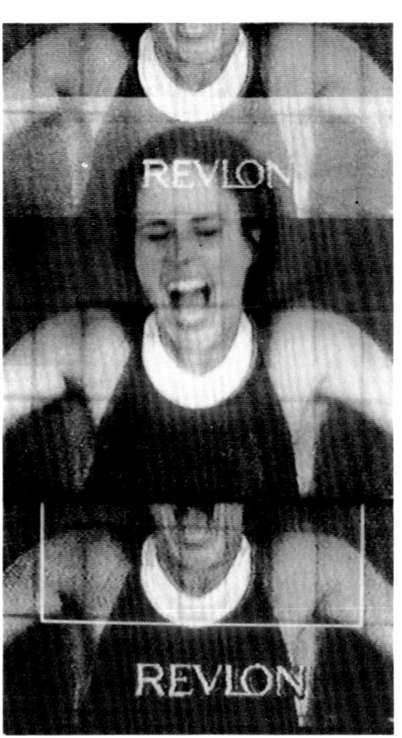

REVLON
REVLON

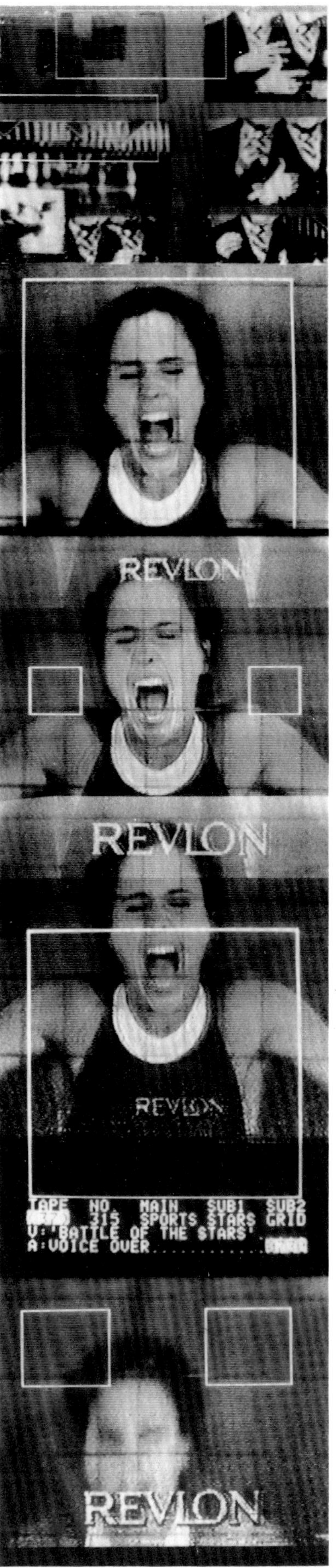

REVLON
REVLON
REVLON
TAPE   NO   MAIN   SUB1   SUB2
       315 SPORTS STARS GRID
V: BATTLE OF THE STARS
A: VOICE OVER
REVLON

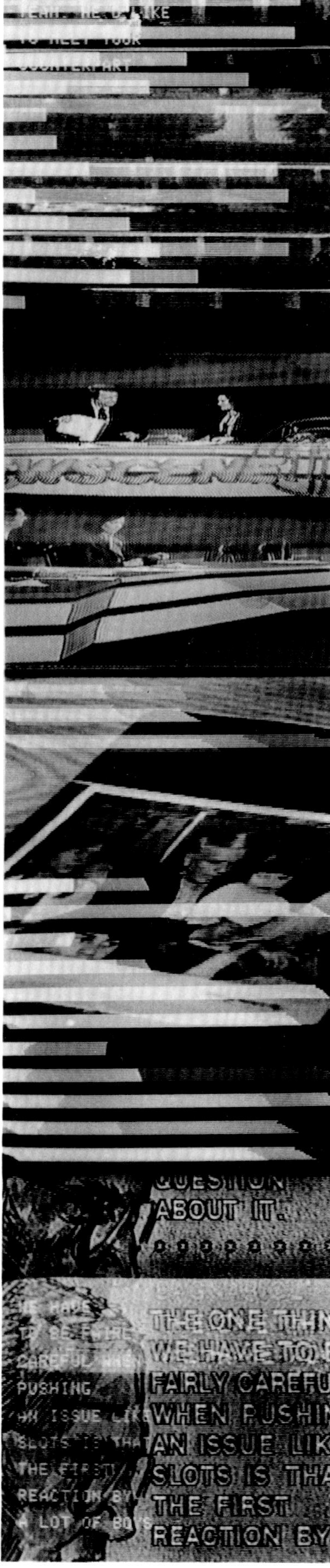

TEAM. HE'D LIKE
TO MEET YOUR
COUNTERPART
QUESTION
ABOUT IT.
THE ONE THING
WE HAVE TO BE
FAIRLY CAREFUL
WHEN PUSHING
AN ISSUE LIKE
SLOTS IS THAT
THE FIRST
REACTION BY
A LOT OF BOYS

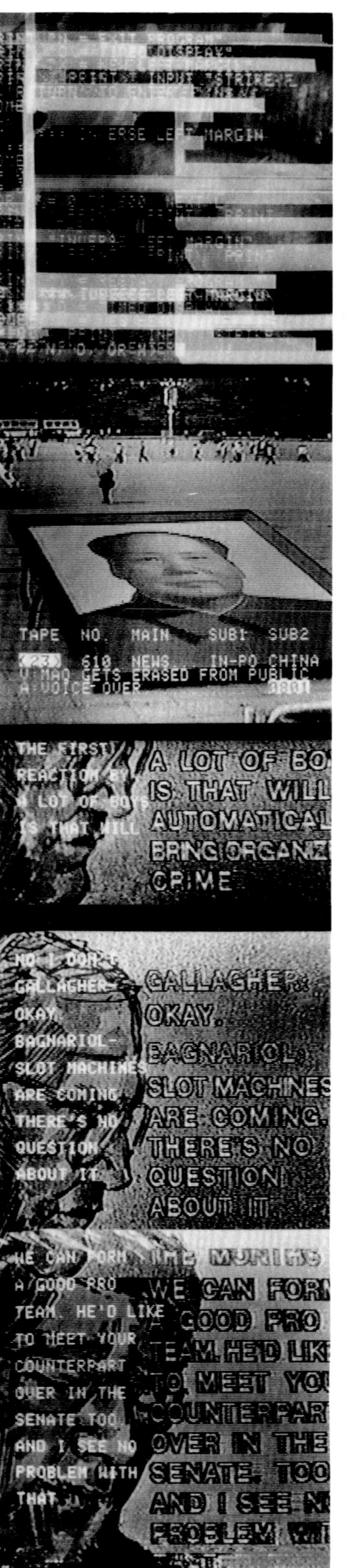

ERSE LEFT MARGIN
TAPE NO. MAIN SUB1 SUB2
(23) 610 NEWS IN-PO CHINA
V. MAO GETS ERASED FROM PUBLIC
A VOICE OVER 0801
THE FIRST
REACTION BY
A LOT OF BOYS
IS THAT WILL
A LOT OF BO
IS THAT WILL
AUTOMATICAL
BRING ORGANIZ
CRIME
NO I DON'T
GALLAGHER—
OKAY.
BAGNARIOL—
SLOT MACHINES
ARE COMING
THERE'S NO
QUESTION
ABOUT IT
GALLAGHER:
OKAY.
BAGNARIOL:
SLOT MACHINES
ARE COMING.
THERE'S NO
QUESTION
ABOUT IT
WE CAN FORM THE MONTHS
A GOOD PRO
TEAM. HE'D LIKE
TO MEET YOUR
COUNTERPART
OVER IN THE
SENATE TOO.
AND I SEE NO
PROBLEM WITH
THAT.
WE CAN FORM
A GOOD PRO
TEAM. HE'D LIK
TO MEET YOU
COUNTERPAR
OVER IN THE
SENATE. TOO
AND I SEE N
PROBLEM WIT

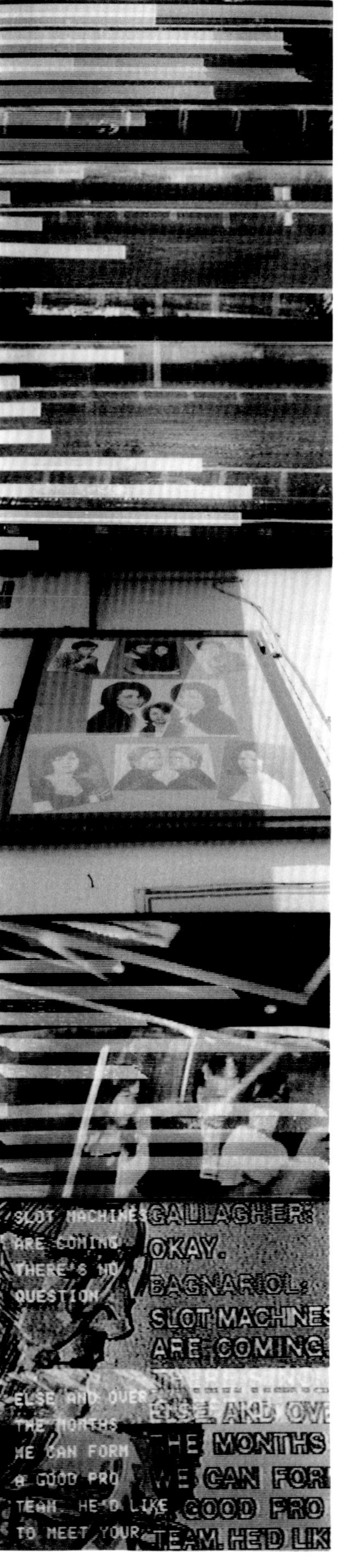

SLOT MACHINES
ARE COMING
THERE'S NO
QUESTION
ELSE AND OVER
THE MONTHS
WE CAN FORM
A GOOD PRO
TEAM. HE'D LIKE
TO MEET YOUR
GALLAGHER:
OKAY.
BAGNARIOL:
SLOT MACHINES
ARE COMING
ELSE AND OVE
THE MONTHS
WE CAN FOR
A GOOD PRO
TEAM. HE'D LIK

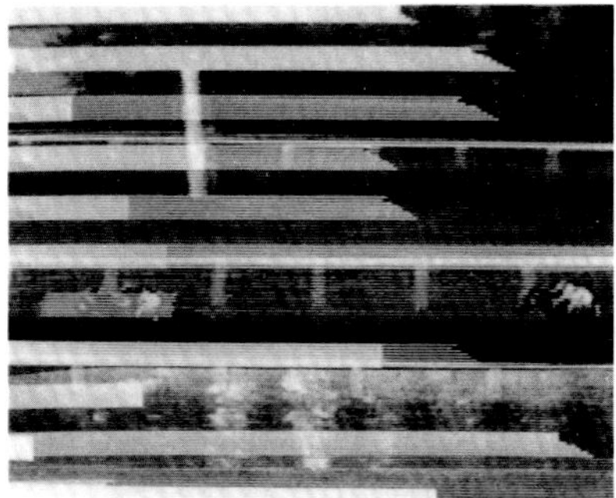
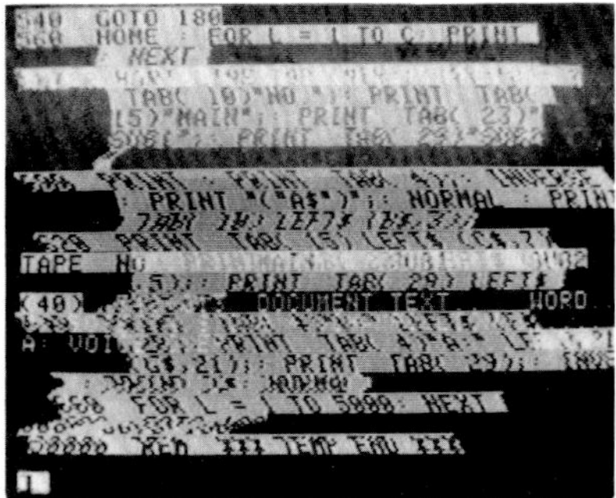
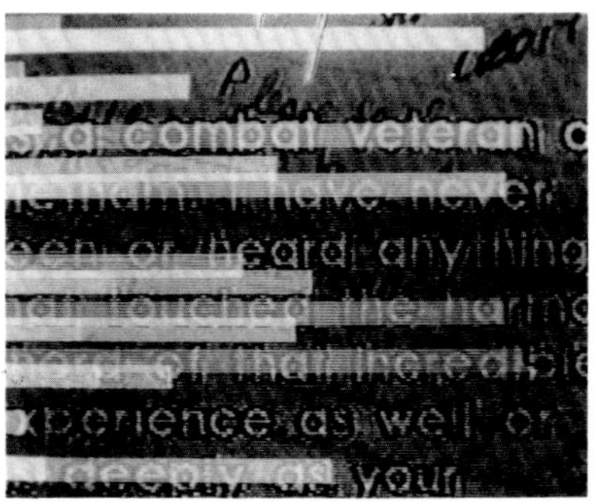

Writing

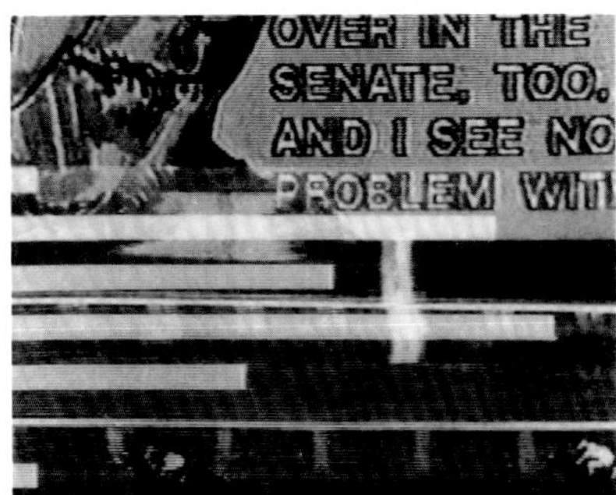

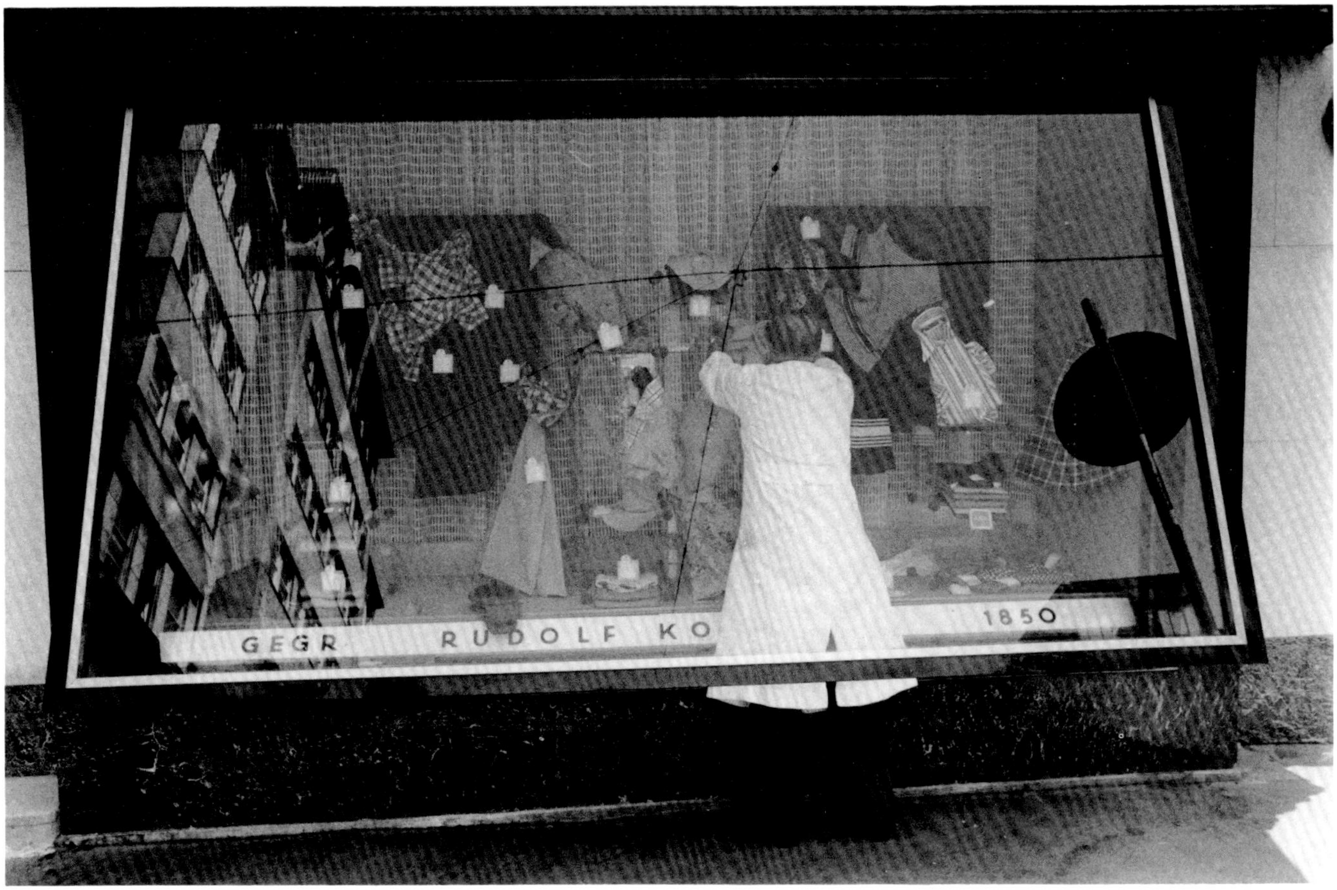

"Most people who use computer displays are familiar with windows...The trouble with windowing systems is that windows

compete with each other... Kay's idea was to allow the windows to overlap... The screen is portrayed as the surface of a desk, and the windows as overlapping sheets of paper... A partly covered sheet peeks from behind others... you can... uncover... that sheet..."

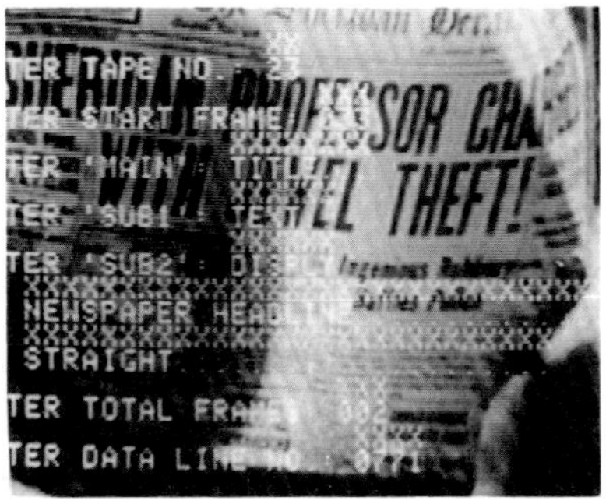

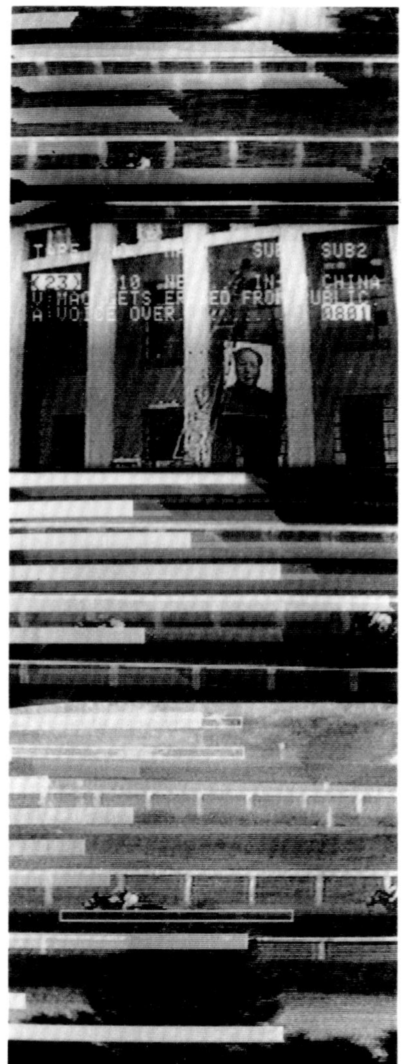

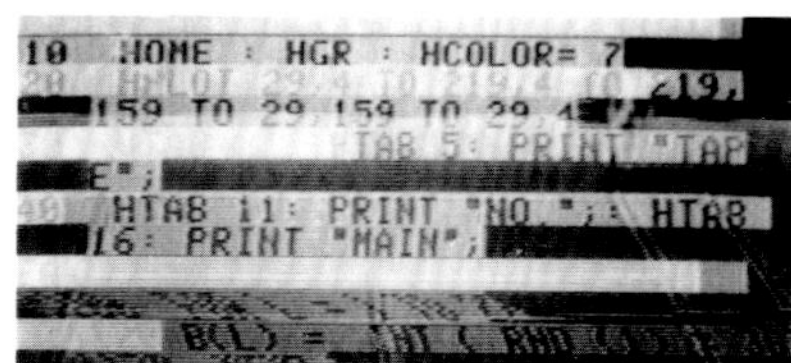

Writing

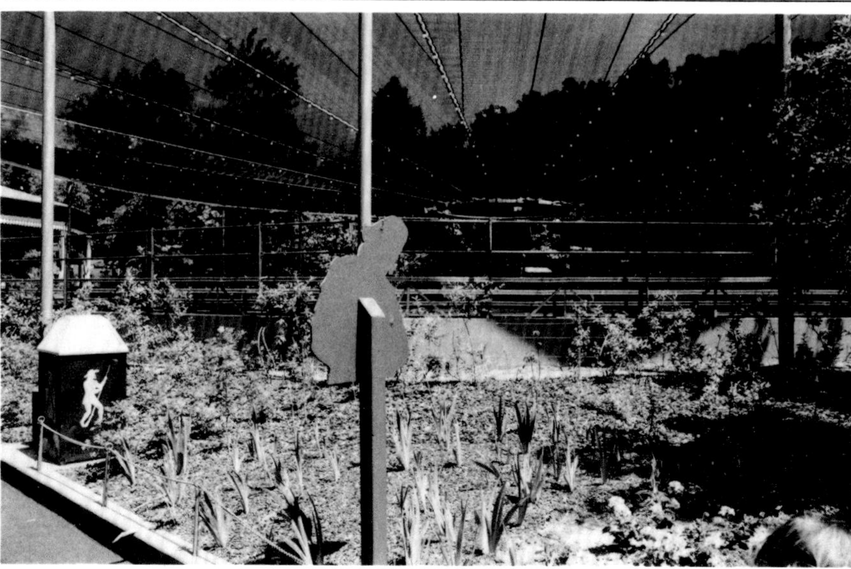

"The screen is portrayed as the surface of a desk, and the windows as overlapping sheets of paper. Partly covered sheets peek out from behind sheets that obscure them. With the aid of a pointing device... you can... uncover that sheet."

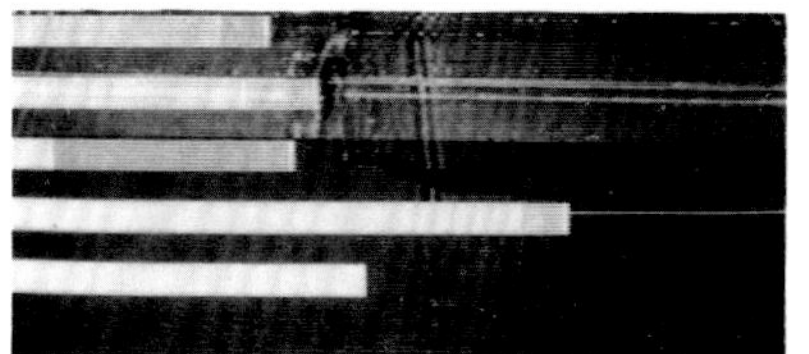

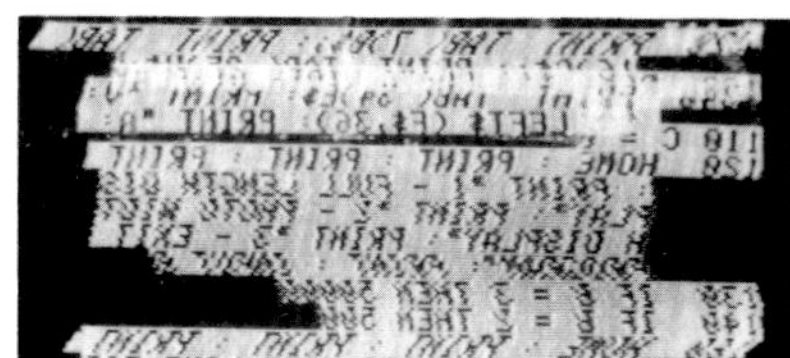

Display

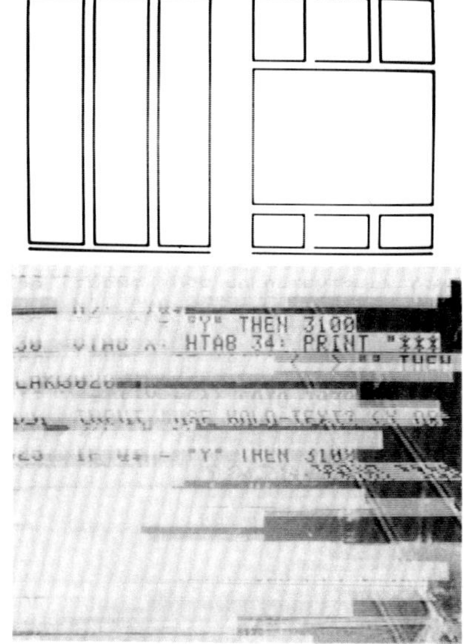

TAPE NO.	MAIN	SUB1	SUB2	
(10) 298+006	TITLE	TEXT	SHOWTI	
V: INTRO TO SHOWTIME MOVIE-TEXT-RATING				
A: LION MGM LOGO MOVIE INTRO....			R-1702	
(47) 279+001	TITLE	TEXT	TV	
V: SIGN OFF-LOGO OF NAT'L TELEVISION C				
A: ODE SEAL OF GOOD PRACTICE....			R-1737	
(54) 808+005	TITLE	TEXT	DIAGNL	
V: INTRO CREDITS TO B LEE FILM-MOSTLY				
A: IN CHINESE CHARACTERS COLLAGE			R-2060	
(56) 368+010	TITLE	TEXT	FRIDAY	
V: END THEME & SX-70'S AT END OF FRIDA				
A: MUSIC & VOICE OVER....			R-2109	
(57) 480+005	TITLE	TEXT	CRAWL	
V: FR SNL-CRAWL TEXT INTRO EXPLANATION				
A: OF HUGH HEFNER SKIT....			R-2178	
(19) 348+002	TITLE	TEXT	CRAWL	
V: ROLLING TEXT INTRO TO MOVIE				
A: PSA ABOUT FED HOTLINE SERVICE			R-0577	
(22) 620+001	TITLE	TEXT	CPTION	
V: END OF SHOW CREDITS TO 'WRITE ON'				
A: AMIX....			R-0754	
(22) 677+001	TITLE	TEXT	CPTION	
V: AIRLINE AD W/ CITIES OVER LANDING				
A: STRAIGHT....			R-0758	
(23) 033+002	TITLE	TEXT	DISPLY	
V: NEWSPAPER HEADLINE....				
A: STRAIGHT....			R-0771	
(23) 827+004	TITLE	TEXT	CPTION	
V: MUSIC ALBUM AD-CRAWL OF SONGS				
A: COUNTRY MUSIC....			R-0811	
342+003	TITLE	TEXT	CRAWL	
V: CRAWL RE VIDEO COPYWRITE FOR CABLE				
A: BROADCAST OF F-BALL GAME....			R-1292	
(36) 377+005	TITLE	TEXT	CRAWL	
V: END OF ROCK CONCERT-CREDITS CRAWL				
A: MUSIC....			R-1295	
(39) 250+009	TITLE	TEXT	SPACE	
V: CREDITS TO NEWS OVER SPACE SHUTTLE				
A: LANDING.... A-MUSIC....			R-1453	
(59) 663+002	TITLE	TEXT	DIAGNL	
V: TITLE (END)-'OFFICE OF WAR INFORMAT				
A: ION -MOTION PICTURE DIVISION'			R-2326	
(60) 343+004	TITLE	TEXT	INTRO	
V: FR OLD C CHAPLIN FILM-INTRO TITLE P				
A: AGES (2) RE TITLES IN FILM...			R-2339	
(61) 200+010	TITLE	TEXT	DIAGNL	
V: FR 'HUNCHBACK'- 'THE END'- & 'RKO R				
A: ADIO PICTURES'-CAST CREDITS..			R-2390	

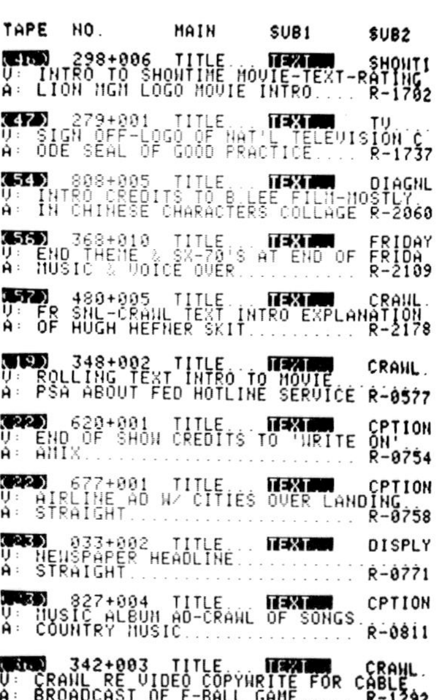

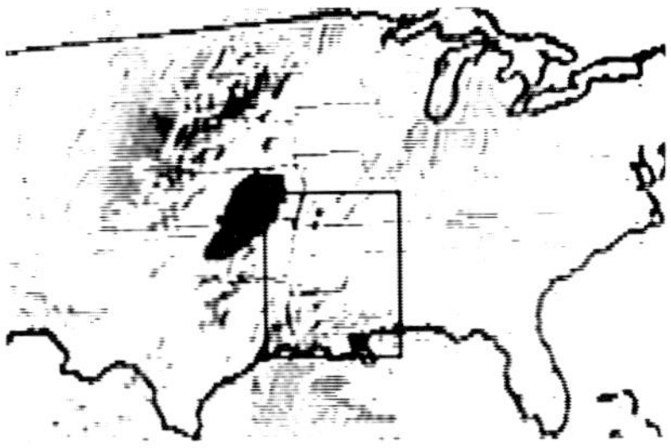

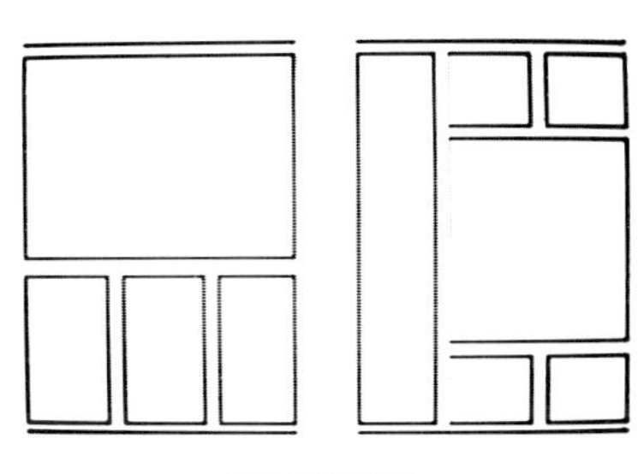
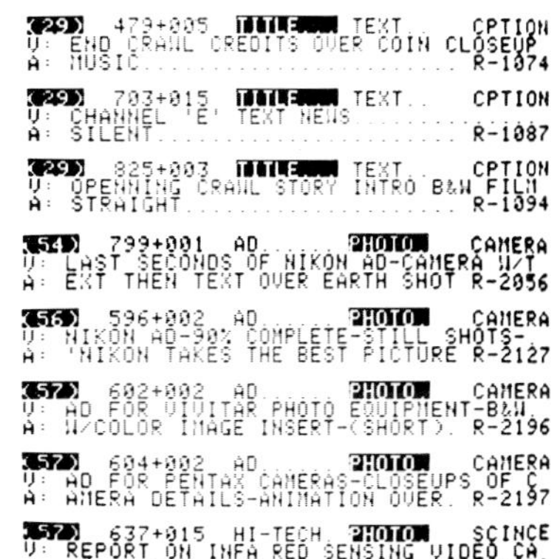
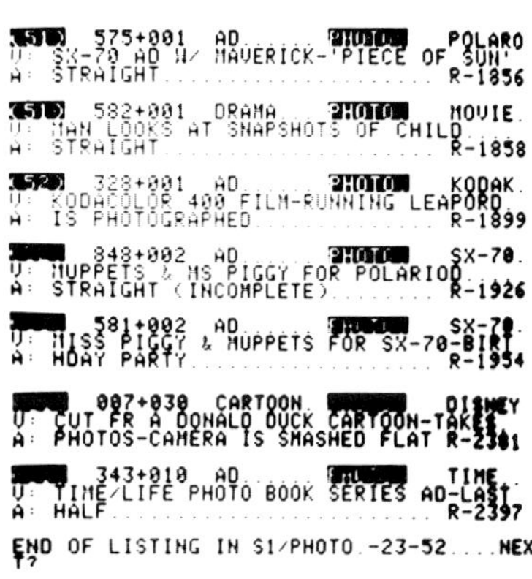

TAPE   NO.   MAIN   SUB1   SUB2

(53) 718+003 AD........PHOTO   CAMERA
V: CANON AE-1 CAMERA-SPACE AGE MOTIF-
A: 'YOUR BEST COMPOSITIONS'...... R-1969

(53) 833+001 AD........PHOTO   SX-70.
V: MISS PIGGY FOR POLAROID-SHORT VERSI
A: ON.............A-STRAIGHT...... R-1986

(53) 840+008 AD........PHOTO   TIMELI
V: LIFE MAG AD-GET 'BEST OF LIFE' PHOT
A: O BOOK AS GIFT W/SUBSCRIPTION R-1987

(54) 170+003 AD........PHOTO   SX-70.
V: MAVERICK FOR SX-70-'PIECE OF THE SU
A: N'-AUTO FILL IN FLASH........ R-2007

TAPE   NO.   MAIN   SUB1   SUB2

(10) 324+002 AD......PHOTO   CULTUR
V: PENTAX 110 CAMERA...............
A: STRAIGHT....................... R-0382

(08) 118+002 AD......PHOTO   SX-70.
V: SX-70 SONAR AD-PEOPLE HOLDING STILL
A: STRAIGHT....................... R-0245

(12) 147+004 AD......PHOTO   STAR..
V: MAVERICK POLAROID AD.............
A: STRAIGHT....................... R-0442

(11) 328+002 AD......PHOTO   STAR..
V: OLYMPUS AD W/ C.TIEGS & CAMERAS.
A: STRAIGHT....................... R-0736

(24) 028+032 DRAMA...PHOTO   CULTUR
V: HI-FASHION MODEL-PHOTO SESSION.
A: VOICE OVER.................... R-0817

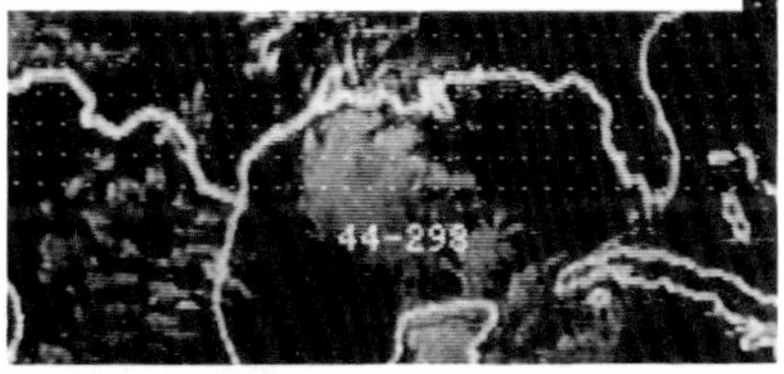

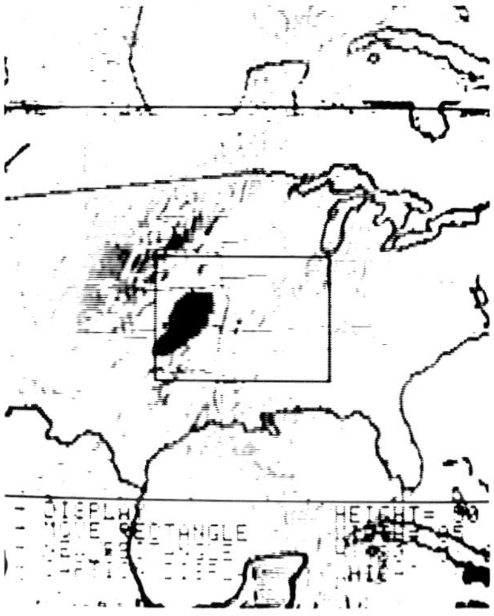

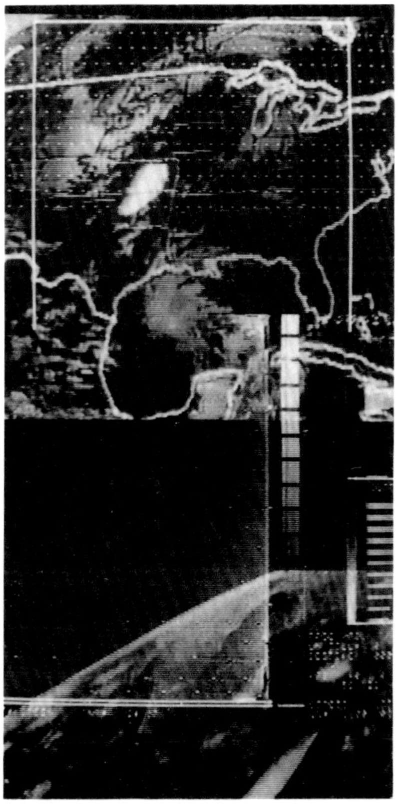

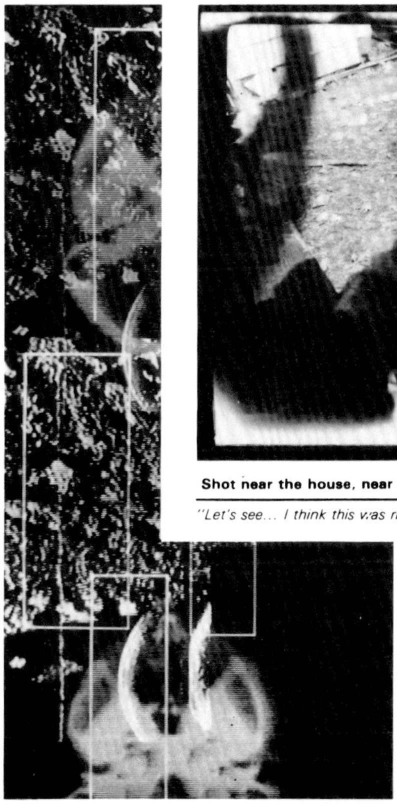

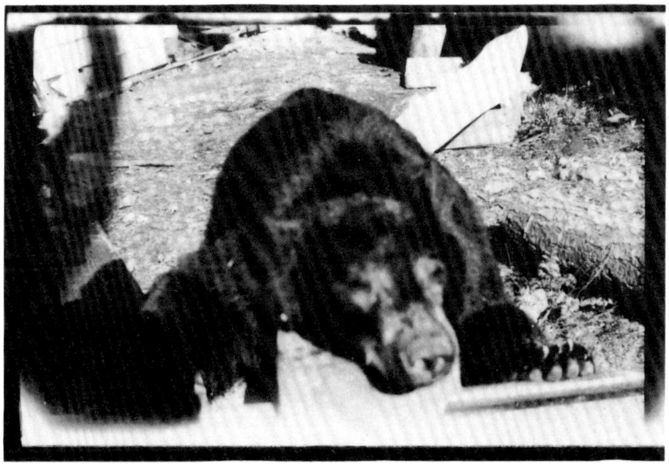

Shot near the house, near The Dalles, Oregon 1937

"Let's see... I think this was right before we moved... No, it was a couple of years before that..."

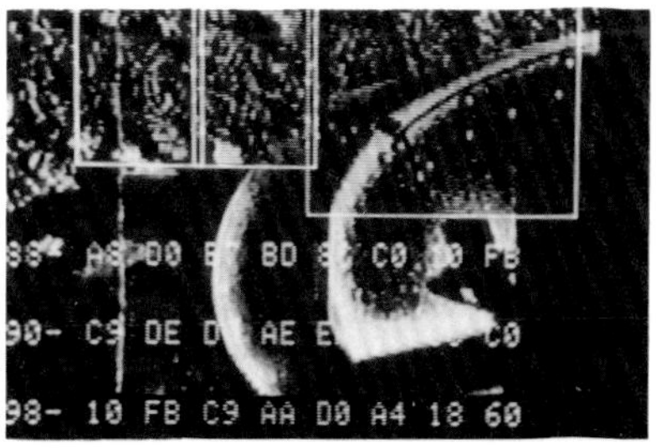

PHOTOGRAPHY: Print D$"Open Photography,L64": Print D$"Read Photography,R"X: For L= 1 to TX: Input Z$(L): Next: Print D$"Cl

61 BD 8C C0 10 FB 49 D5 D0 F4 EA BD 8C C0 10 FB C9 AA D0 F2 A0 56 BD 8C C0 10 FB C9 AD D0 E7 A9 00 88 84 26 BC 8C C0 10 FB 59 00

(29) 479+005 TITLE   TEXT..   CPTION
V: END CRAWL CREDITS OVER COIN CLOSEUP
A: MUSIC........................ R-1074

(29) 703+015 TITLE   TEXT..   CPTION
V: CHANNEL 'E' TEXT NEWS...........
A: SILENT....................... R-1087

(29) 825+003 TITLE   TEXT..   CPTION
V: OPENNING CRAWL STORY INTRO B&W FILM
A: STRAIGHT..................... R-1094

(54) 799+001 AD......PHOTO   CAMERA
V: LAST SECONDS OF NIKON AD-CAMERA W/T
A: EXT THEN TEXT OVER EARTH SHOT R-2056

(56) 596+002 AD......PHOTO   CAMERA
V: NIKON AD-90% COMPLETE-STILL SHOTS-
A: 'NIKON TAKES THE BEST PICTURE R-2127

(57) 602+002 AD......PHOTO   CAMERA
V: AD FOR VIVITAR PHOTO EQUIPMENT-B&W
A: W/COLOR IMAGE INSERT-(SHORT). R-2196

(57) 604+002 AD......PHOTO   CAMERA
V: AD FOR PENTAX CAMERAS-CLOSEUPS OF C
A: AMERA DETAILS-ANIMATION OVER. R-2197

(57) 637+015 HI-TECH PHOTO   SCINCE
V: REPORT ON INFA RED SENSING VIDEO CA.

(51) 575+001 AD......PHOTO   POLARO
V: SX-70 AD W/ MAVERICK-'PIECE OF SUN'
A: STRAIGHT..................... R-1856

(51) 582+001 DRAMA...PHOTO   MOVIE.
V: MAN LOOKS AT SNAPSHOTS OF CHILD.
A: STRAIGHT..................... R-1858

(52) 328+001 AD......PHOTO   KODAK.
V: KODACOLOR 400 FILM-RUNNING LEAPORD.
A: IS PHOTOGRAPHED.............. R-1899

( ) 848+002 AD......PHOTO   SX-70.
V: MUPPETS & MS PIGGY FOR POLARIOD.
A: STRAIGHT (INCOMPLETE)........ R-1926

( ) 581+002 AD......PHOTO   SX-70.
V: MISS PIGGY & MUPPETS FOR SX-70-BIRI
A: HDAY PARTY................... R-1954

( ) 007+030 CARTOON.   DISNEY
V: CUT FR A DONALD DUCK CARTOON-TAKES
A: PHOTOS-CAMERA IS SMASHED FLAT R-2301

( ) 343+010 AD......   TIME.
V: TIME/LIFE PHOTO BOOK SERIES AD-LAST
A: HALF......................... R-2397

END OF LISTING IN S1/PHOTO -23-52....NEX
T?

- PHOTOGRAPHY -

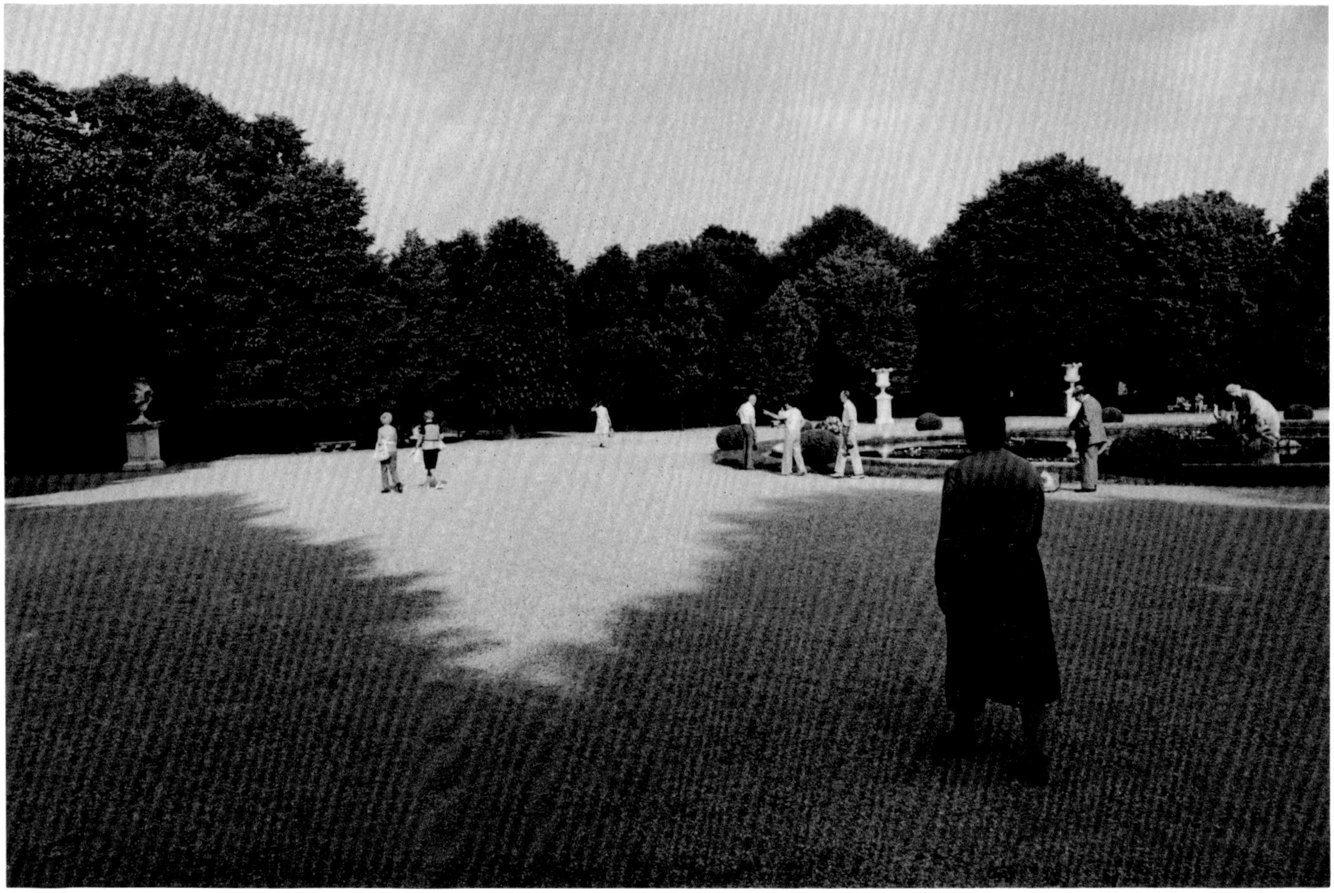

Untitled no. 237 - ''Let's see... it's at a park... in France... no, in Italy... yeah, I think it's in Italy...''

Il dit qu'il l'a prise... en France? (rire)... non, en Italie... Il se rappelle qu'il l'a prise dans un parc, en Italie...

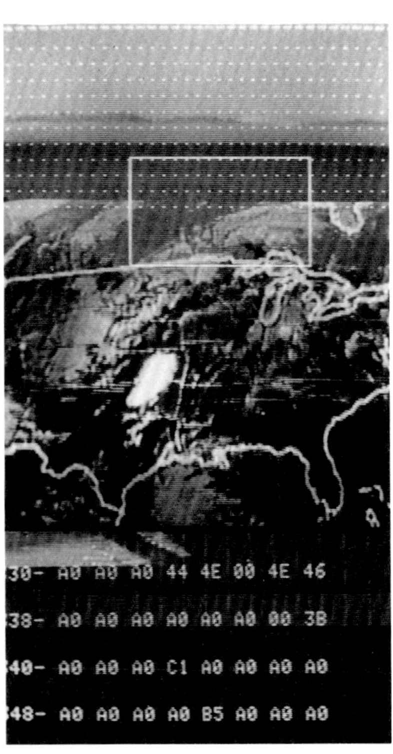

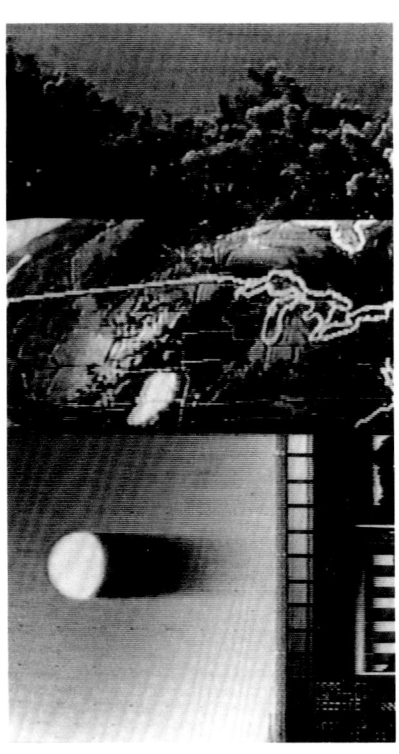

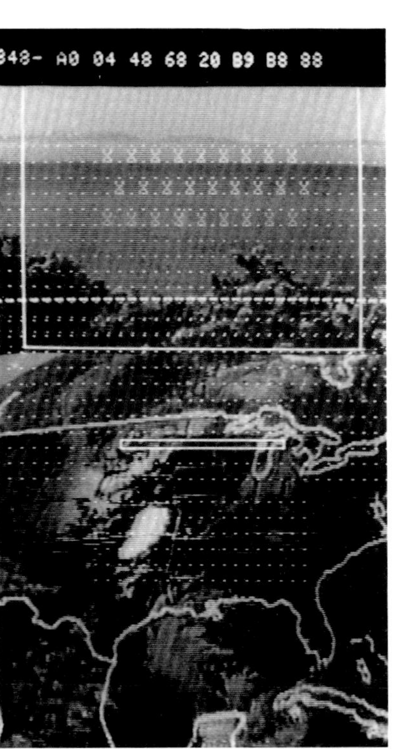

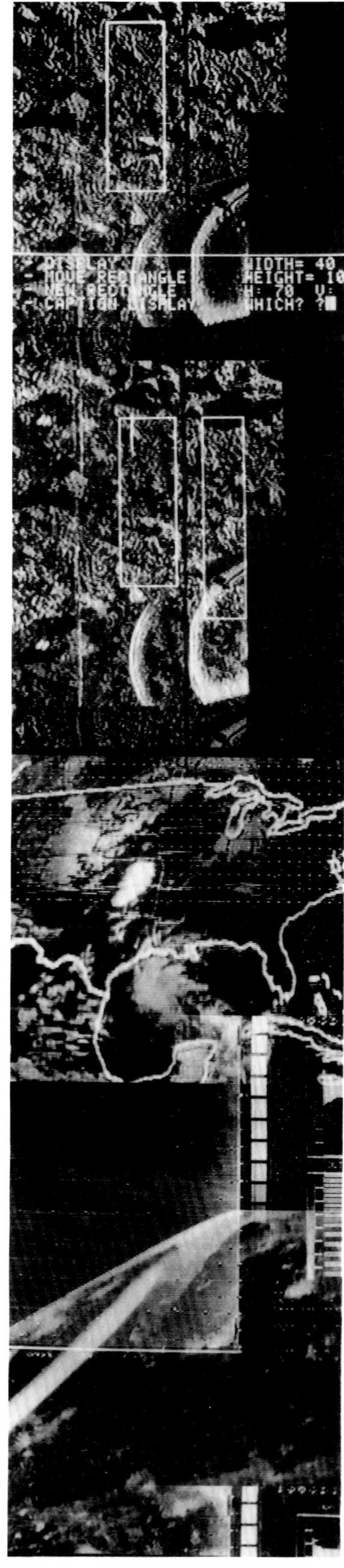

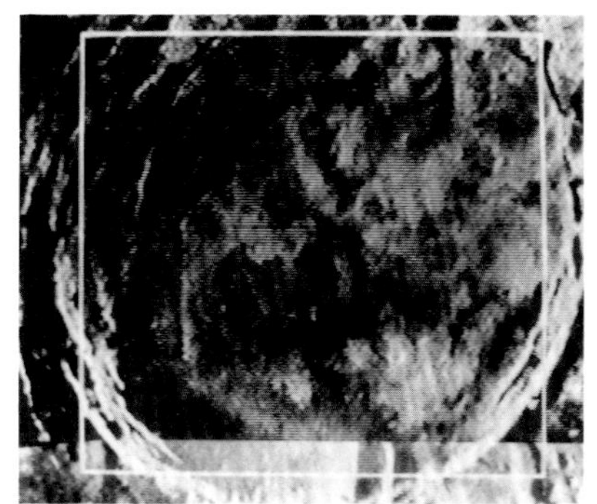

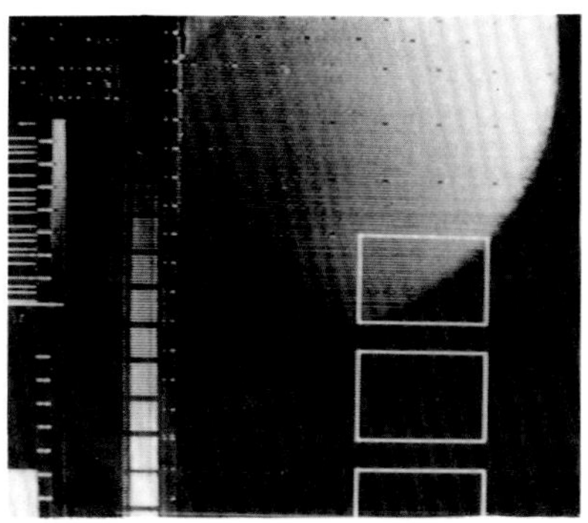

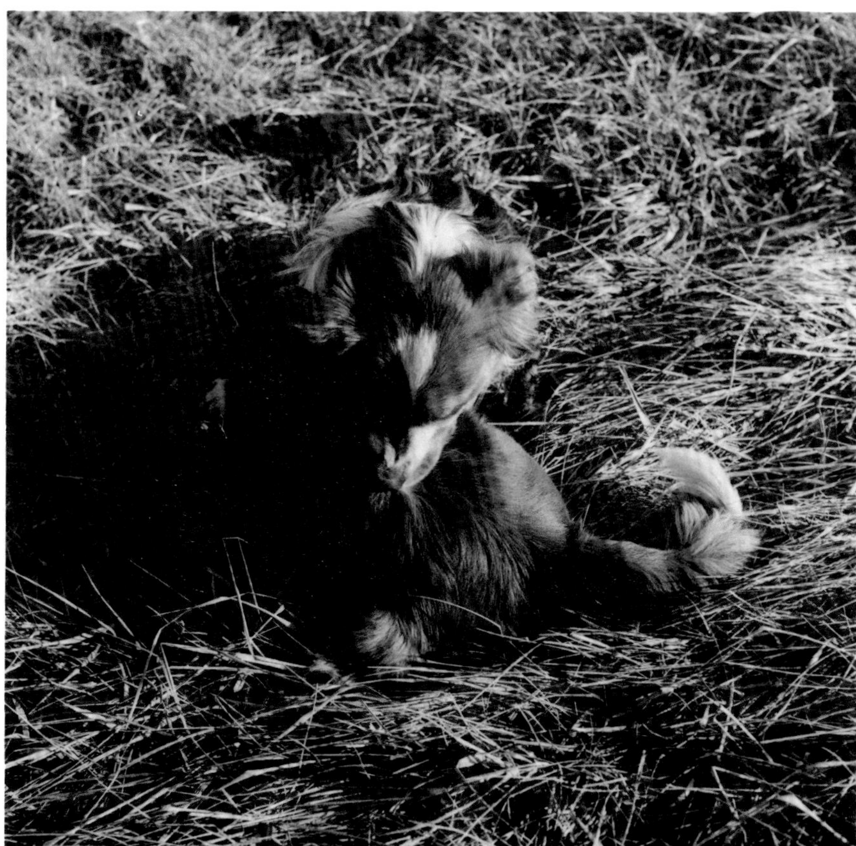

Satellite photo of farmer's dog at 10⁸ magnification, near Urbana, Illinois

CAT scanning your dog from 21,000 miles in space.

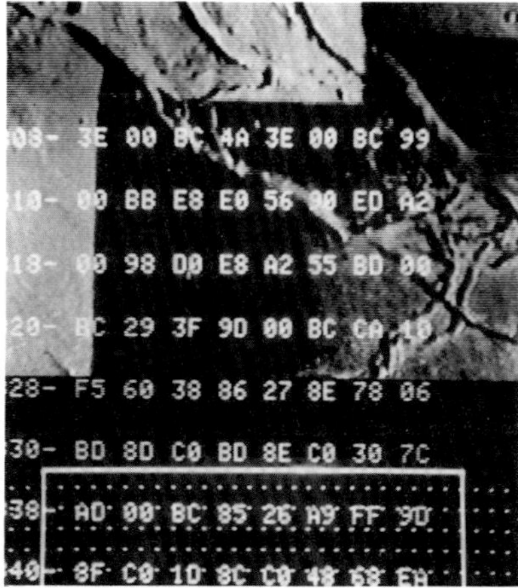

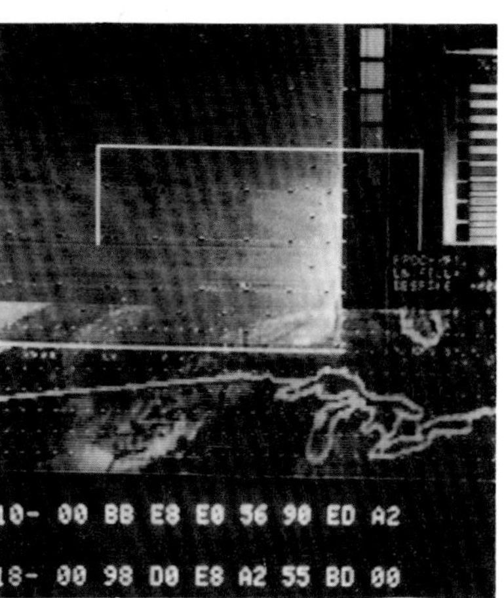

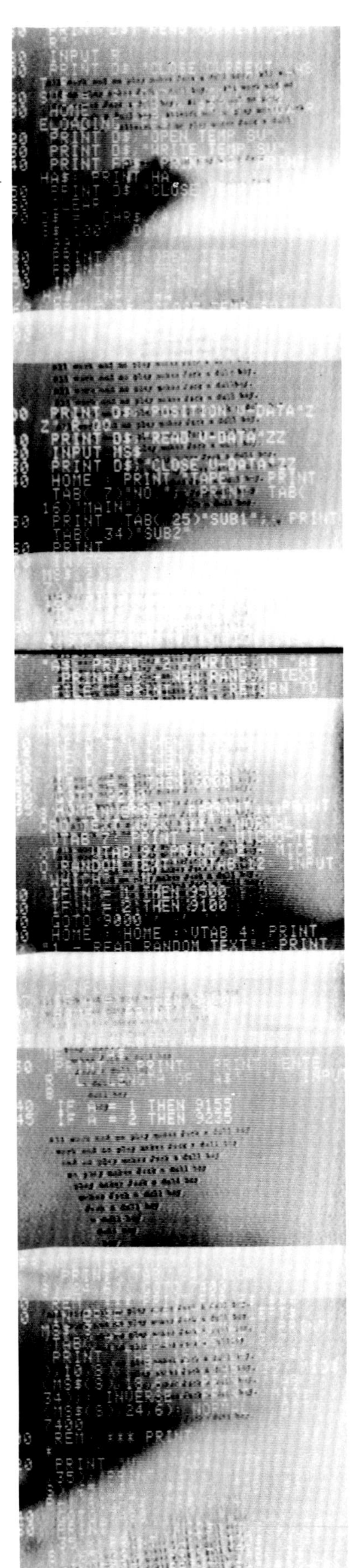

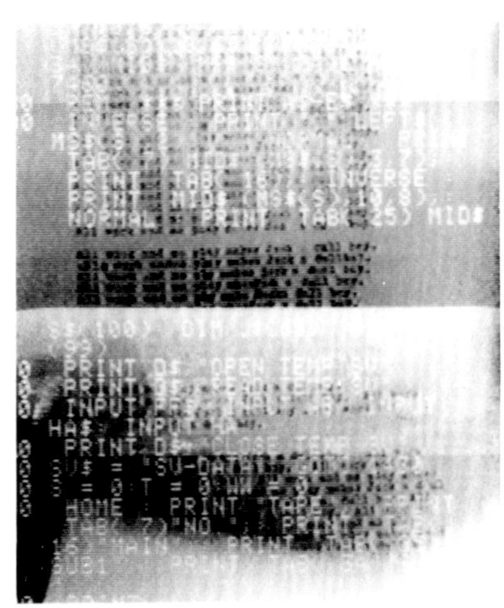

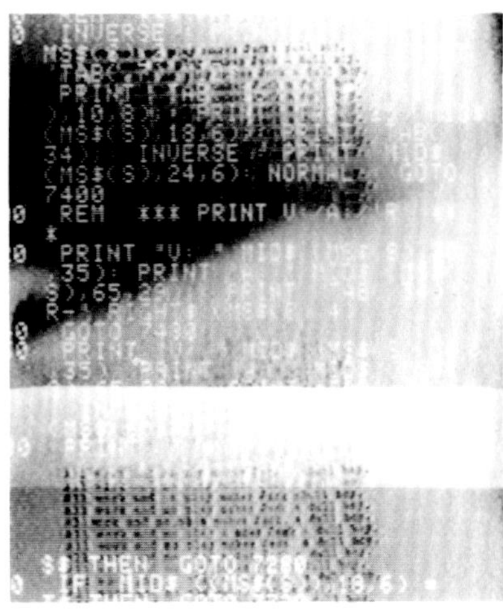

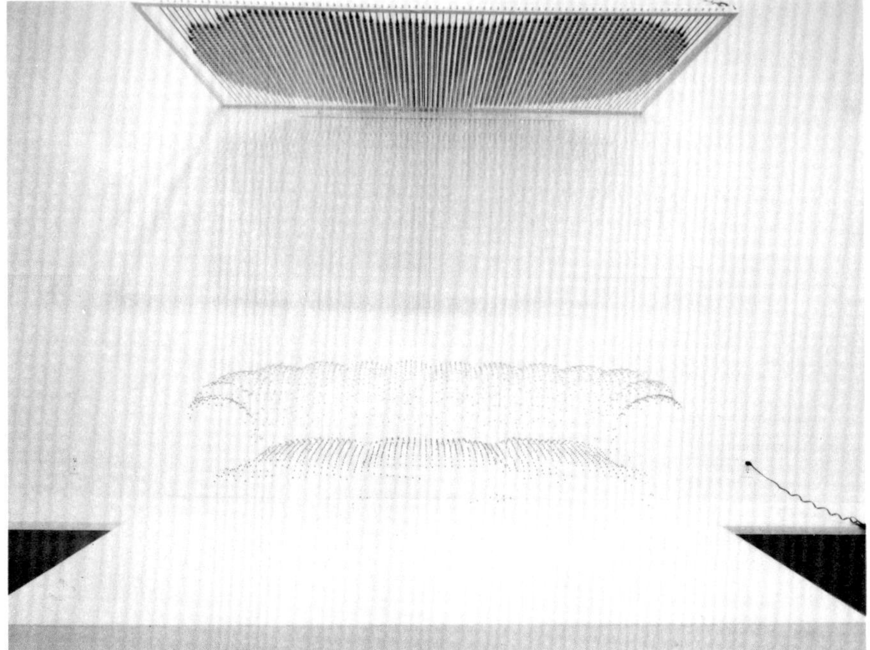

'Couch' - Richard Berger, 1976

When in its presence, our spontaneous recognition of the 'couch' is a perception of both an

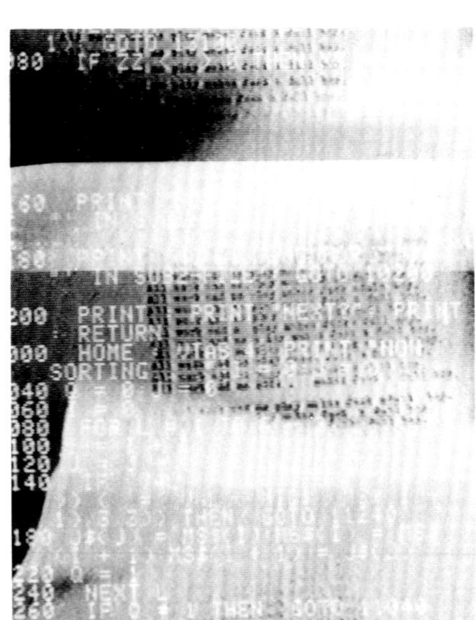

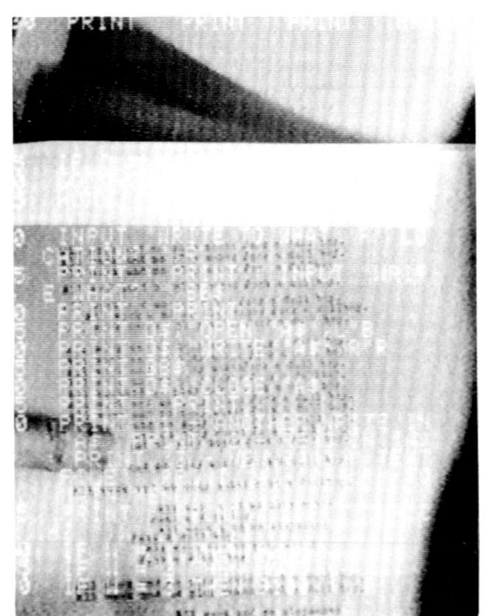

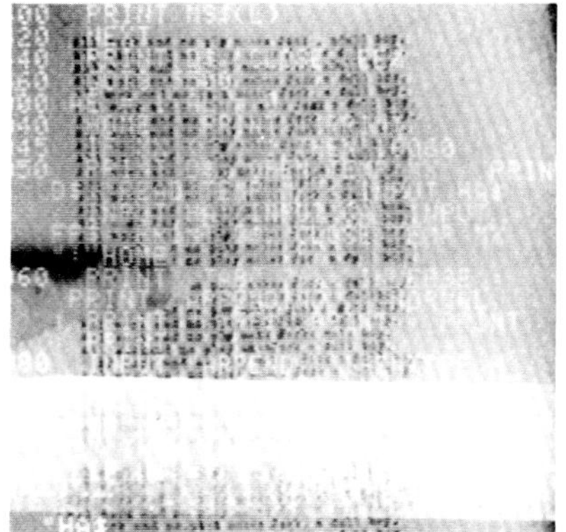
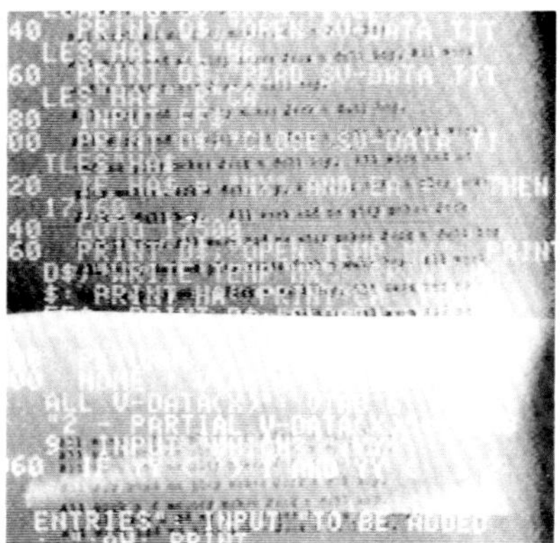
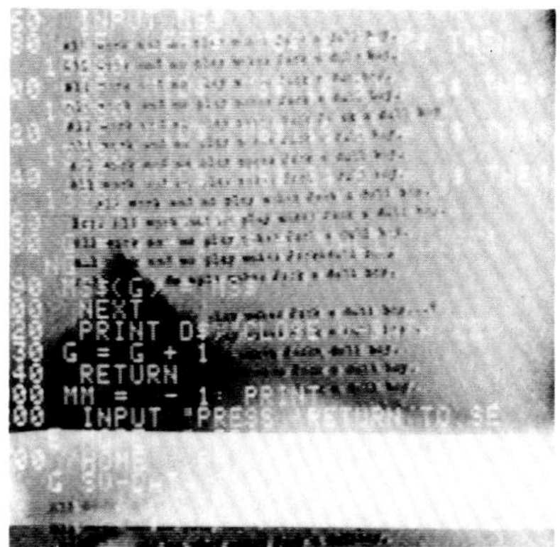

Space

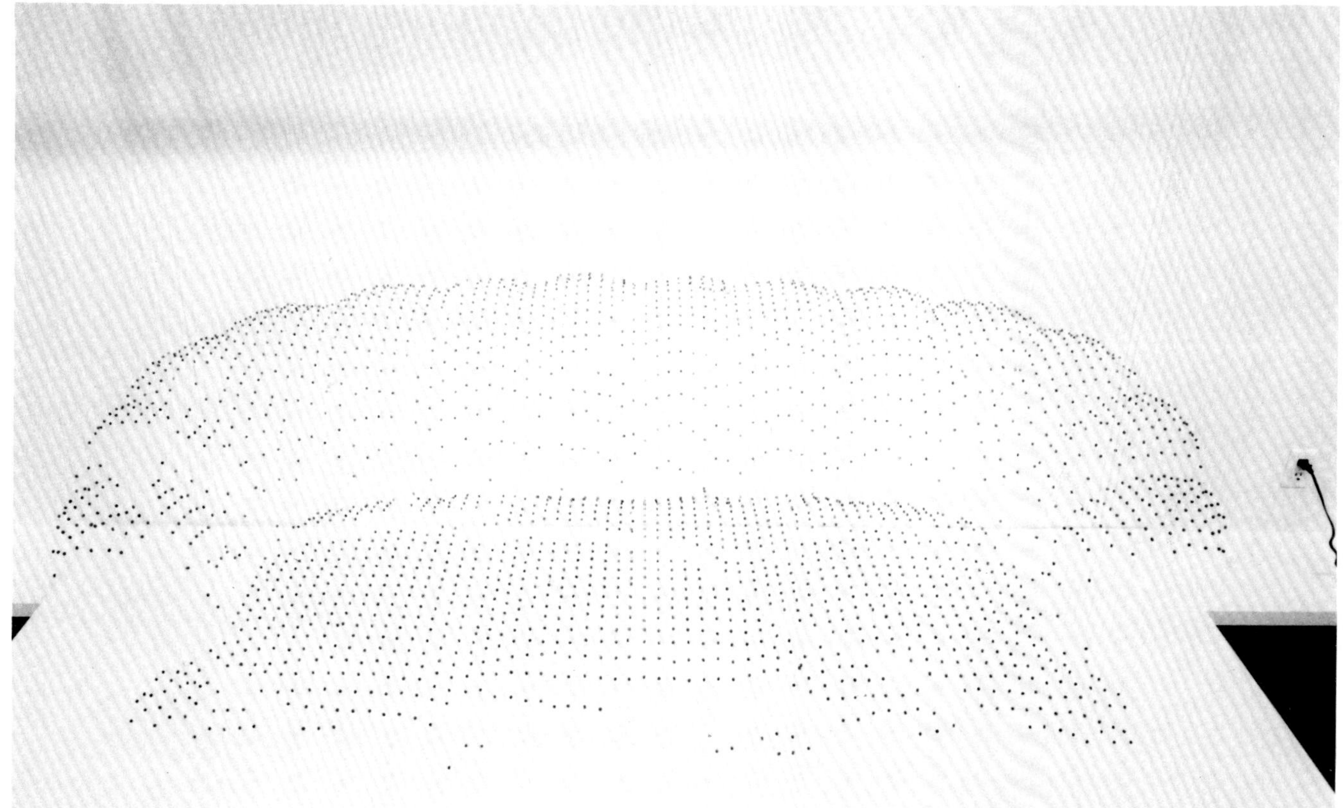

It can't be photographed adequately.

elegant object and our own ability to navigate complex spacial descriptions and their transformations as binocular animals moving in space.

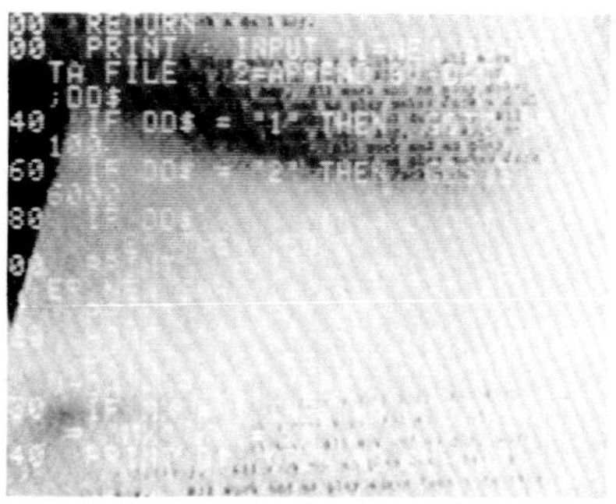
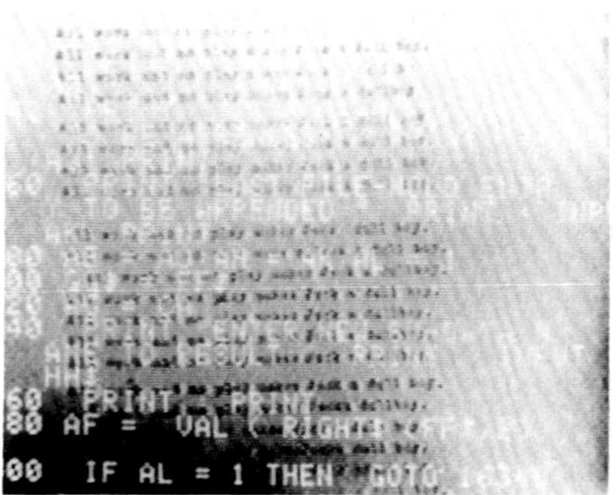

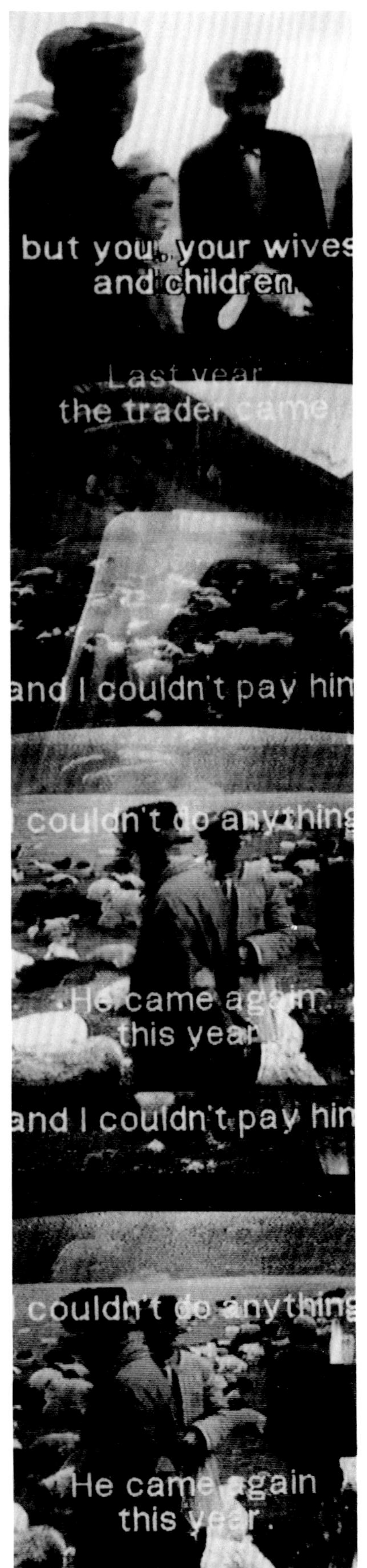

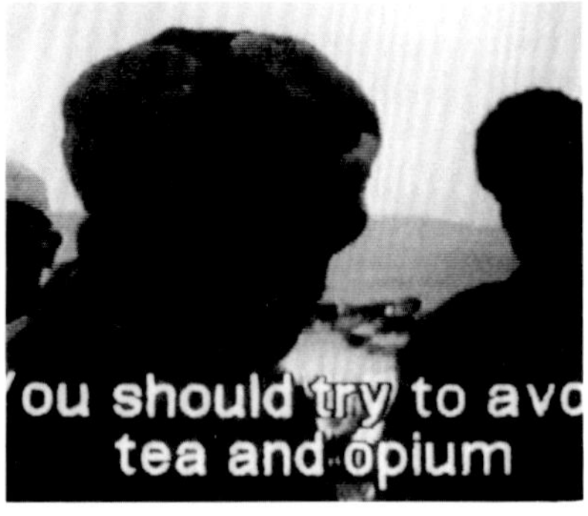

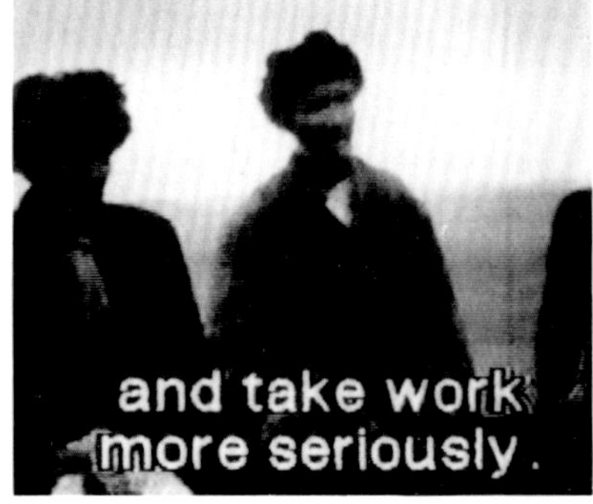

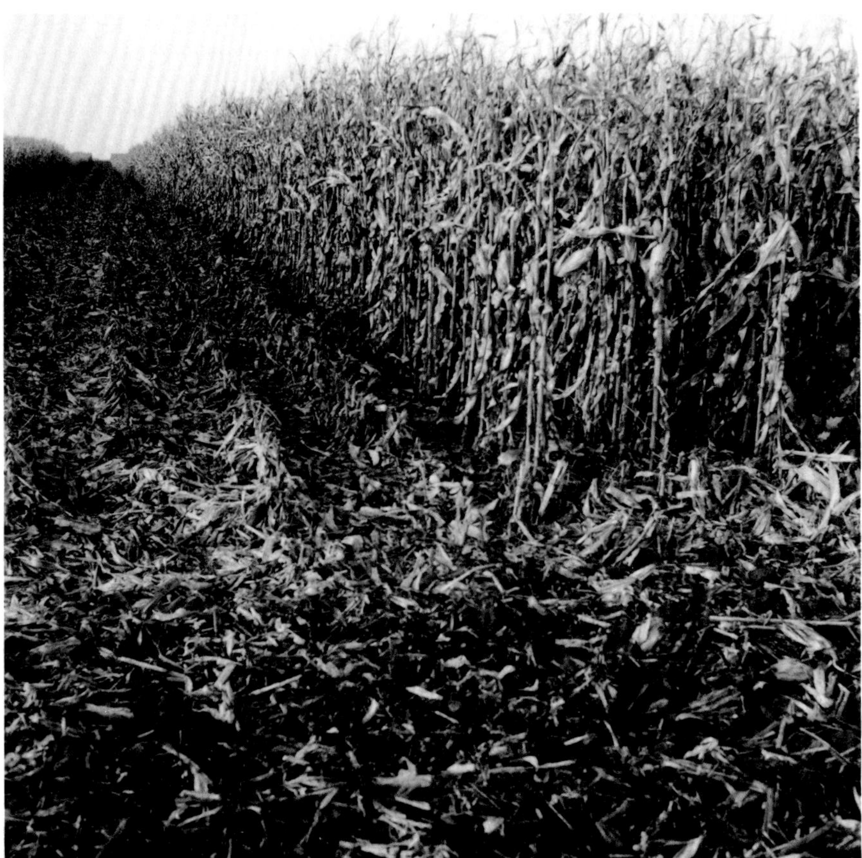

University of Illinois at Champaign/Urbana - Agriculture Program

Ag.En.311 - Instrumentation and Measurements; Ag.Ec.335 - Economics of Food Distribution

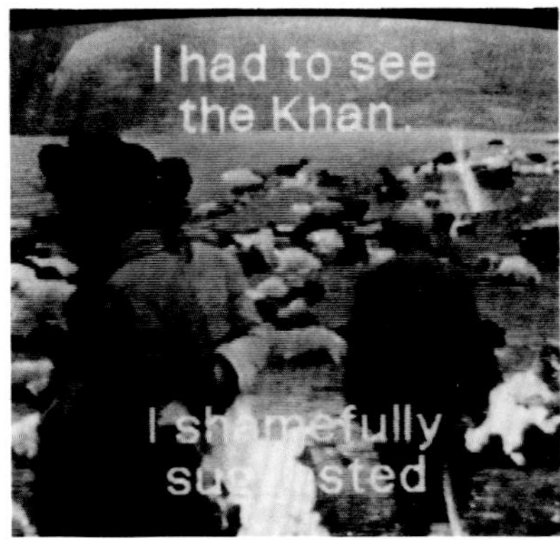

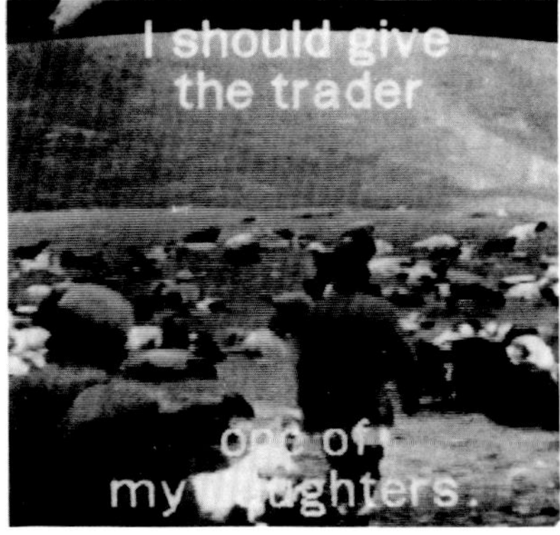

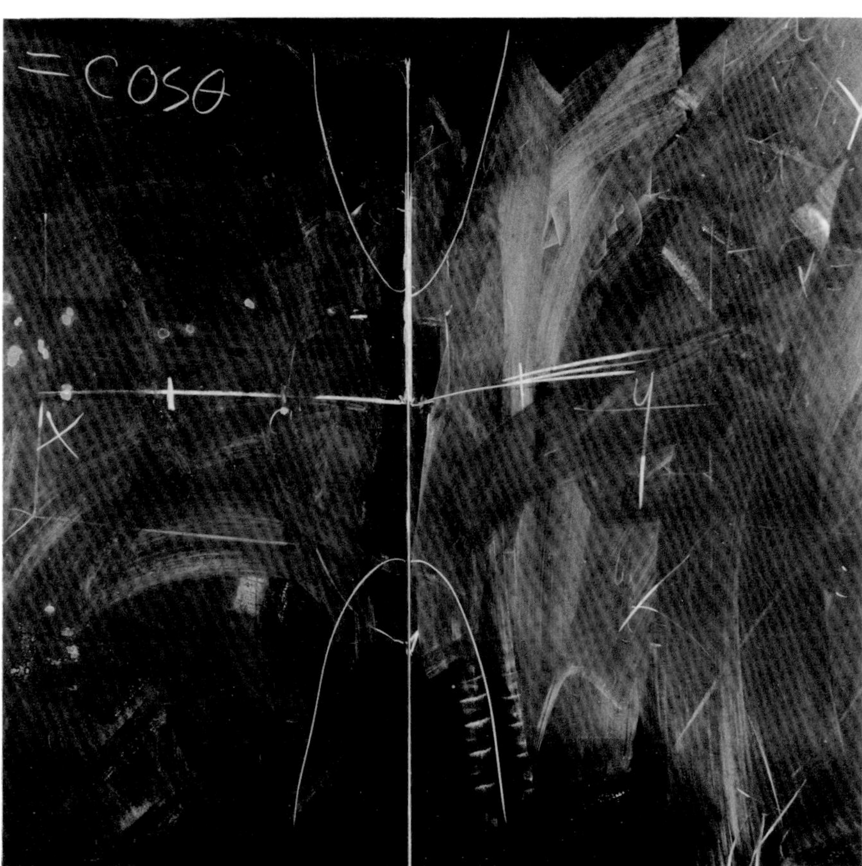

University of Illinois at Urbana/Champaign - Mathematics Program

A forest is an undirected graph which contains no cycles. A connected forest is a tree.

A 'FOREST' IS AN UNDIRECTED GRAPH WHICH CONTAINS NO CYCLES. A CONNECTED FOREST IS A 'TREE'. A 'ROOTED TREE', (T,R), IS A TREE T=(V,E) WITH A DISTINGUISHED VERTEX R(.V. IF I(.V AND I≠R, THE 'FATHER' OF I IN (T,R) IS THE VERTEX J (.V WHICH IS ADJACENT TO I ON THE SHORTEST PATH IN T JOINING I AND R. THEN I IS THE 'SON' OF J

IF J LIES ON THE SHORTEST PATH IN T JOINING I AND R, THEN J IS AN 'ANCESTOR OF I AND I IS A DESCENDANT OF J. IN THIS PAPER, A 'DIRECTED ROOTED TREE' (T,R), IS DEFINED TO BE A DIRECTED GRAPH T=(V,E) WITH A DISTINGUISHED VERTEX R(.V. IN WHICH THERE IS NO EDGE OF E LEAVING R. AND FOR EACH I(.V WITH I≠R, THERE IS A UNIQUE PATH IN T FROM I TO R^2.

DIRECTED ROOTED TREE, (T,R), IS DEFINED TO BE A DIRECTED GRAPH T=(V,E) WITH A DISTINGUISHED VERTEX R*V, IN WHICH THERE IS NO EDGE OF E LEAVING R AND FOR EACH

A 'FOREST' IS AN UNDIRECTED GRAPH WHICH CONTAINS NO CYCLES. A CONNECTED FOREST IS A TREE. A ROOTED TREE, (T,R), IS A TREE T=(V,E) WITH A DISTINGUISHED VERTEX R*V

IF J LIES ON THE SHORTEST PATH IN T JOINING I AND R, THEN J IS AN 'ANCESTOR OF I AND I IS A DESCENDANT OF J. IN THIS PAPER, A 'DIRECTED ROOTED TREE', (T,R), IS DEFINED TO BE A DIRECTED GRAPH T=(V,E) WITH A DISTINGUISHED VERTEX R(.V. IN WHICH THERE IS NO EDGE OF E LEAVING R AND FOR EACH I(.V WITH I≠R, THERE IS A UNIQUE PATH IN T FROM I TO R^2.

(I,J)(.E. J IS THE 'FATHER' OF I I IS THE 'SON' OF J. IF THERE IS H IN T FROM I TO J THEN I IS A SCENDANT' OF J ('PROPER DESCENDANT I≠J). AND J IS AN 'ANCESTOR' OF ROPER ANCESTOR' IF I≠J). A 'DIRE FOREST' IS A UNION OF DIRECTED ROO TREES WITH PAIRWISE DISJOINT VERTE S.

IF THERE IS A PATH IN T FROM I TO J THEN I IS A 'DESCENDENT' OF J ('PROPER ANCESTOR' IF I≠J). A 'DIRECTED FOREST' IS A UNION OF DIRECTED ROOTED TREES WITH PAIRWISE DISJOINT VERTEX SETS.

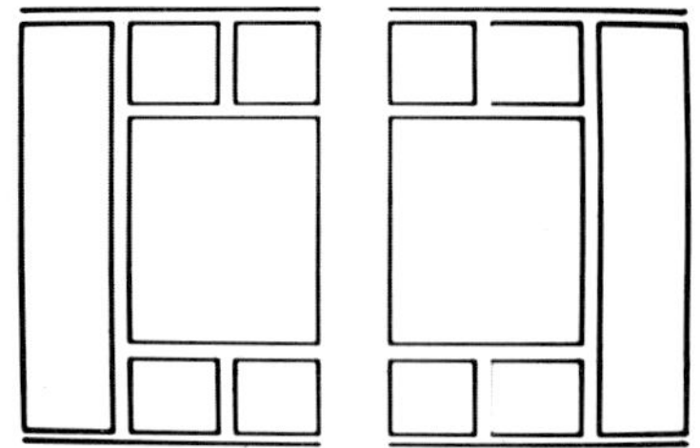

244+176 DOCUMENT ANTHRO   CPTION
V: NOVA-AFGANI TRIBE-DIALOG CPTION-HIG
A: H MT.PAMIR-LATER MOVED TO PAK R-1944

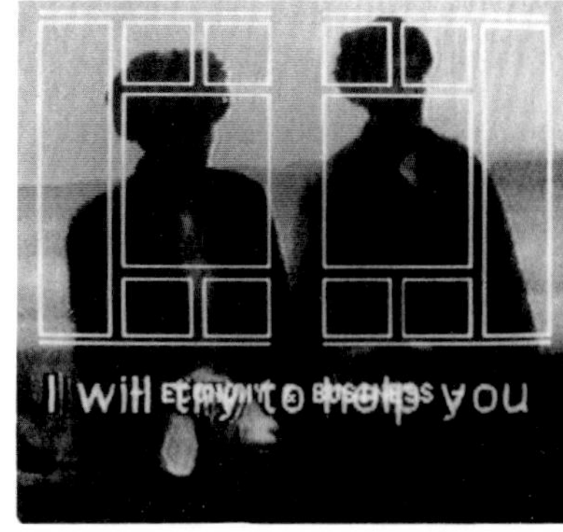

479+005 TITLE   TEXT   CPTION
V: END CRAWL CREDITS OVER COIN CLOSEUP
A: MUSIC............................ R-1074

703+015 TITLE   TEXT   CPTION
V: CHANNEL 'E' TEXT NEWS............
A: SILENT........................... R-1087

825+003 TITLE   TEXT   CPTION
V: OPENNING CRAWL STORY INTRO B&W FILM
A: STRAIGHT......................... R-1094

779+003 CULTURE   TEXT   CPTION
V: LETTERS TO 60-MINUTES-TEXT ON CARDS
A: AIR FORCE NARRATOR............... R-1213

248+011 TITLE   TEXT   CPTION
V: INTRO TO 'MAGIC CHRISTIAN'-FOLLOW
A: BOUNCING BALL-CPTIONOVERMONEY R-1638

124+006 C-NEWS   MONEY   FAMILY
V: PROBLEMS OF HOME BUYING.........
A: VOICE OVER....................... R-0327

018+004 C-NEWS   MONEY   HOME..
V: HOME MORGAGES (B&W TRANS).....
A: VOICE OVER....................... R-0434

END OF LISTING IN M/C-NEWS-4-92....NEXT?

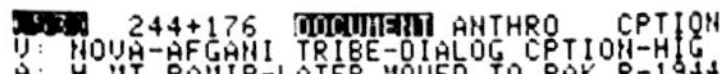

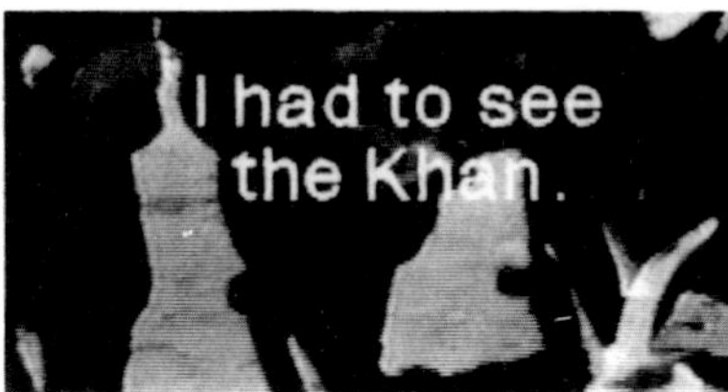

Economy & Business

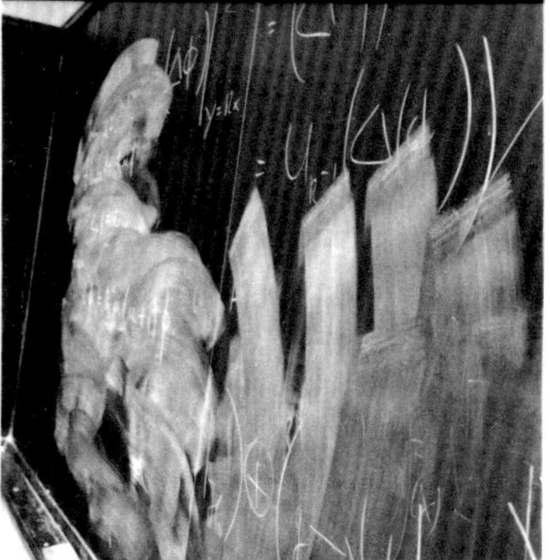

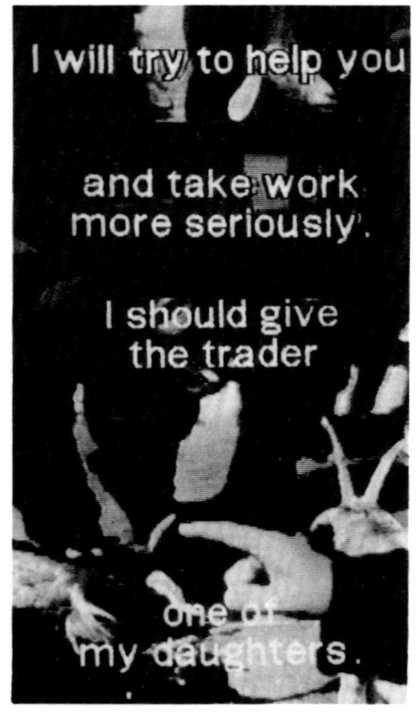

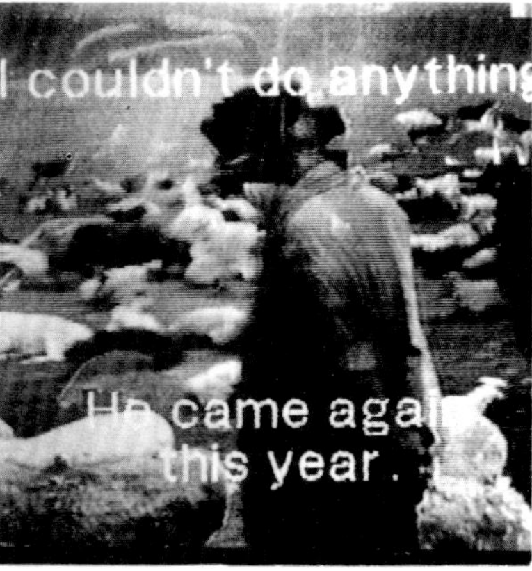

A "directed forest" is a union of directed rooted trees with pairwise disjoint vertex sets.

Last year the trader came and I couldn't pay him. I couldn't do anything. He came again this year. I still couldn't do anything. I had to see the Khan. I shamefully suggested I should give the trader one of my daughters. "I won't marry him", she said, "I'll die if I do".

ECONOMY & BUSINESS: Print D$"Open Econ/Biz,L198": Print D$"Read Econ/Biz,R"X: For L=1 to EB: Input Z$(L): Next: Print D$"Close Econ

A0 04 48 68 20 B9 B8 88 D0 F8 A9 D5 20 B8 B8 A9 AA 20 B8 B8 A9 AD 20 B8 B8 98 A0 56 D0 03 B9 00 BC 59 FF BB AA BD 29 BA A6 27 9D 8D C0

```
      A 'FOREST' IS AN UNDIRECTED GRAPH WHICH
      CONTAINS NO CYCLES. A CONNECTED FOREST
      IS A 'TREE'. A 'ROOTED TREE', (T,R), IS
      A TREE T=(V,E) WITH A DISTINGUISHED
3120  ON I GOTO 3300,3400,3500,10
      0
3300  HOME : VTAB 3
3310  PRINT "A 'FOREST' IS AN UND
      IRECTED GRAPH WHICH": PRINT
3320  PRINT "CONTAINS NO CYCLES.
      A CONNECTED FOREST": PRINT
3330  PRINT "IS A 'TREE'. A 'ROOT
      ED TREE', (T,R), IS": PRINT
3335  PRINT "A TREE T=(V,E) WITH
      A DISTINGUISHED": PRINT
3340  PRINT "VERTEX R < V. IF I <
      V AND I/=R, THE": PRINT
3345  PRINT "'FATHER' OF I IN (T
```

```
      prefer our Afghan ways
3430  PRINT "OF I AND I IS A DESC
      ENDANT OF J. IN": PRINT
3435  PRINT "THIS PAPER, A 'DIREC
      TED ROOTED TREE',": PRINT
3440  PRINT "(T,R), IS DEFINED TO
      BE A DIRECTED GRA-": PRINT
3445  PRINT "PH T=(V,E) WITH A DI
      STINGUISHED VERTEX": PRINT
3450  PRINT "R < V, IN WHICH THER
      E IS NO EDGE OF E": PRINT
3455  PRINT "LEAVING R AND FOR EA
      CH I < V WITH I/=R,": PRINT
3460  PRINT "THERE IS A UNIQUE PA
      TH IN T FROM I TO ": PRINT
3465  PRINT "R^2."
3470  GOTO 3365
```

```
3335  PRINT "A TREE T=(V,E) WITH
      A DISTINGUISHED": PRINT
3340  PRINT "VERTEX R < V. IF I <
      V AND I/=R, THE": PRINT
3345  PRINT "'FATHER' OF I IN (T,
      R) IS THE VERTEX J": PRINT
3350  PRINT "(V WHICH IS ADJACENT
      TO I ON THE SHORT-": PRINT
3355  PRINT "EST PATH IN T JOININ
      G I AND R. THEN I": PRINT
3360  PRINT "IS THE 'SON' OF J."
3365  FOR L = 1 TO 5000: NEXT : GOTO
      3000
3400  HOME : VTAB 3
3420  PRINT "IF J LIES ON THE SHO
      RTEST PATH IN T": PRINT
3425  PRINT "JOINING I AND R, THE
      N J IS AN 'ANCESTOR": PRINT
3430  PRINT "OF I AND I IS A DESC
      ENDANT OF J. IN": PRINT
3435  PRINT "THIS PAPER, A 'DIREC
```

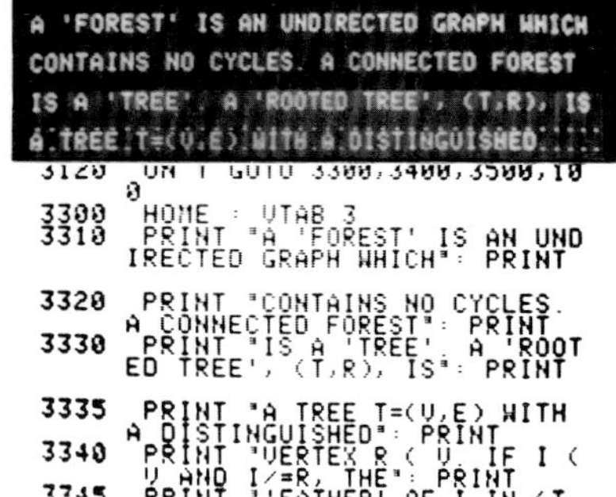

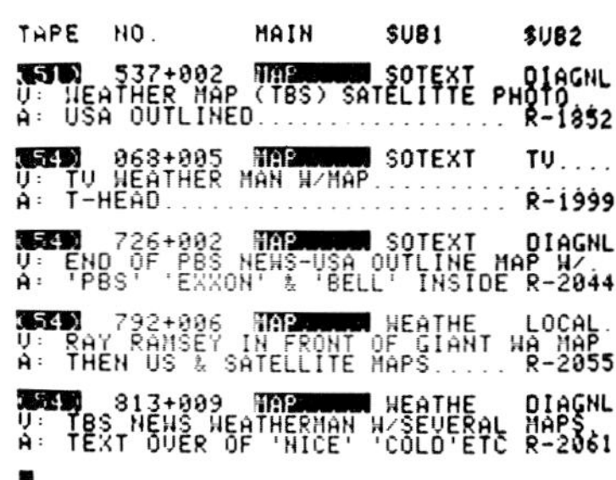

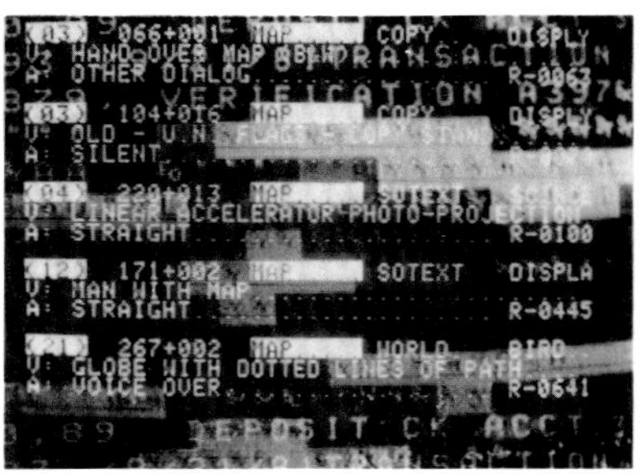

Display

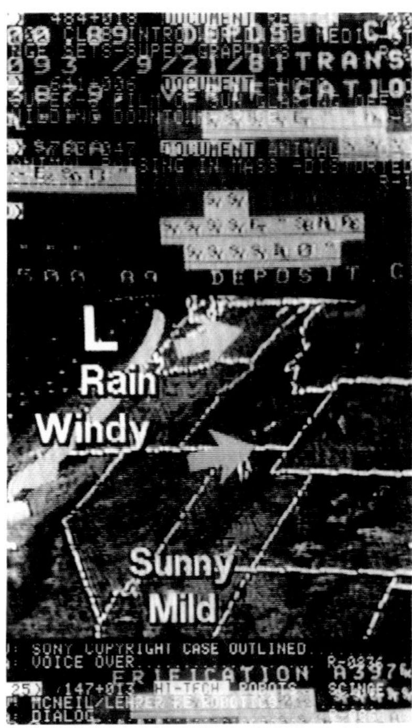

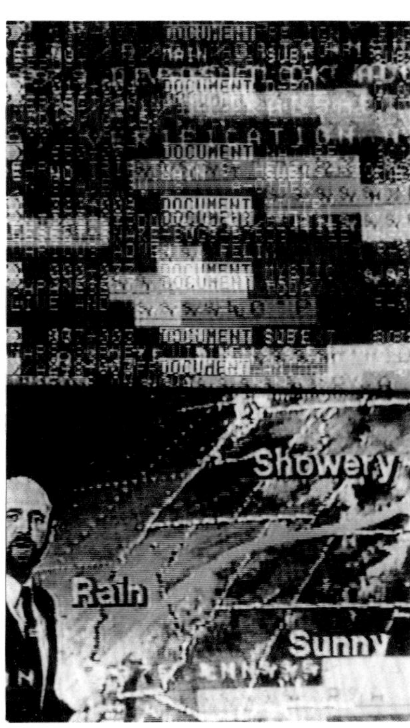

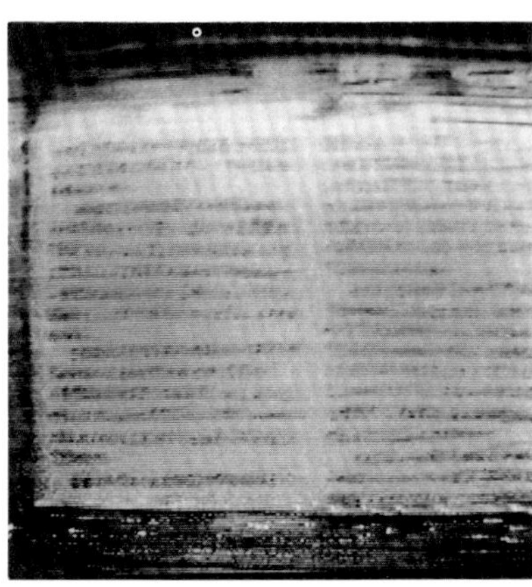

The Map and its Plan

Books and their pages.

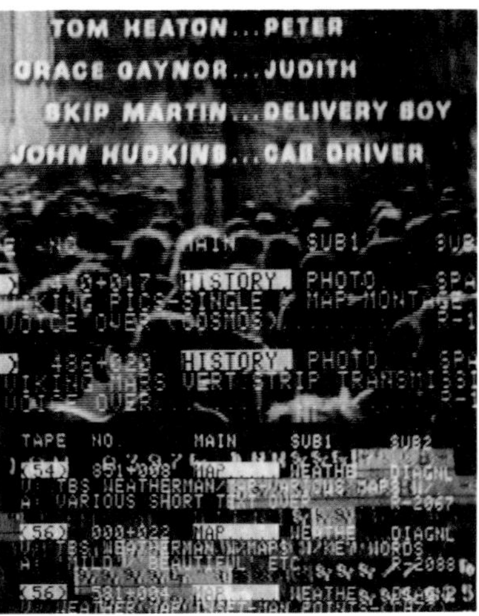

Map & Plan

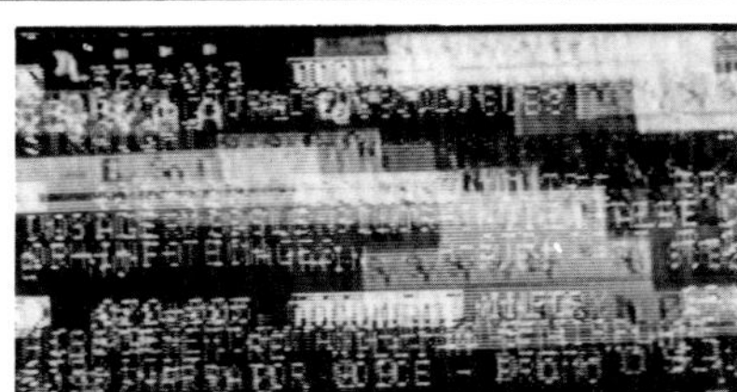

MAP & PLAN: Print D$"Open Map/Plan,L180": Print D$"Read Map/Plan,R"X: For L=1 to XY: Input Z$(L): Next: Print D$"Close Map/Plan"

00 98 D0 E8 A2 55 BD 00 BC 29 3F 9D 00 BC CA 10 F5 60 38 86 27 8E 78 06 BD 8D C0 BD 8E C0 30 7C AD 00 BC 85 26 A9 FF 9D 8F C0 1D 8C C0

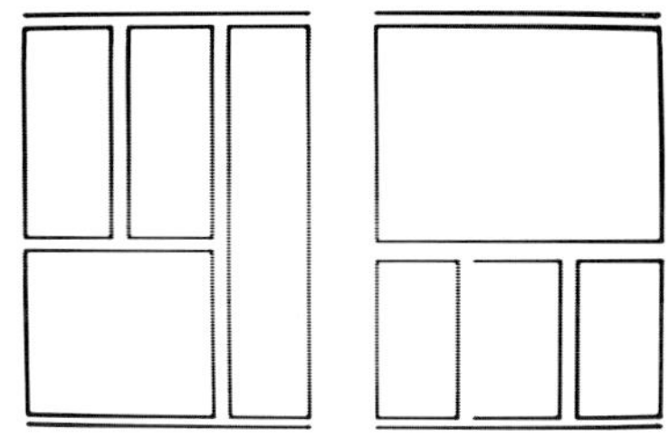

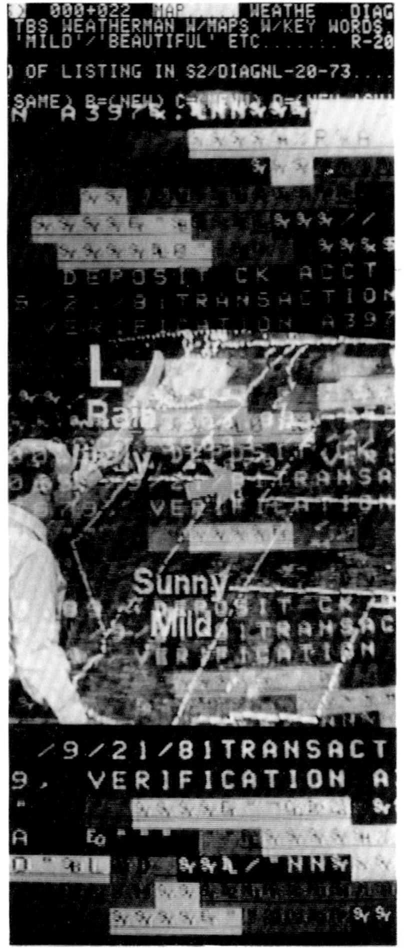

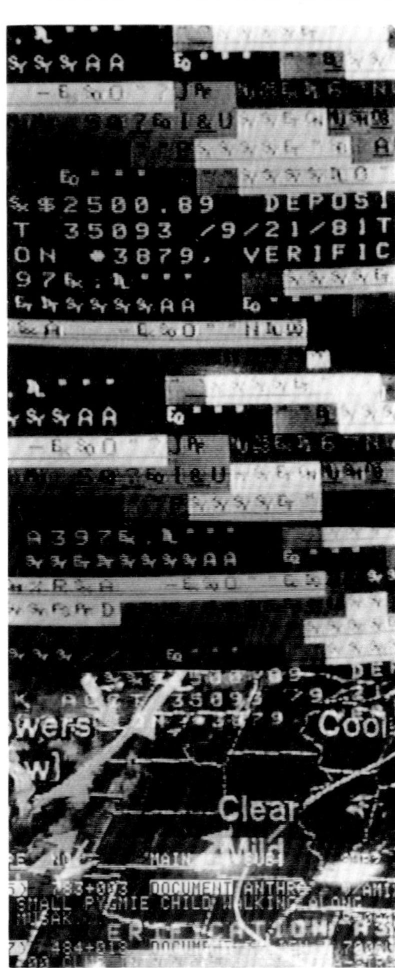

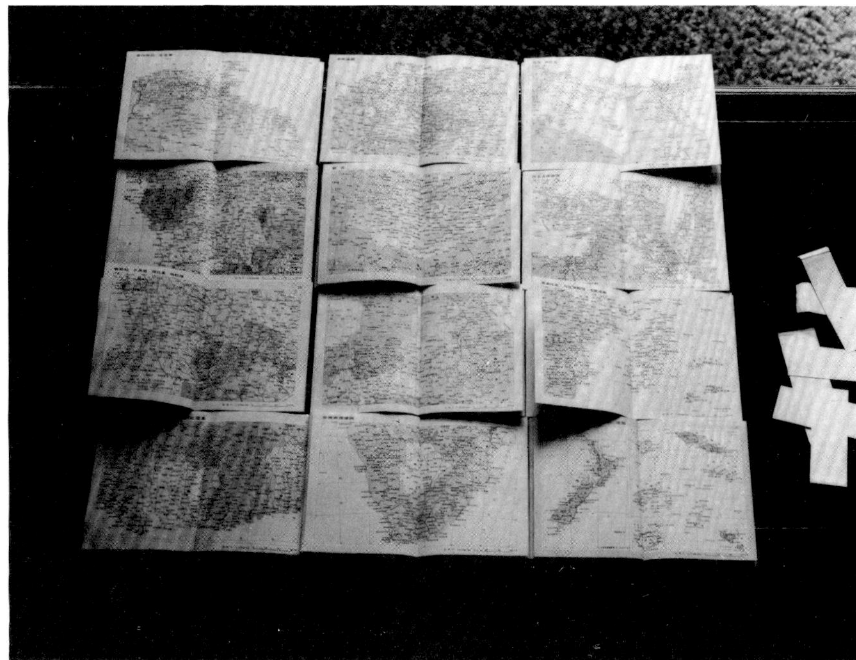

MX Missile 'shellgame' Atlas

sequenced daily by the National Bureau of Encryptation, Washington, D.C.

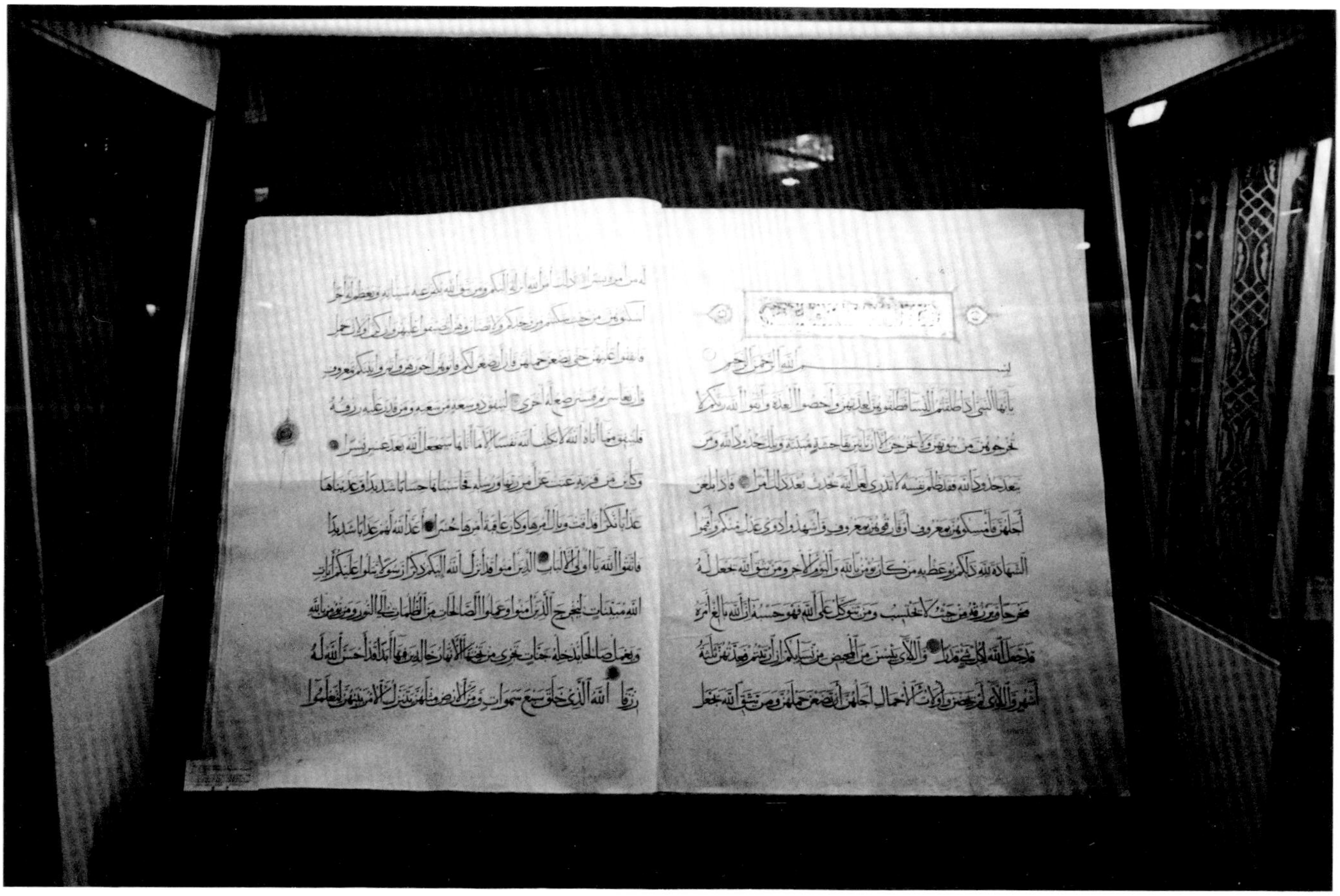

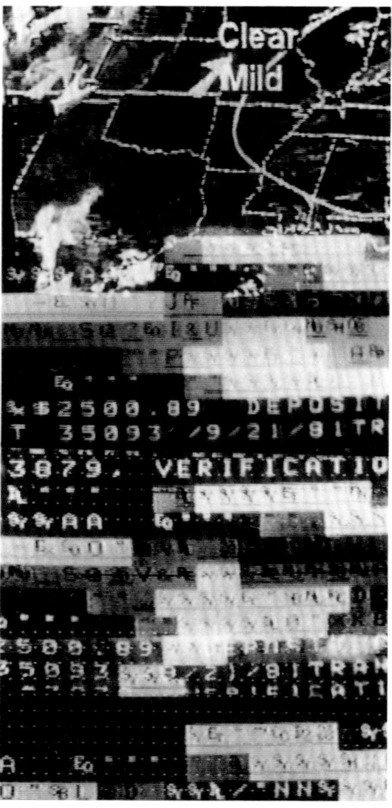

Giant Koran inside a glass case, inside the British Museum.

The Koran ('the reading' or 'book to be read') assembled the numerous original revelations to Mohammed in roughly the order of their length, without regard to content. Thus the Book has 'neither beginning, middle, nor end'.

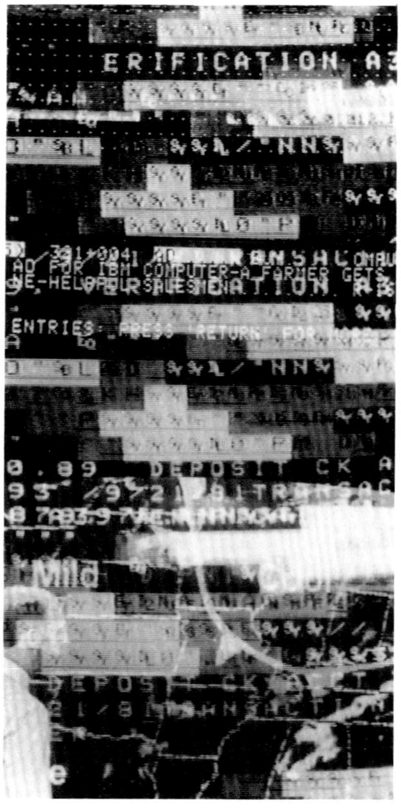

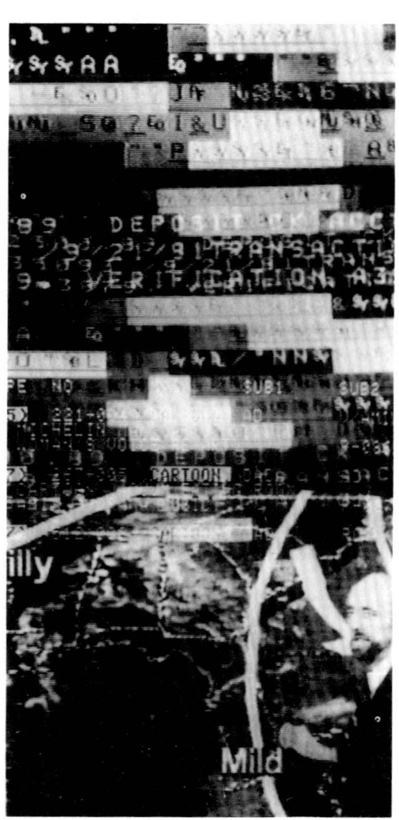

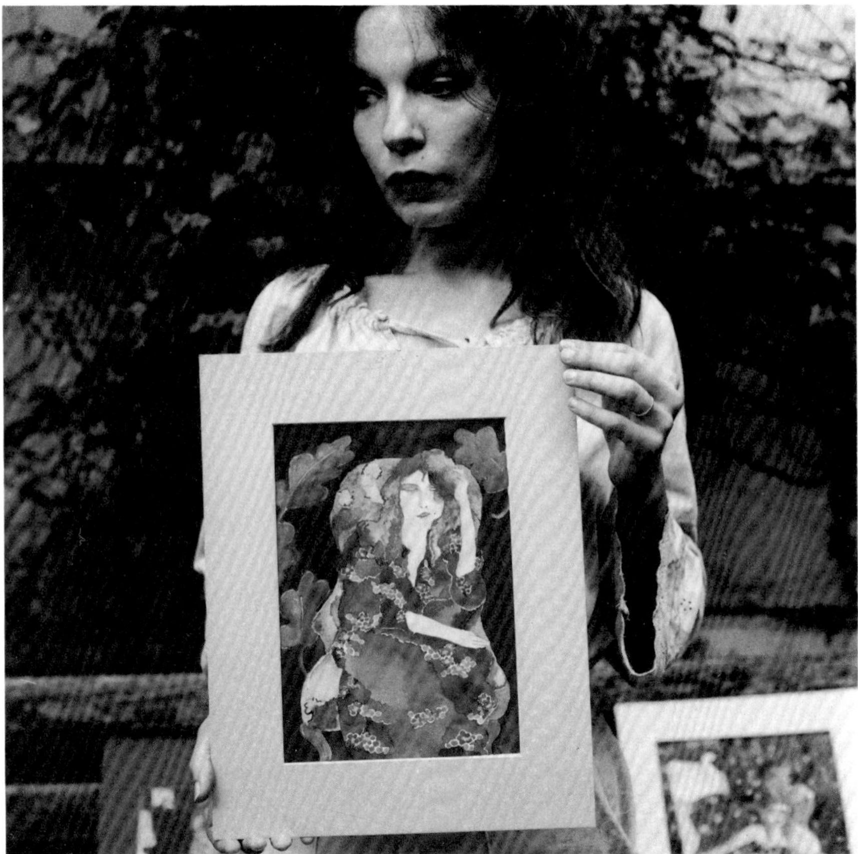

My guardian angel, who folowed you by hanging on the jet's wing, has found his

way back here. We see you now from afar. I must hold him back occasionally, but always successfully. ''How did this happen?,'' I say to the angel, then to you.

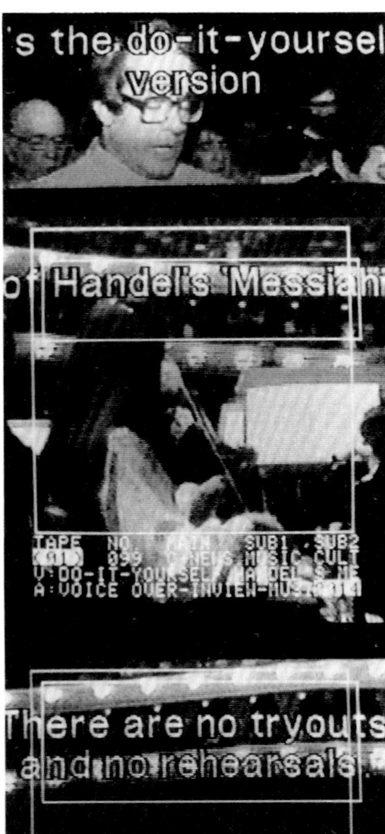

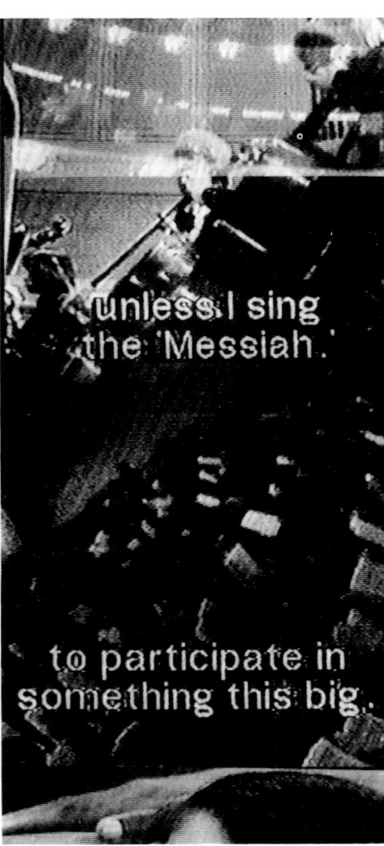

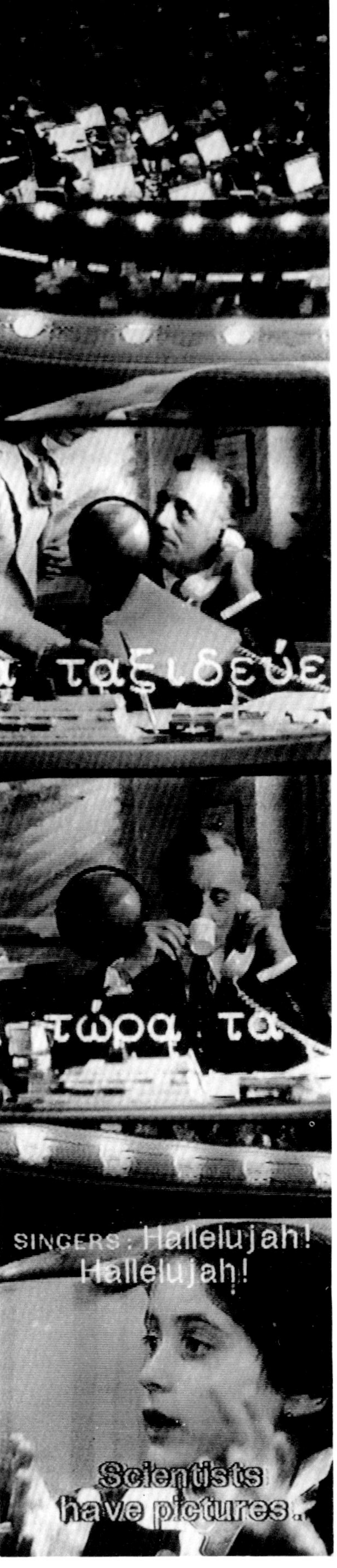

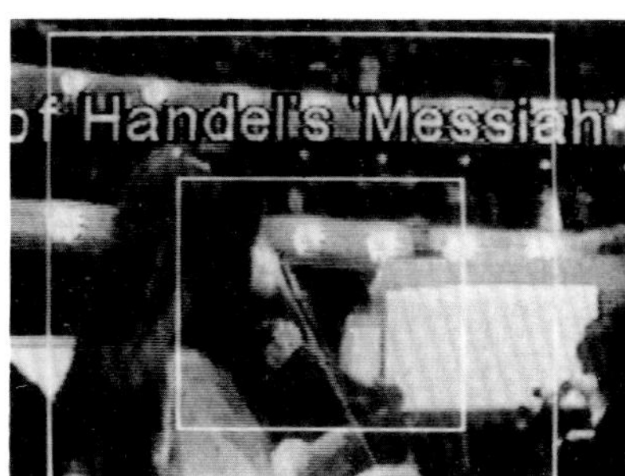

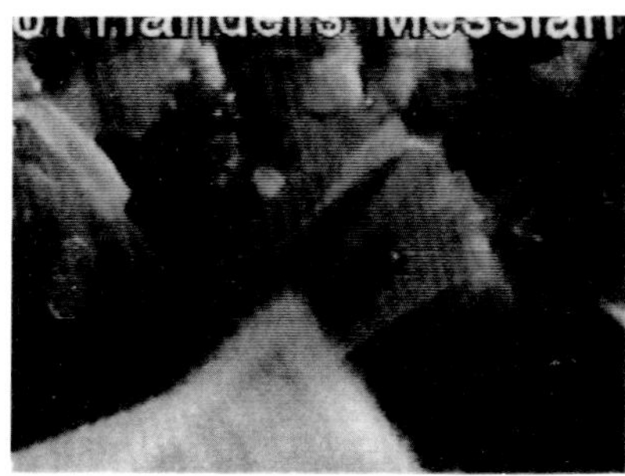

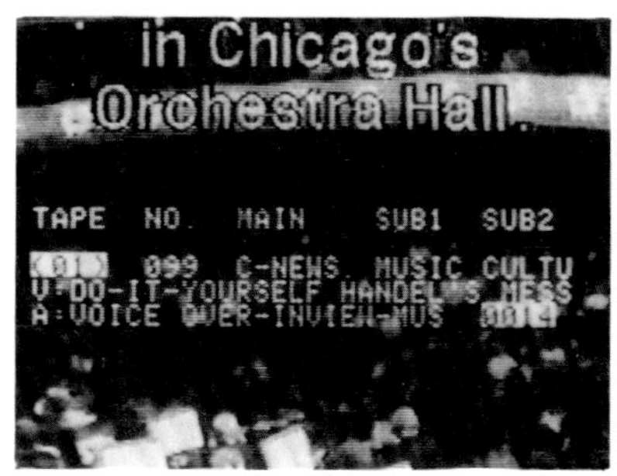

Memory

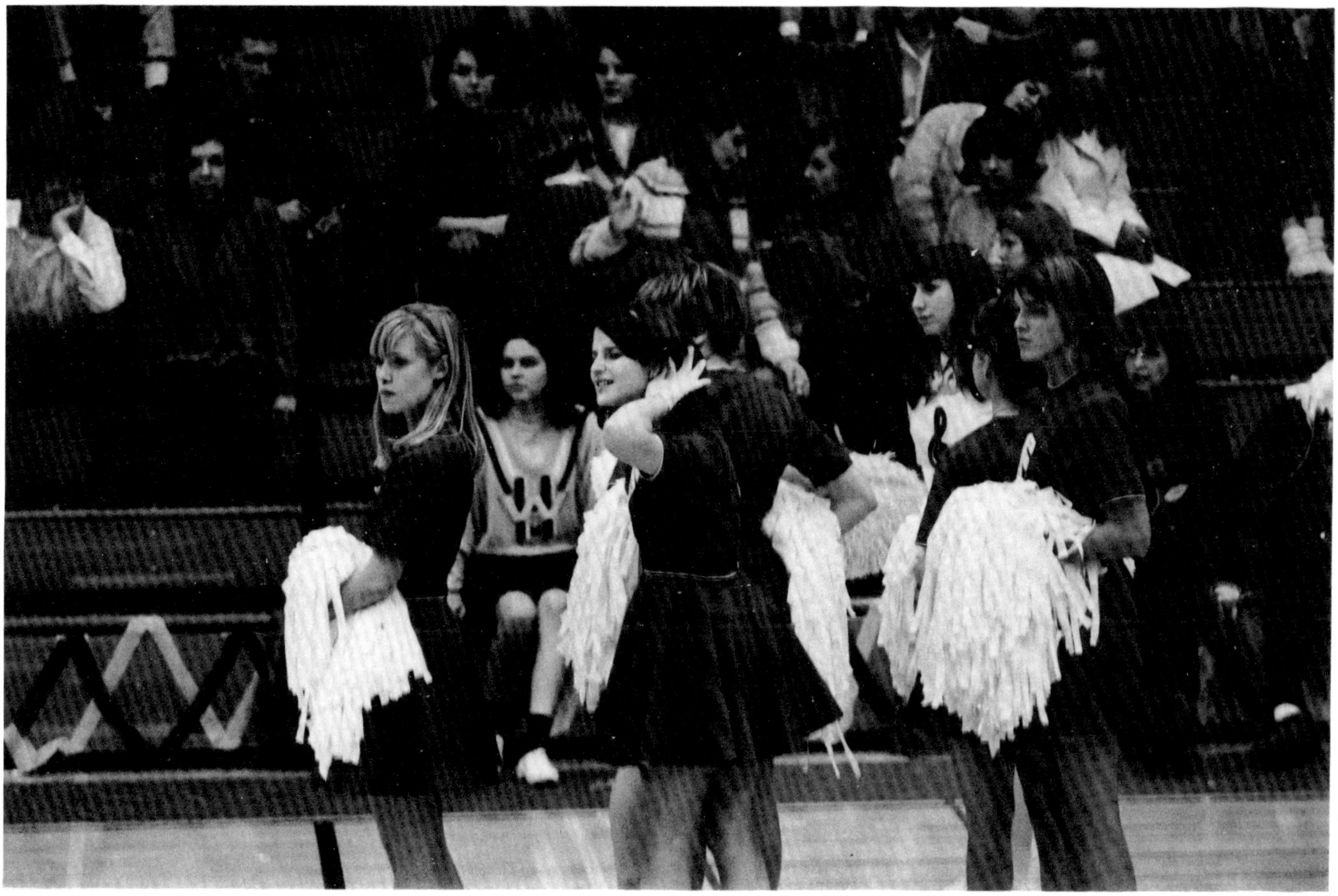

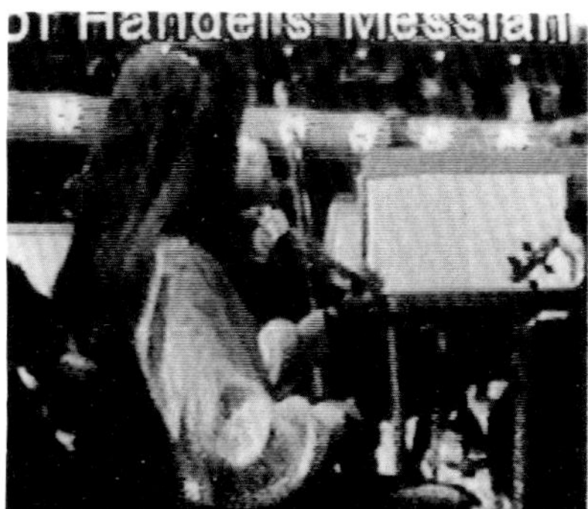

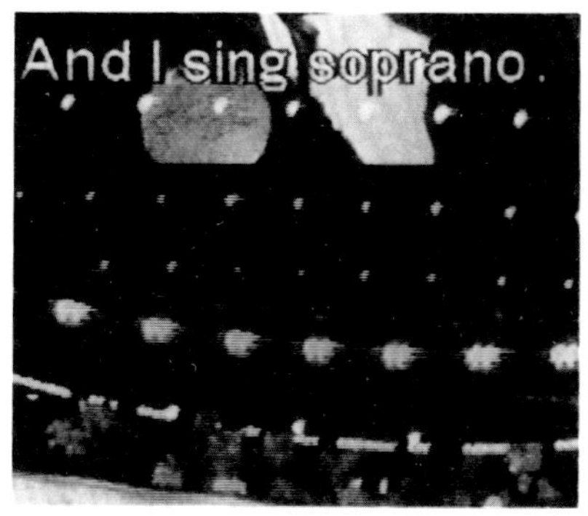

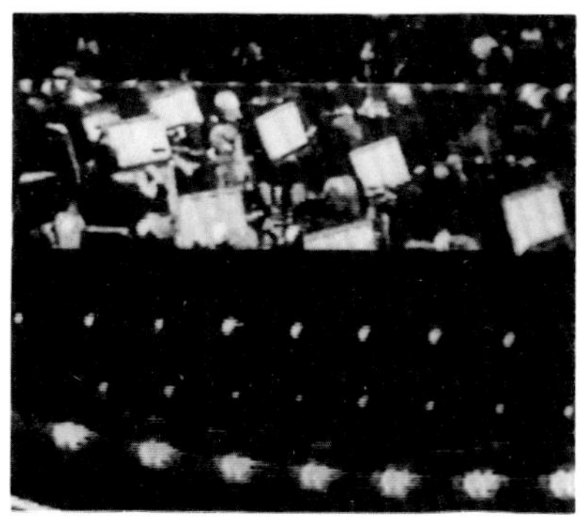

She remembers the exact moment she figured out subtraction, sitting on the small ledge dividing the backyard into lawn and

concrete, staring at the paper in her hand and the numbers on it, thinking of subtraction as another kind of addition and both as ways of counting.

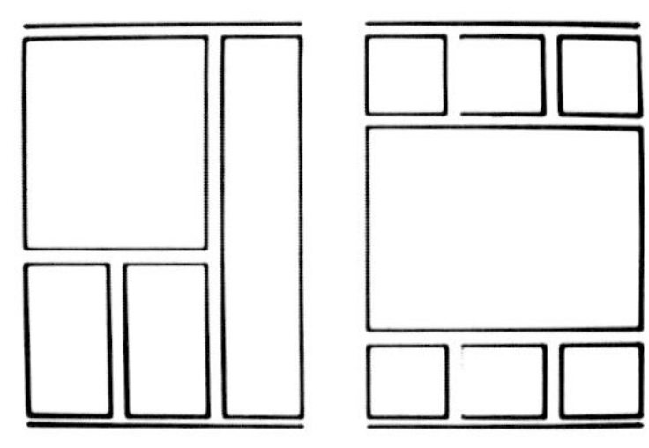

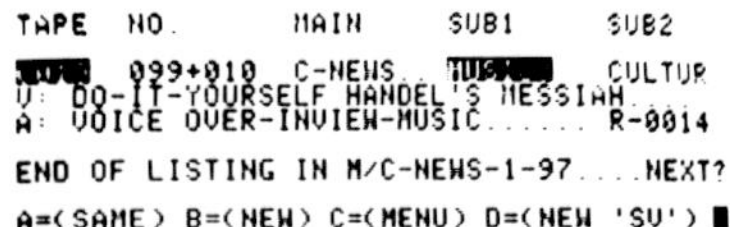

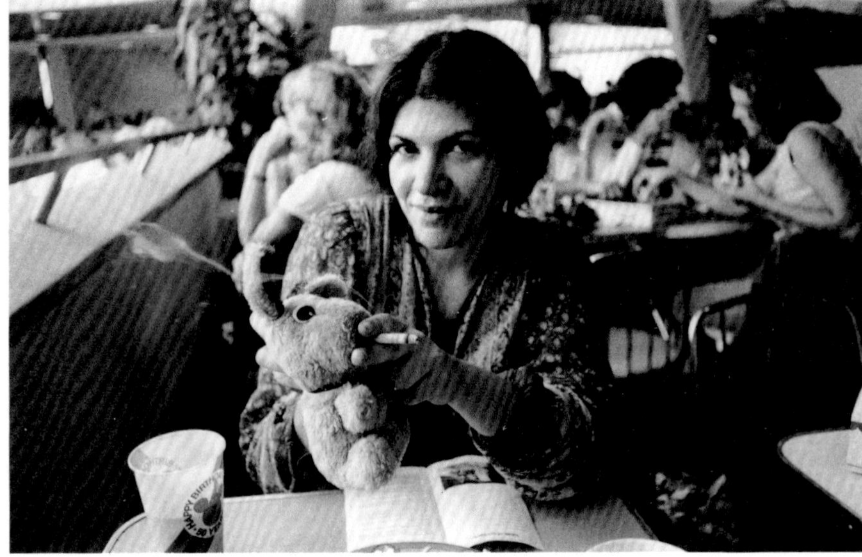

Our trip to Disneyland, August 1978

"Don't look at me so triumphantly", said the steady rabbit to the pouncing fox. "I can talk".

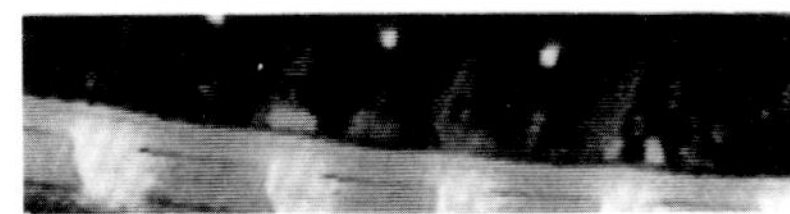

Memory

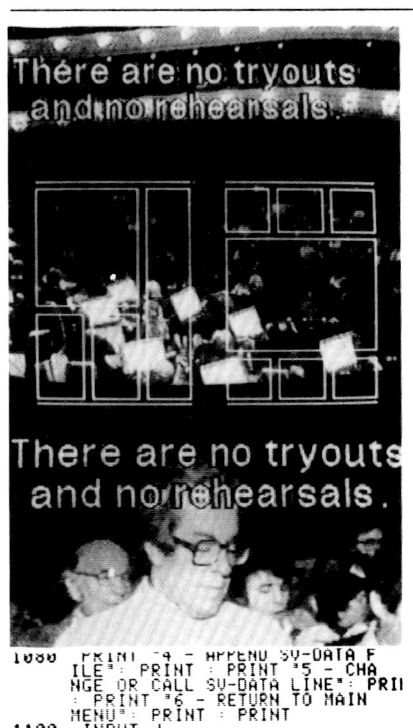

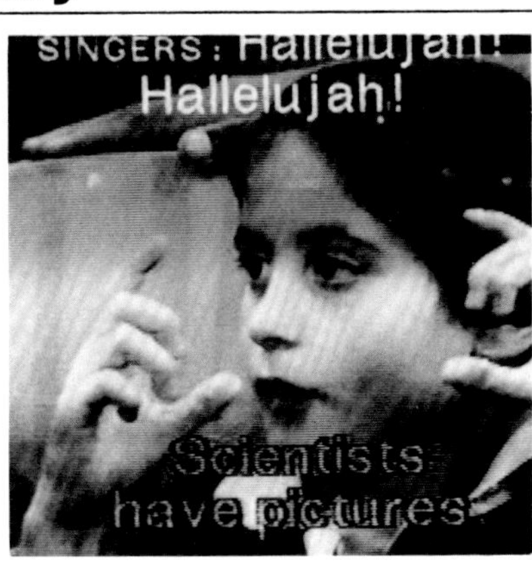

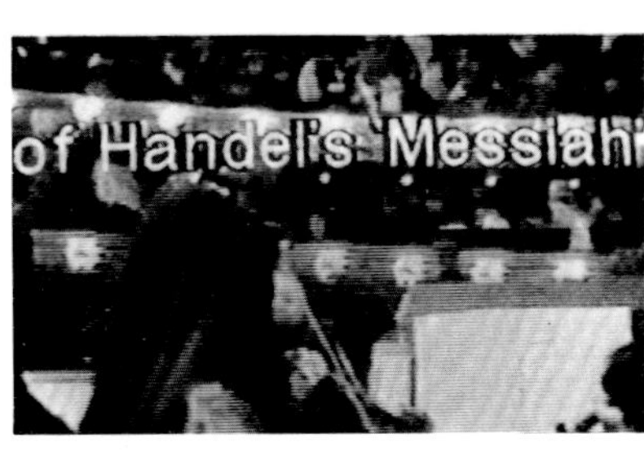

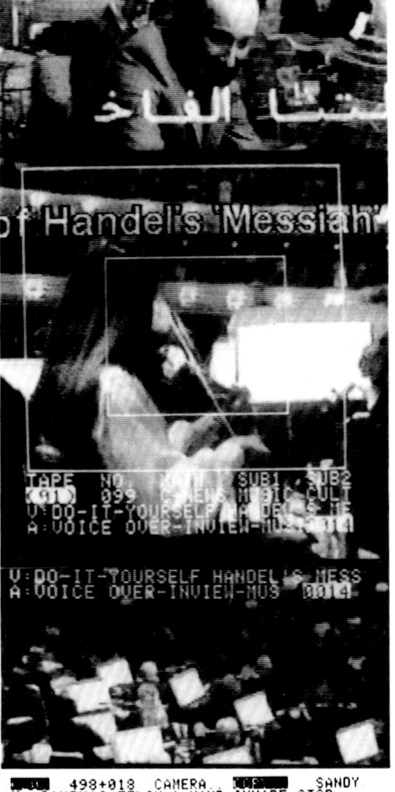

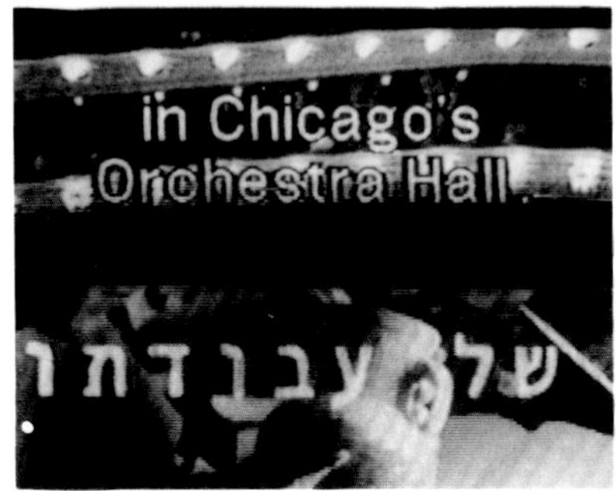

MEMORY: Print D$"Open Memory,L99": Print D$"Read Memory,R"X: For L=1 to RM: Input Z$(L): Next: Print D$"Close Memory": Return

88 D0 EB A5 26 EA 59 00 BB AA BD 29 BA AE 78 06 9D 8D C0 BD 8C C0 B9 00 BB C8 D0 EA AA BD 29 BA A6 27 20 BB B8 A9 DE 20 B8 B8 A9 AA

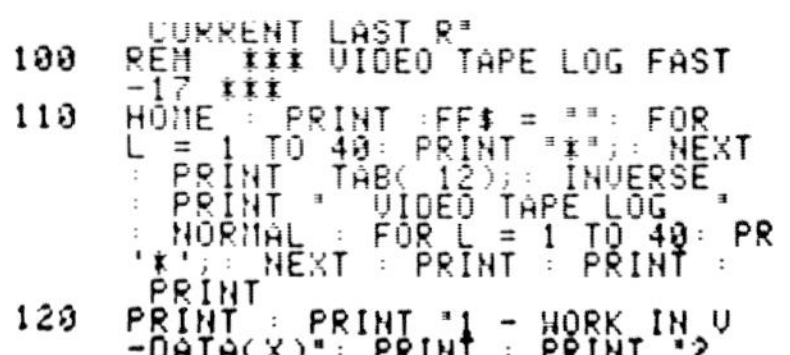

```
            CURRENT LAST R"
100    REM  *** VIDEO TAPE LOG FAST
       -17 ***
110    HOME : PRINT :FF$ = "": FOR
       L = 1 TO 40: PRINT "*";: NEXT
       : PRINT  TAB( 12);: INVERSE
       : PRINT " VIDEO TAPE LOG ":
       NORMAL : FOR L = 1 TO 40: PR
       '*';: NEXT : PRINT : PRINT :
       PRINT
120    PRINT : PRINT "1 - WORK IN V
       -DATA(X)": PRINT : PRINT "2
```

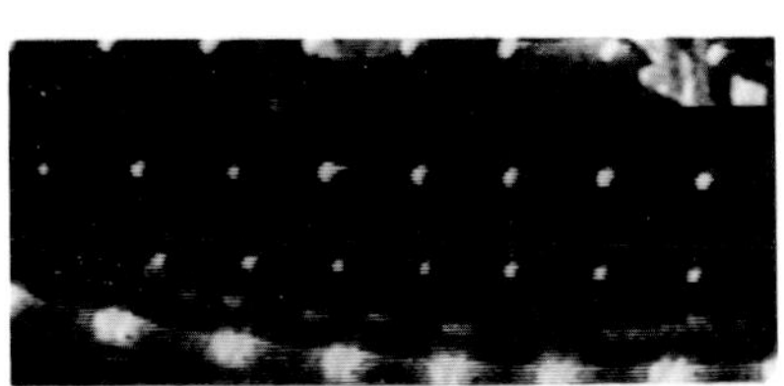

```
       }   HOME : VTAB 4: PRINT "RECORD
           ING NEW V-DATA....":ZZ = INT
           ((R + 1) / 100):QQ = ((R + 1
           ) - (ZZ * 100)): PRINT D$"OP
           EN V-DATA"ZZ: PRINT D$"POSIT
           ION V-DATA"ZZ",R"QQ: PRINT D
           $"WRITE V-DATA"ZZ
448    FOR L = 1 TO BB: PRINT MS$(L
       ): NEXT : PRINT D$;"CLOSE V-
       DATA"ZZ
456    IF  VAL ( RIGHT$ (MS$(BB),4)
       ) > R THEN  GOSUB 3000
```

TREE IN WHICH EACH VERTEX HAS AT
MOST TWO SONS. A VERTEX OF T WHICH
HAS NO SONS IS CALLED A 'LEAF'. TH
'HEIGHT' OF T IS THE LENGTH OF THE
LONGEST SIMPLE PATH IN T BETWEEN
THE ROOT OF T AND A LEAF OF T. NOT
THAT A BINARY TREE OF HEIGHT H CAN

```
10 REM      **** VIDEO TAPE LOG *
    ********                      *
20 HOME : PRINT : PRINT : PRINT
   "LOADING CURRENT 'R' NUMBER.
30 D$ =  CHR$ (4): DIM MS$(100): DI
   J$(65): DIM CC$(99): DIM SD$
   (24)
40 PRINT D$"OPEN CURRENT LAST R"
   : PRINT D$"READ CURRENT LAST
   R": INPUT R: PRINT D$"CLOSE
   CURRENT LAST R"
100 REM  *** VIDEO TAPE LOG FAST
```

World

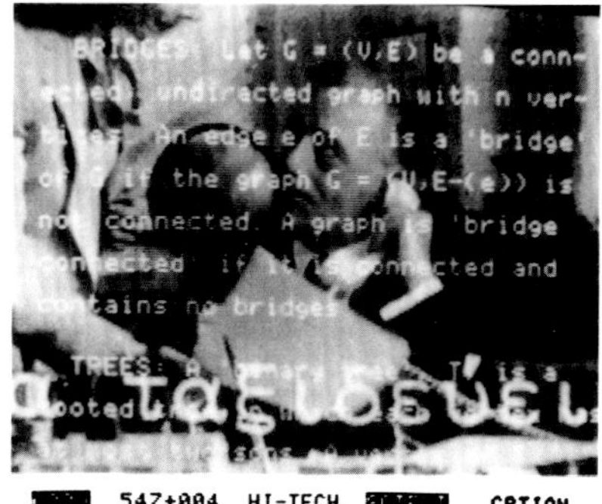

547+004 HI-TECH ... CPTION
V: IBM TYPEWRITER AD-OTHER LANGUAGES
A: BACKGROUND MUSIC R-0750

SHE REMEMBERS THE EXACT MOMENT SHE
FIGURED OUT SUBTRACTION, SITTING O
THE SMALL LEDGE DIVIDING THE BACK-
YARD INTO LAWN AND CONCRETE, STARI
AT THE PAPER IN HER HAND AND THE
NUMBERS ON IT, THINKING OF SUBTRACT
ION AS ANOTHER KIND OF ADDITION AN
BOTH AS WAYS OF COUNTING.

```
1060   PRINT : PRINT "1 - LIST EXI
       STING SV-DATA FILE TITLES": PRI
       : PRINT "2 - RETRIEVE FROM S
       V-DATA FILES": PRINT : PRINT
       "3 - CREATE NEW SV-DATA FILE
```

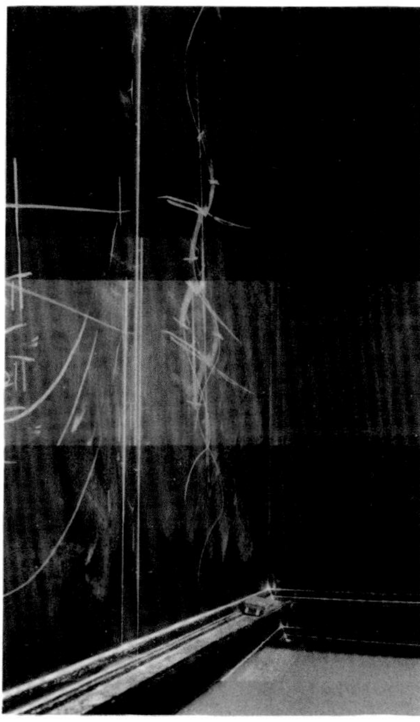

Display

THE SMALL LEDGE DIVIDING THE BACK-
YARD INTO LAWN AND CONCRETE, STARING
AT THE PAPER IN HER HAND AND THE
NUMBERS ON IT, THINKING OF SUBTRACT-
ION AS ANOTHER KIND OF ADDITION AND
BOTH AS WAYS OF COUNTING.

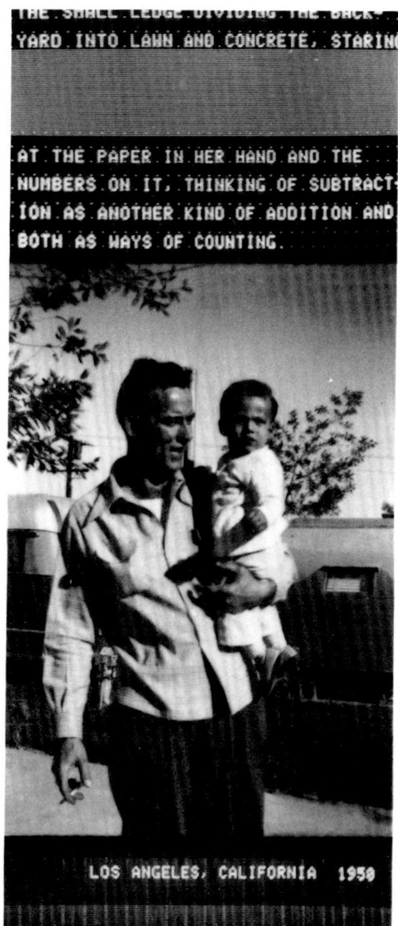

A 'FOREST' IS A
WHICH CONTAINS
ECTED FOREST IS
TREE', (T,R), IS
WITH A DISTINGUI
IF I @ V AND I≠
I IN (T,R) IS T
WHICH IS ADJACE
SHORTEST PATH I
THEN I IS THE

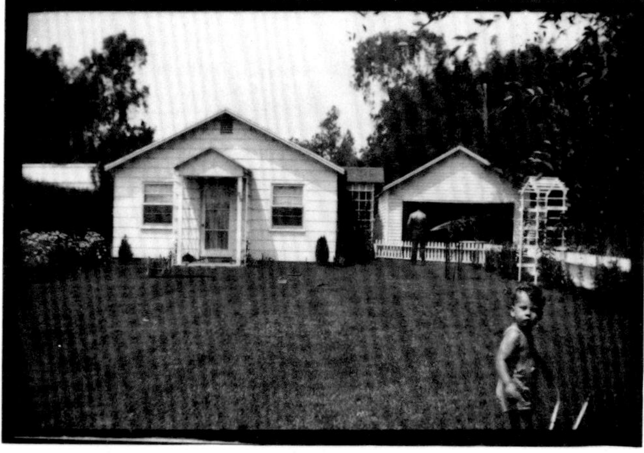

November, 1945 - Richard with Glen in the background, Burbank, CA

The garage was finished. The road had still not been paved. The house is there today

IF (I,J) @ E, J IS THE 'FATHER' OF
I AND I IS THE 'SON' OF J. IF THERE
IS A PATH IN T FROM I TO J THEN I
IS A 'DESCENDANT' OF J ('PROPER DE-
SCENDANT' IF I≠J) AND J IS AN 'AN-
CESTOR' OF I ('PROPER ANCESTOR' IF
I≠R).

A 'DIRECTED FOREST' IS A UNION OF
OF DIRECTED ROOTED TREES WITH PAIR-
WISE DISJOINT VERTEX SETS.

a 'forest' is an undirected graph
which contains no cycles. a connected forest is a 'tree'. a 'rooted'
tree', (t,r), is a tree t=(v,e)
with a distinguished vertex r @ v.

that a binary tree of height h can
have at most 2^h leaves...The follow-

if ... and ... the father of
i in (t,r) is the vertex j @ v
which is adjacent to i on the
shortest path in t joining i and r.
then i is the 'son' of j

WORLD: Print D$"Open World,L360": Print D$"Read World,R"X: For L=1 to LN: Input Z$(L): Next: Print D$"Close World": Return

EB 20 B8 B8 A9 FF 20 B8 B8 BD 8E C0 BD 8C C0 60 18 48 68 9D 8D C0 1D 8C C0 60 A0 00 A2 56 CA 30 FB B9 00 BB 5E 00 BC 2A 5E 00 BC 2A 91

PARALLEL ALGORITHMS FOR GRAPH
THEORETIC PROBLEMS

Carla Diane Savage
August, 1977

FOREST: A 'forest' is an undirected
graph which contains no cycles. A
connected forest is a 'tree'. A
'rooted tree', (T,r), is a tree T =
(V,E) with a distinguished vertex r
@ V. If i @ V and i/=r, the 'father'

TREES: A 'binary tree', T, is a
rooted tree in which each vertex has
at most two sons. A vertex of T
which has no sons is called a 'leaf'

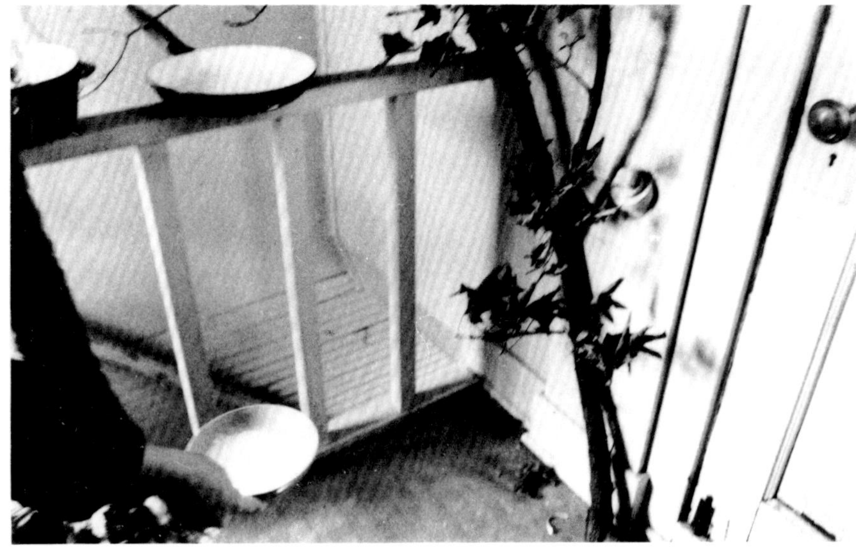

The 'height' of T is the length of
the longest simple path in T between
the root of T and a leaf of T. Note

that a binary tree of height h can
have at most 2^h leaves...The following properties are nontrivial, mono-

World

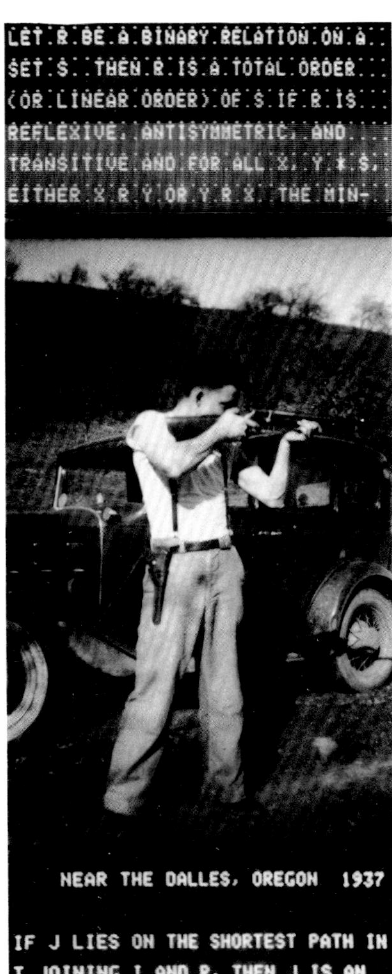

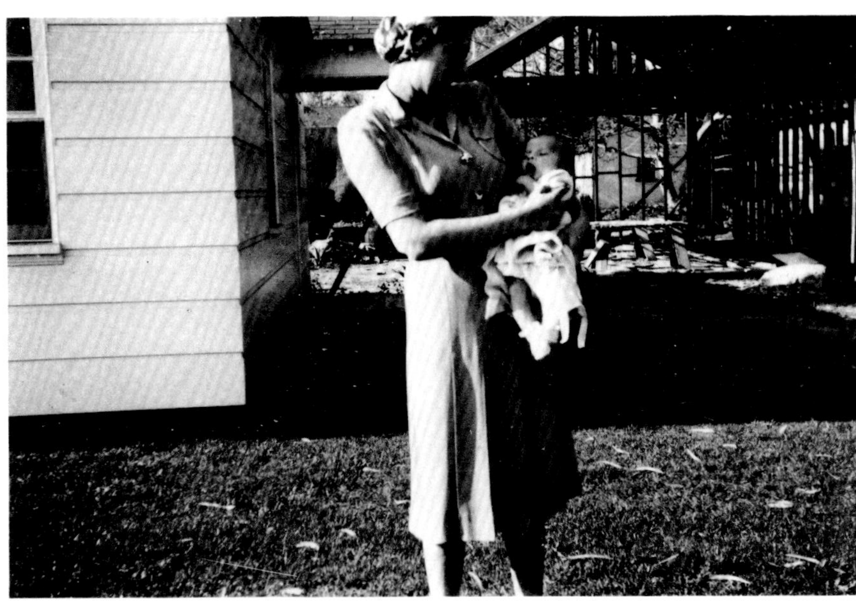

January, 1945 - Virginia with infant Richard, Burbank, CA

The lot was large. We were adding a garage. The city hadn't finished the road in front.

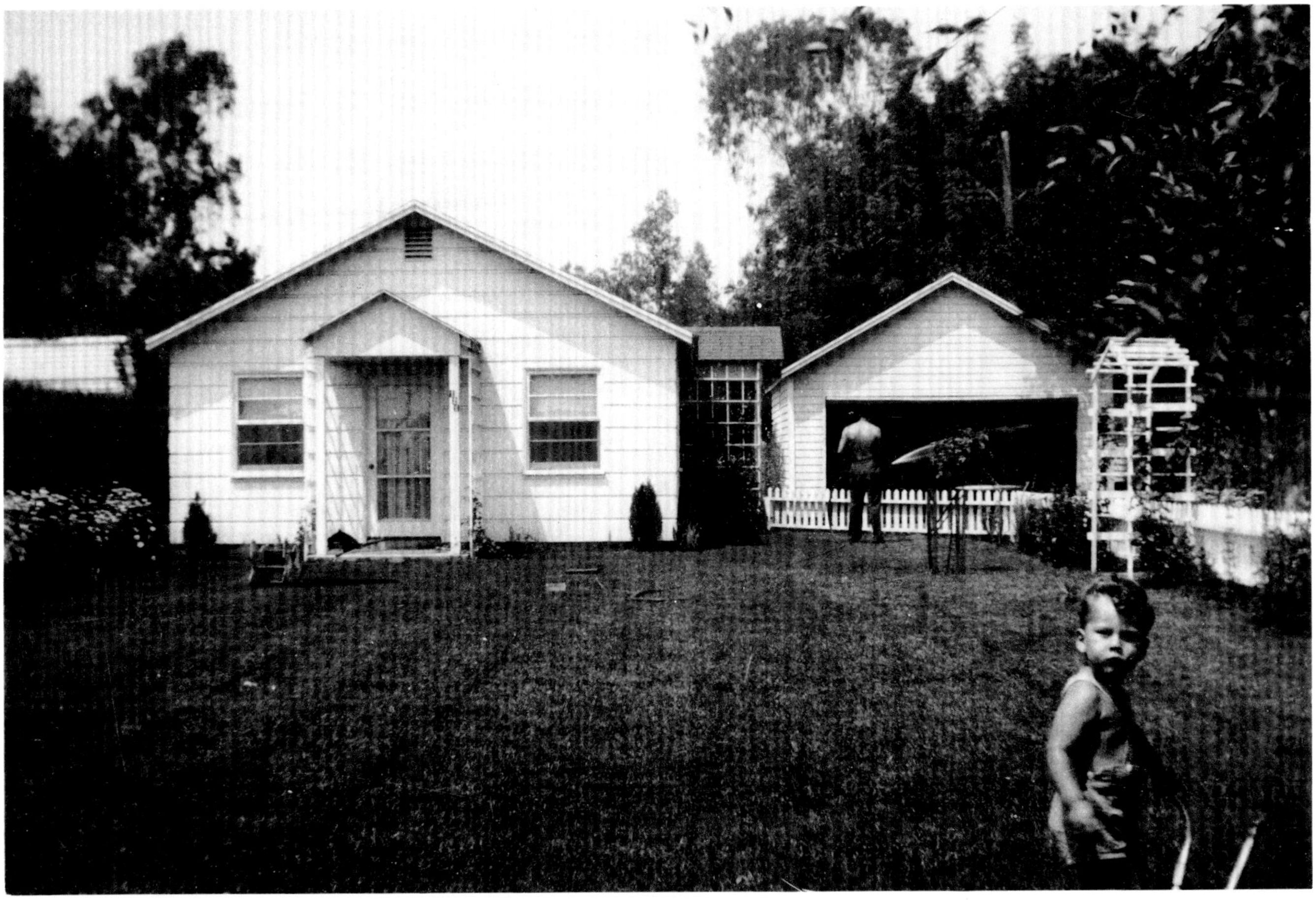

November, 1945 - Richard with Glen in the background, Burbank, CA

The garage was finished. The road had still not been paved. The house is there today.

AT THE PAPER IN HER HAND AND THE
NUMBERS ON IT, THINKING OF SUBTRAC
ION AS ANOTHER KIND OF ADDITION AN
BOTH AS WAYS OF COUNTING.

a 'binary tree', t, is a rooted
tree in which each vertex has at
most two sons. a vertex of t which
has no sons is called a 'leaf'. the
'height' of t is the length of the
longest simple path in t between
the root of t and a leaf of t.

a 'forest' is an undirected graph
which contains no cycles. a connected forest is a 'tree'. a 'rooted'
tree, (t,r), is a tree t=(v,e)
with a distinguished vertex r @ v.
if i @ v and i≠r, the 'father' of
i in (t,r) is the vertex j @ v
which is adjacent to i on the

tices. An edge e of E is a 'bridge'
of G if the graph G = (V,E-(e)) is
not connected. A graph is 'bridge
connected' if it is connected and
contains no bridges.

a 'directed forest' is a union of
of directed rooted trees with pairwise disjoint vertex sets.

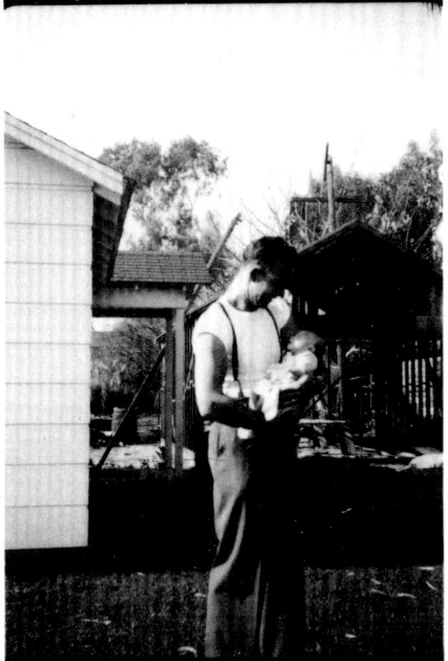

i in (t,r) is the vertex j @ v
which is adjacent to i on the
shortest path in t joining i and r.
then i is the 'son' of j

GLEN WITH INFANT RICHARD
JAN. 1945

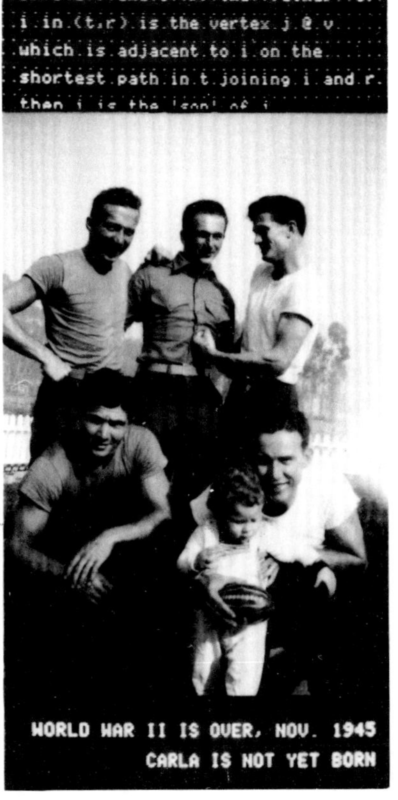